pasta prim p. 27
garlic shrimp 110
cuc. salad 141

Great Beginnings

&

Happy Endings

Hors d'oeuvres and Desserts
for Standing Ovations

by Renny Darling

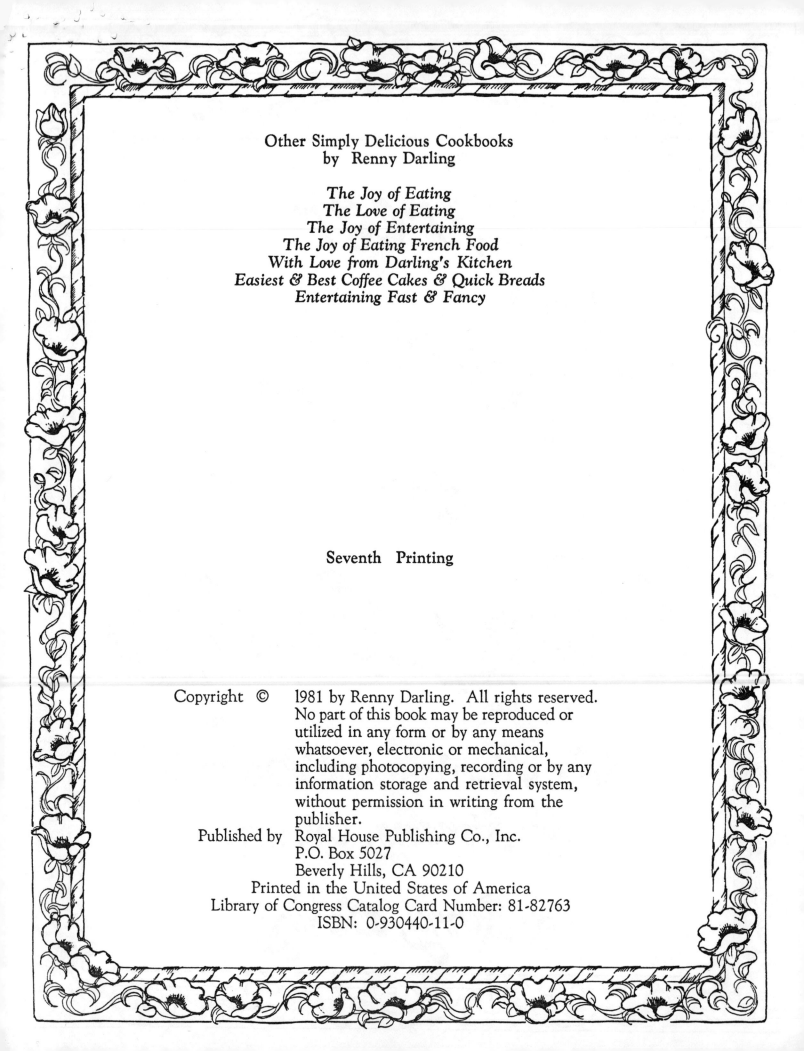

Other Simply Delicious Cookbooks
by Renny Darling

The Joy of Eating
The Love of Eating
The Joy of Entertaining
The Joy of Eating French Food
With Love from Darling's Kitchen
Easiest & Best Coffee Cakes & Quick Breads
Entertaining Fast & Fancy

Seventh Printing

Published by Royal House Publishing Co., Inc.
P.O. Box 5027
Beverly Hills, CA 90210
Printed in the United States of America
Library of Congress Catalog Card Number: 81-82763
ISBN: 0-930440-11-0

The Introduction

This book is for people who like people. It is a book for people who care about people . . . for, after all, cooking is the gentle art of pleasing others. It is for those who make everyday a celebration . . . who bring excitement and glamor into their lives by preparing food in an exciting and unpredictable manner. This book is not only for the occasional party. The recipes can be used everyday, for it is only the size of the portion that makes a dish an hors d'oeuvre or a small entree or a main dish for lunch or dinner. The word "hors d'oeuvre" literally means, "outside the main course," which explains the inclusion of breads and soups and salads.

This is a book for the days when you invite friends to "Come for dessert after the theatre." or "Come for a bite before the game." It is especially helpful for those times, when a simple dinner is planned and a smashing beginning and ending is necessary, to add sparkle and enchantment to the meal.

"Come for hors d'oeuvres and desserts." is a simple way to entertain larger groups. There are many advantages to this kind of entertaining. To begin with, everybody loves desserts and hors d'oeuvres. Also, these are stand-up parties, so mingling is easier and you can comfortably accommodate many more guests. So often, at parties, a certain momentum in gaiety and conversation is developing, and how nice to continue this without interruption.

This is a book for busy people; people, who are hard at work and hard at play and who do not choose to spend inordinate amounts of time in the kitchen for preparation. Although the recipes sound glamorous, please be assured they are the essence of simplicity to prepare. There are a few shortcuts using the prepared puff pastry and frozen pie shells. But the results are very good, indeed.

For the most part, ingredients used are basically inexpensive, except for the occasional splurge with crabmeat or caviar. Other than these, I have used ordinary ingredients that produce extraordinary results. The recipes cover many themes. There are hors d'oeuvres and desserts for the most formal occasions, to a family chili for a picnic in your garden.

"Great Beginnings" stimulate conversation and make guests happy and animated. "Happy Endings" leaves them with a delicious memory of good times spent with family and friends.

You will find the recipes astonishingly quick to prepare, amazingly easy to execute and above all, joyously delicious.

So, have a banquet! . . . Have a ball! And while you're at it, give yourself a kiss. You deserve it.

Renny Darling
Beverly Hills, California
July, 1981

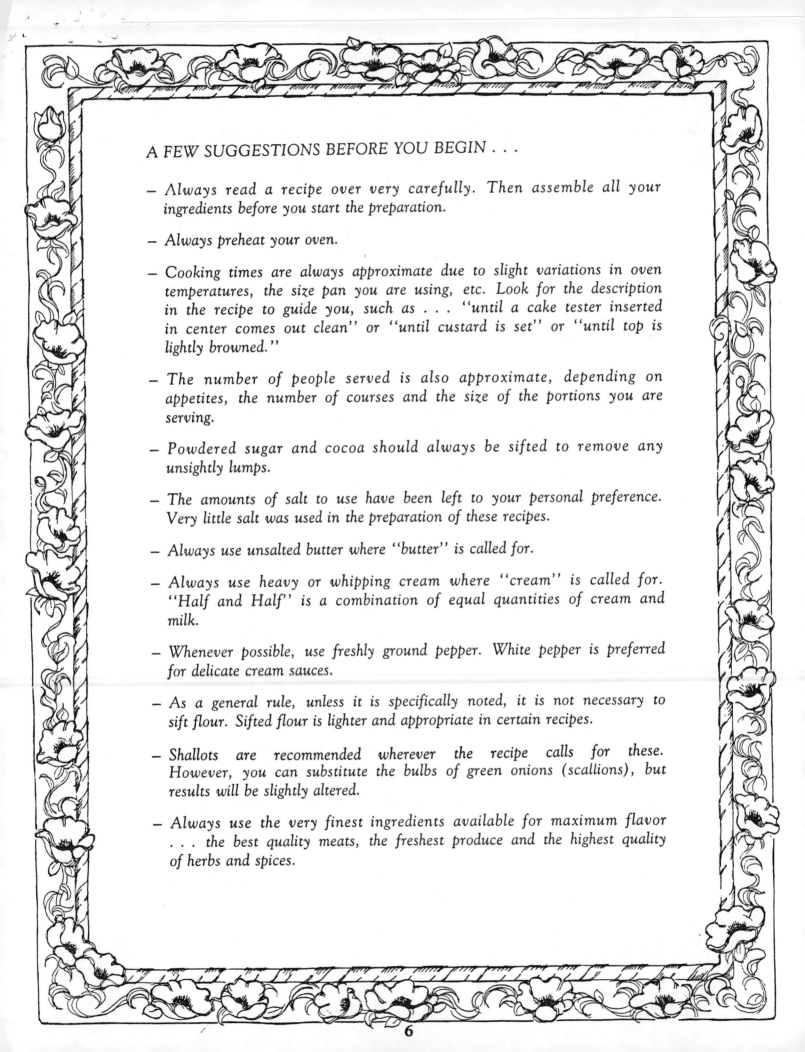

A FEW SUGGESTIONS BEFORE YOU BEGIN . . .

— *Always read a recipe over very carefully. Then assemble all your ingredients before you start the preparation.*

— *Always preheat your oven.*

— *Cooking times are always approximate due to slight variations in oven temperatures, the size pan you are using, etc. Look for the description in the recipe to guide you, such as . . . "until a cake tester inserted in center comes out clean" or "until custard is set" or "until top is lightly browned."*

— *The number of people served is also approximate, depending on appetites, the number of courses and the size of the portions you are serving.*

— *Powdered sugar and cocoa should always be sifted to remove any unsightly lumps.*

— *The amounts of salt to use have been left to your personal preference. Very little salt was used in the preparation of these recipes.*

— *Always use unsalted butter where "butter" is called for.*

— *Always use heavy or whipping cream where "cream" is called for. "Half and Half" is a combination of equal quantities of cream and milk.*

— *Whenever possible, use freshly ground pepper. White pepper is preferred for delicate cream sauces.*

— *As a general rule, unless it is specifically noted, it is not necessary to sift flour. Sifted flour is lighter and appropriate in certain recipes.*

— *Shallots are recommended wherever the recipe calls for these. However, you can substitute the bulbs of green onions (scallions), but results will be slightly altered.*

— *Always use the very finest ingredients available for maximum flavor . . . the best quality meats, the freshest produce and the highest quality of herbs and spices.*

The Contents

For Harry
With All My Love

Breads & Muffins

Cinnamon Zucchini Bread with Raisins & Orange

1 cup grated zucchini
1 cup sugar
1/2 orange, grated. Remove any large pieces of
     membrane.
2 eggs
1/2 cup butter, softened

1 1/2 cups flour
1 teaspoon baking powder
1/2 teaspoon baking soda
1/4 teaspoon salt
2 teaspoons cinnamon

1 cup raisins
1 teaspoon vanilla

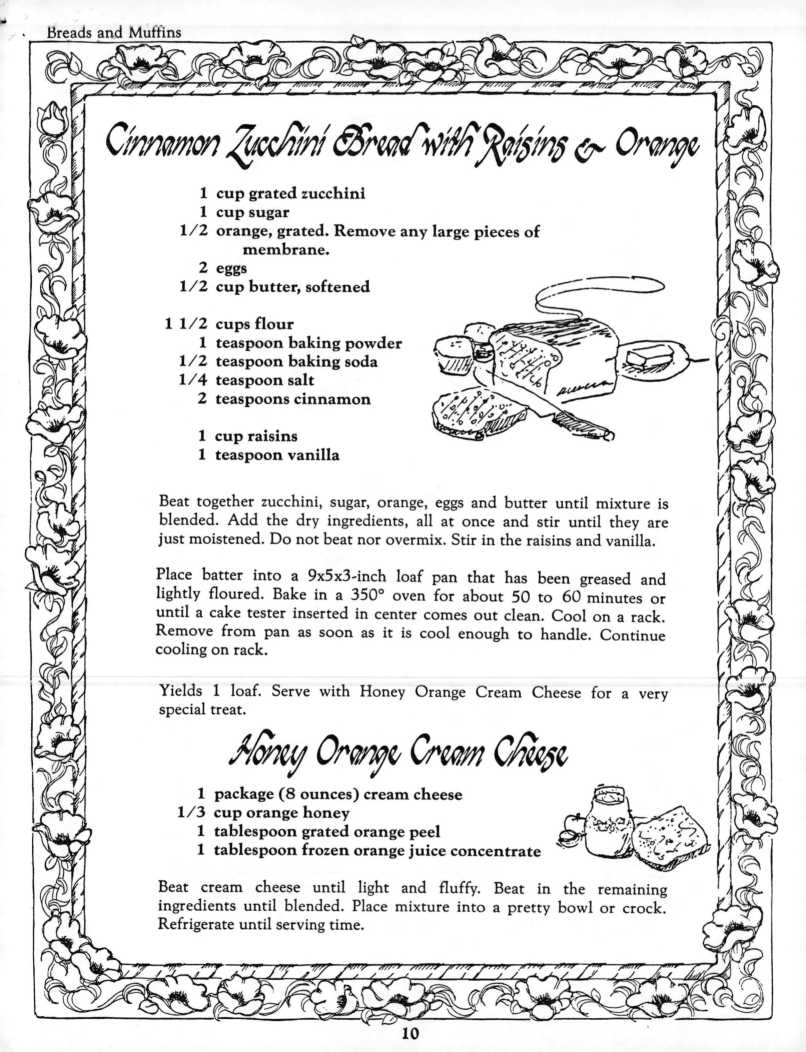

Beat together zucchini, sugar, orange, eggs and butter until mixture is blended. Add the dry ingredients, all at once and stir until they are just moistened. Do not beat nor overmix. Stir in the raisins and vanilla.

Place batter into a 9x5x3-inch loaf pan that has been greased and lightly floured. Bake in a 350° oven for about 50 to 60 minutes or until a cake tester inserted in center comes out clean. Cool on a rack. Remove from pan as soon as it is cool enough to handle. Continue cooling on rack.

Yields 1 loaf. Serve with Honey Orange Cream Cheese for a very special treat.

Honey Orange Cream Cheese

1 package (8 ounces) cream cheese
1/3 cup orange honey
1 tablespoon grated orange peel
1 tablespoon frozen orange juice concentrate

Beat cream cheese until light and fluffy. Beat in the remaining ingredients until blended. Place mixture into a pretty bowl or crock. Refrigerate until serving time.

Thanksgiving Spiced Pumpkin Bread with Orange & Apple

The fragrance of this bread baking in the oven will absolutely bring a crowd to your door. The aromas of spice and apples and orange and raisins is very enticing, so be sure not to eat it all before the great feast.

2 cups sugar 1³⁄4
2 eggs
1 cup canned pumpkin

1/2 cup oil

2 1/2 cups flour
1 1/2 teaspoons baking soda
1 1/2 teaspoons pumpkin pie spice
1 teaspoon cinnamon
1/2 teaspoon salt

1/2 orange, grated. Use the peel, juice and fruit.
1 apple, peeled, cored and grated
1/2 cup yellow raisins

In the large bowl of an electric mixer, beat together sugar, eggs and pumpkin until blended. Beat in the oil. Beat in the remaining ingredients until blended.

Pour batter into 4 3x5-inch greased loaf pans and bake in a 350° oven for 45 to 50 minutes or until a cake tester, inserted in center, comes out clean. Cool for 10 minutes and then remove breads from pans and continue cooling on a rack. Place breads back into pans for storing. Yields 4 loaves.

Note: - Breads freeze beautifully. Wrap in double thicknesses of plastic wrap and then foil. Remove wrappers when defrosting.
- If you are serving this bread for other than Thanksgiving, add 1/2 cup yellow raisins and 1 cup chopped walnuts. As Thanksgiving dinner is such a huge feast, keeping the bread a little less rich is more advisable.
- If you are planning to give this bread as a gift from your kitchen, then brush the top with a thin coat of honey (when cool) and sprinkle with a few chopped toasted walnuts.

Spiced Pumpkin Bread with Dates, Nuts & Raisins

4 tablespoons sour cream
1 teaspoon soda

1 1/2 cups flour mixed with 1/4 teaspoon salt

1/2 cup butter (1 stick)
1 1/4 cups sugar
1 teaspoon vanilla
2 eggs, beaten

1 cup canned pumpkin
1/2 cup finely chopped dates
1/2 cup chopped walnuts
1/2 cup golden raisins (plumped in orange juice)

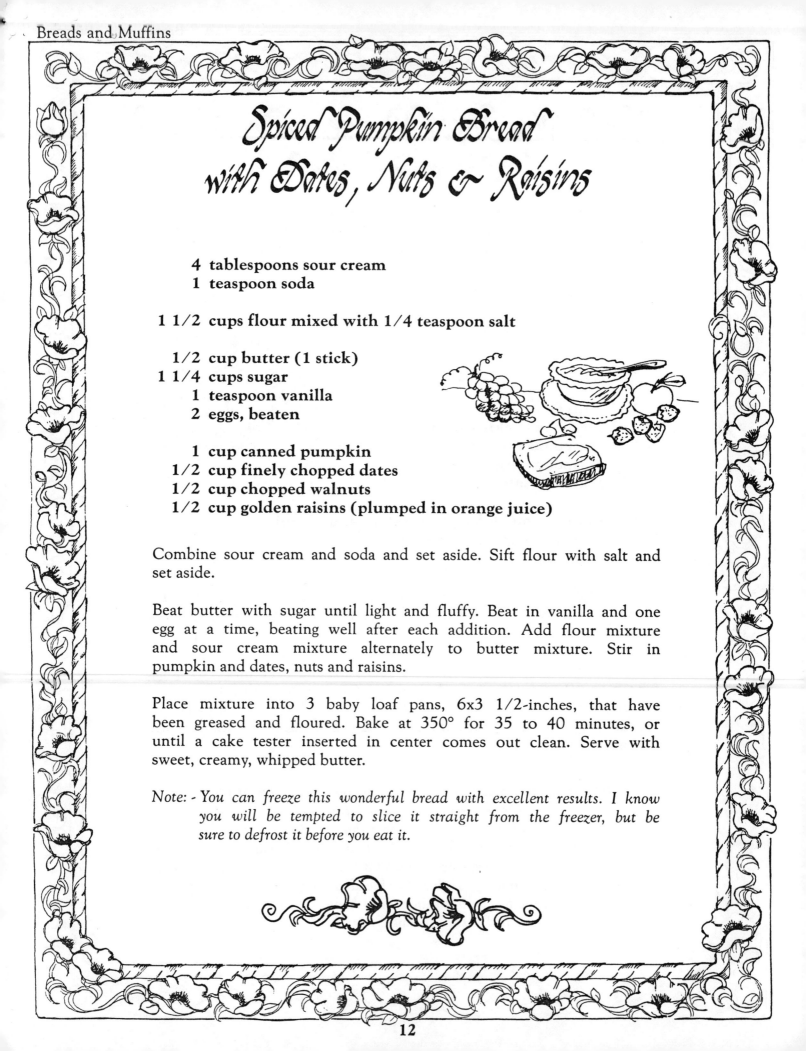

Combine sour cream and soda and set aside. Sift flour with salt and set aside.

Beat butter with sugar until light and fluffy. Beat in vanilla and one egg at a time, beating well after each addition. Add flour mixture and sour cream mixture alternately to butter mixture. Stir in pumpkin and dates, nuts and raisins.

Place mixture into 3 baby loaf pans, 6x3 1/2-inches, that have been greased and floured. Bake at 350° for 35 to 40 minutes, or until a cake tester inserted in center comes out clean. Serve with sweet, creamy, whipped butter.

Note: - You can freeze this wonderful bread with excellent results. I know you will be tempted to slice it straight from the freezer, but be sure to defrost it before you eat it.

Spiced Orange Bread with Sour Cream & Nutmeg

This is a very easy, but very special bread. It is deeply fragrant and a lovely accompaniment to a Thanksgiving banquet. While this bread is not sweet, after spreading it with creamy sweet butter, everyone declared that it was just like cake.

2	cups flour
1	tablespoon grated orange zest
4	tablespoons sugar
2	tablespoons butter
1	teaspoon salt
1	package dry yeast
2	tablespoons warm water (105° to 110°)
2	teaspoons sugar
3	ounces sour cream
3	ounces milk
1/2	teaspoon nutmeg
1	tablespoon oil

In the large bowl of an electric mixer, place first 5 ingredients and beat for a few seconds until mixture is blended.

In a glass measuring cup, place yeast, water and sugar and allow to stand about 5 minutes or until yeast starts to foam up. (If yeast does not foam, then it is not active and should be discarded.) Stir in the sour cream, milk and nutmeg.

Pour yeast mixture into mixer bowl and beat for 2 minutes. Dough should be soft. Place 1 tablespoon oil in a 1-quart souffle dish. Place dough into the bowl and turn it so that the top is nicely covered with oil. Cover bowl with plastic wrap and let it rise in a warm place for about 1 hour or until it has doubled in bulk. Bake in a 350° oven for about 40 minutes or until top is golden brown. Allow to stand for 10 minutes and then remove bread from pan and cool on a rack. Yields 1 loaf.

Note: - A lovely addition would be 1/2 cup chopped walnuts and 1/2 cup yellow raisins. Beat this in at the end.

- For other than Thanksgiving, glaze this delightful bread with a mixture of 1/2 small orange, grated (about 2 tablespoons) 1/3 cup chopped walnuts, 2 tablespoons chopped raisins and about 1 cup powdered sugar (sifted) until mixture is thick enough to spread.

Honey Cinnamon Sticky Rolls with Walnuts & Raisins

This is a very easy breakfast bread and just right for Sunday brunch. It is fun to pull off a few "bouchees" (bites) at a time, all lavished with honey and cinnamon and nuts and raisins.

2 packages (8 ounces, each) refrigerated biscuits.
    Cut each biscuit into fourths.
1/3 cup butter, melted
3/4 cup brown sugar
3 teaspoons cinnamon
1/2 cup chopped raisins
3/4 cup chopped walnuts or pecans

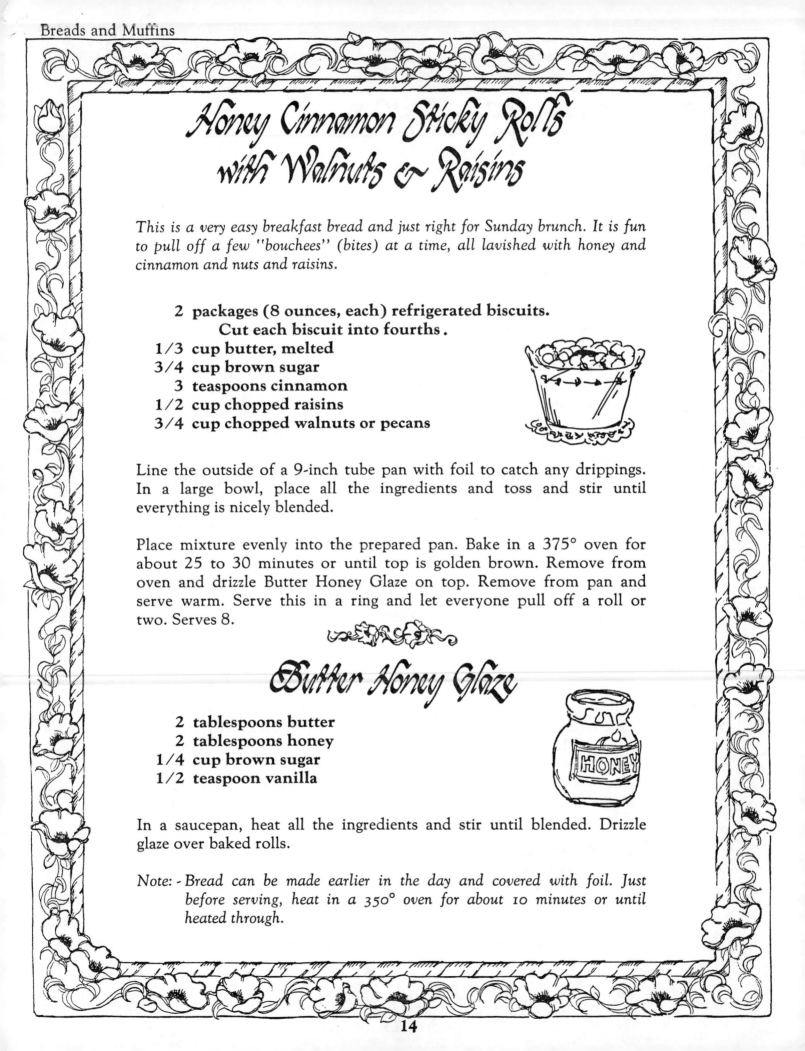

Line the outside of a 9-inch tube pan with foil to catch any drippings. In a large bowl, place all the ingredients and toss and stir until everything is nicely blended.

Place mixture evenly into the prepared pan. Bake in a 375° oven for about 25 to 30 minutes or until top is golden brown. Remove from oven and drizzle Butter Honey Glaze on top. Remove from pan and serve warm. Serve this in a ring and let everyone pull off a roll or two. Serves 8.

Butter Honey Glaze

2 tablespoons butter
2 tablespoons honey
1/4 cup brown sugar
1/2 teaspoon vanilla

In a saucepan, heat all the ingredients and stir until blended. Drizzle glaze over baked rolls.

Note: - Bread can be made earlier in the day and covered with foil. Just before serving, heat in a 350° oven for about 10 minutes or until heated through.

14

Farmhouse Lemon Nut Bread with Lemon Glaze

1/2 **cup butter, melted**
1 1/4 **cups sugar**
3 **tablespoons grated lemon (grate the whole lemon
and use the fruit, juice and peel)**
2 **eggs**

2 **cups flour**
1 **teaspoon baking powder**
1/2 **teaspoon salt**

1/2 **cup milk**

1 **cup walnuts or pecans, coarsely chopped**

In the large bowl of an electric mixer, beat together butter, sugar, lemon and eggs until nicely blended. Combine flour, baking powder and salt, and add this alternately with the milk to the egg mixture. Beat very little, and just enough to blend, no more. Stir in the nuts.

Butter and flour 2 8x4-inch loaf pans and divide batter between the pans. Bake for about 1 hour in a 350° oven, or until a cake tester, inserted in center, comes out clean. Leave loaves in pans.

Drizzle Lemon Glaze over the warm breads and let them set in the refrigerator for about 24 hours before cutting. Yields 2 loaves.

Lemon Glaze:
4 **tablespoons lemon juice**
1/2 **cup sugar**

In a bowl, stir together lemon juice and sugar until sugar is dissolved. Combine these ingredients before you start the breads, to allow enough time.

*Note: - These can be frozen. Wrap in double thicknesses of plastic wrap and
then foil. Remove wrappers when defrosting.*

Burgundian Cheese Ring with Bacon & Onions

3/4 cup milk
4 tablespoons butter

3/4 cup flour
pinch salt

3 eggs

3 tablespoons grated Parmesan cheese
4 slices bacon, cooked crisp, drained and crumbled
1 tablespoon minced parsley
3 tablespoons minced green onions

In a saucepan, heat milk and butter until mixture comes to a boil. Add the flour and salt and cook and stir until dough forms a ball and leaves the side of the pan, about 2 minutes. Beat in eggs, one at a time, beating well after each addition. Beat in the remaining ingredients.

Drop dough by the tablespoonful, on a greased cookie sheet, and form a 12-inch circle. Mounds of dough should be about 1/2-inch apart but dough will spread while baking. Bake in a 400° oven for 15 minutes. Lower heat to 350° and continue baking for about 25 minutes or until pastry is puffed and golden brown. Place ring on a large platter and serve warm with cheese or pate. A glass of wine is just lovely with this. Also wonderful to serve with soup or salad. Yields about 16 servings.

Note: - Batter can be made earlier in the day and spooned onto the cookie sheet. Store in the refrigerator until ready to bake. Bake as described above, but add a few minutes to baking time.
- Ring can be baked earlier in the day and reheated at time of serving.
- To serve, allow guests to pull puffs apart and spread with a soft cheese or pate.

Sour Cream Onion & Poppy Seed Bread

If you are looking for a recipe that will produce a delicious and honest loaf of bread that will delight your family and friends (and delight you too), I hope you try this moist bread, flavored with onions. It can be assembled in minutes in a food processor and rises and bakes in the same dish. You can vary it with herbs or cheese or bacon, but do try it with the onion and poppy seeds to start.

2 cups flour
1 teaspoon salt
2 tablespoons cold butter
2 tablespoons dry onion flakes
1 tablespoon poppy seeds

1/2 tablespoon (1/2 package) dry yeast
2 tablespoons water (105° to 110°)
2 teaspoons sugar

3 ounces sour cream
3 ounces milk

1/4 cup additional flour, if needed
1 tablespoon oil

Place first 5 ingredients in processor bowl and process for a few seconds until butter is distributed.

In a glass bowl, stir together yeast, water and sugar and allow mixture to stand until yeast is dissolved, about 5 minutes. Add sour cream and milk and stir until blended.

Now, pour yeast mixture into the processor bowl and process for about 40 seconds to 1 minute. (Dough will have formed a ball. If necessary, add a little flour to accomplish this; but not too much. You want the dough soft.)

Place 1 tablespoon oil in a 1-quart souffle dish. Place dough into the bowl and turn it so that the top is nicely covered with oil. Cover bowl with plastic wrap and let it rise in a warm place for about 1 hour or until it has doubled in bulk. Bake in a 350° oven for about 40 minutes or until top is golden brown. Remove from pan and cool on a rack. Yields 1 loaf.

Giant Popovers with Onions, Dill & Cheese

What a lovely accompaniment to a creamed zucchini or cauliflower soup. Serve these with sweet, creamy butter and watch the excitement it generates.

- 3 **eggs**
- 1 **cup flour**
- 1 **cup milk**
- 1/4 **teaspoon salt**
- 1 **tablespoon dried onion flakes**
- 1/2 **teaspoon dried dill weed**

    grated Parmesan cheese

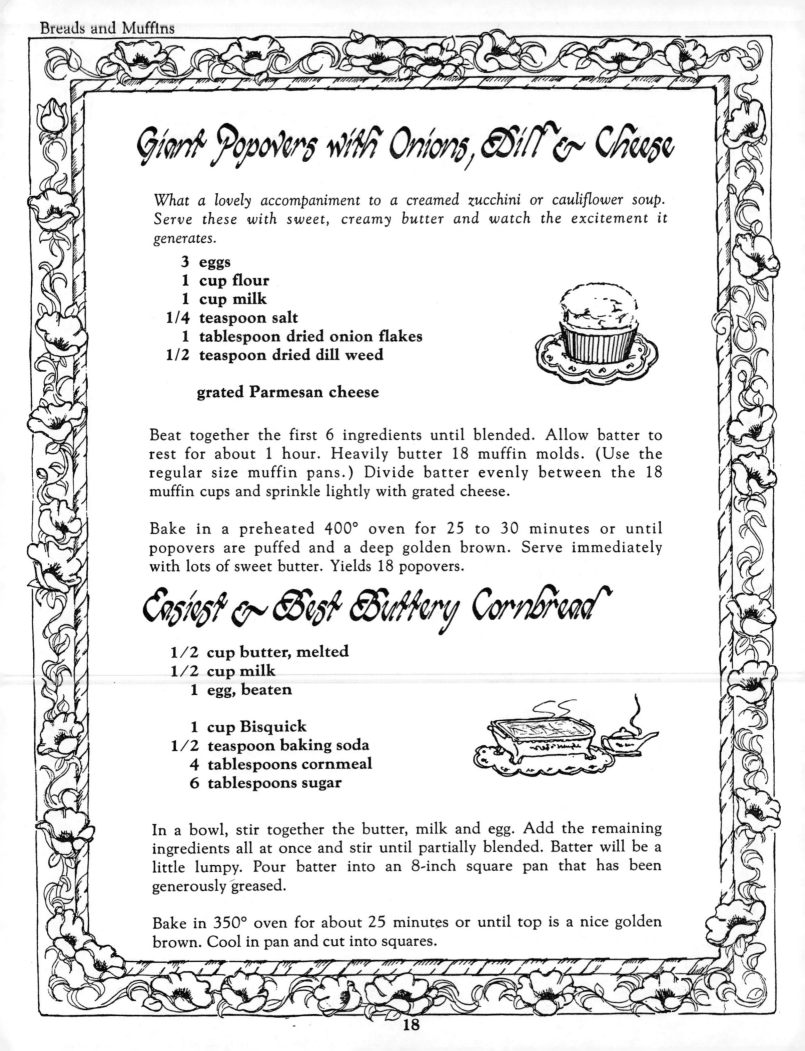

Beat together the first 6 ingredients until blended. Allow batter to rest for about 1 hour. Heavily butter 18 muffin molds. (Use the regular size muffin pans.) Divide batter evenly between the 18 muffin cups and sprinkle lightly with grated cheese.

Bake in a preheated 400° oven for 25 to 30 minutes or until popovers are puffed and a deep golden brown. Serve immediately with lots of sweet butter. Yields 18 popovers.

Easiest & Best Buttery Cornbread

- 1/2 **cup butter, melted**
- 1/2 **cup milk**
- 1 **egg, beaten**

- 1 **cup Bisquick**
- 1/2 **teaspoon baking soda**
- 4 **tablespoons cornmeal**
- 6 **tablespoons sugar**

In a bowl, stir together the butter, milk and egg. Add the remaining ingredients all at once and stir until partially blended. Batter will be a little lumpy. Pour batter into an 8-inch square pan that has been generously greased.

Bake in 350° oven for about 25 minutes or until top is a nice golden brown. Cool in pan and cut into squares.

Monkey Bread with Cheese, Onions & Poppy Seeds

This delicious bread is very easy to prepare and an excellent choice when you are planning a simple meal with soup or salad. It serves in a ring and can even be quite festive for a dinner party.

2   **packages (8 ounces, each) buttermilk refrigerated biscuits. Cut each biscuit into fourths.**
1/2 **cup butter, melted**
1/2 **cup grated Parmesan cheese**
3   **tablespoons onion flakes**
1   **tablespoon poppy seeds**

Line the outside of a 9-inch tube pan with foil to catch any drippings. In a large bowl, place all the ingredients and toss and stir until everything is evenly coated.

Place mixture into prepared pan. Bake in a 375° oven for about 25 minutes or until top is golden brown. Remove from pan and serve warm. Serve it in a ring and let everyone pull off a "bouche" (a bite) or two. Serves 8.

Note: - Bread can be made earlier in the day and covered with foil. Heat in a 350°oven for about 10 minutes or until heated through. Remove foil and serve.

Monkey Bread with Cheese, Dill & Herbs

Follow the recipe for the above bread with the following considerations: delete poppy seeds and add 1 tablespoon dill weed or oregano or thyme. Use the herb that best harmonizes with your meal.

Holiday Spiced Corn Muffins

If you are thinking of serving corn muffins with your turkey this year, try these moist, fragrant (and delicious) spicy muffins. They whip up in seconds and will disappear before your very eyes.

1/2 cup butter, melted
1/3 cup sour cream
1/3 cup milk
  1 egg

  1 cup Bisquick
1/2 teaspoon baking soda
  4 tablespoons cornmeal
  6 tablespoons sugar
  1 teaspoon pumpkin pie spice

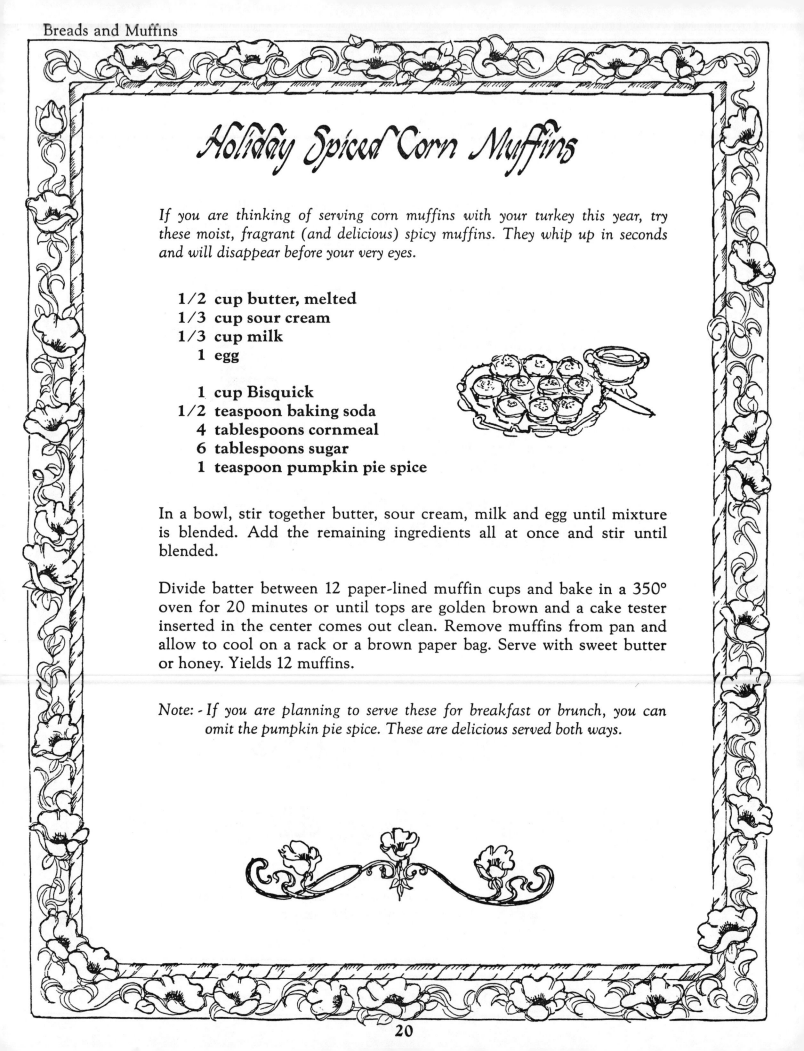

In a bowl, stir together butter, sour cream, milk and egg until mixture is blended. Add the remaining ingredients all at once and stir until blended.

Divide batter between 12 paper-lined muffin cups and bake in a 350° oven for 20 minutes or until tops are golden brown and a cake tester inserted in the center comes out clean. Remove muffins from pan and allow to cool on a rack or a brown paper bag. Serve with sweet butter or honey. Yields 12 muffins.

Note: - If you are planning to serve these for breakfast or brunch, you can omit the pumpkin pie spice. These are delicious served both ways.

Old~Fashioned Chewy Pretzels with Onions, Sesame & Cheese

1 1/2 cups warm water (105°)
   1 envelope dry yeast
   2 teaspoons sugar

   4 cups flour
3/4 teaspoon salt
   1 tablespoon sesame seeds
   1 tablespoon dried onion flakes

   1 egg beaten
   grated Parmesan cheese

Place water, yeast, and sugar in the large bowl of an electric mixer and stir. When yeast has softened, add 3 1/2 cups flour and salt and beat mixture for 5 minutes. Beat in the remaining flour, sesame seeds and onion flakes until blended.

Divide dough into 16 pieces. Roll each piece out, between your hands, to form a 1/4-inch thick rope. Shape this into a pretzel, pinch ends down, and place, seam-side down on a lightly greased cookie sheet. Brush tops with beaten egg and sprinkle with grated Parmesan cheese. Bake in a 400° oven for about 15 minutes or until lightly browned. Yields 16 pretzels.

Note: - *By following the above instructions, you will eliminate kneading. However, if you own a mixer with a dough hook, then add the flour all at once and knead for about 5 minutes. Please note that dough does not have to rest or rise.*

Country Kitchen Gingerbread with Raisins

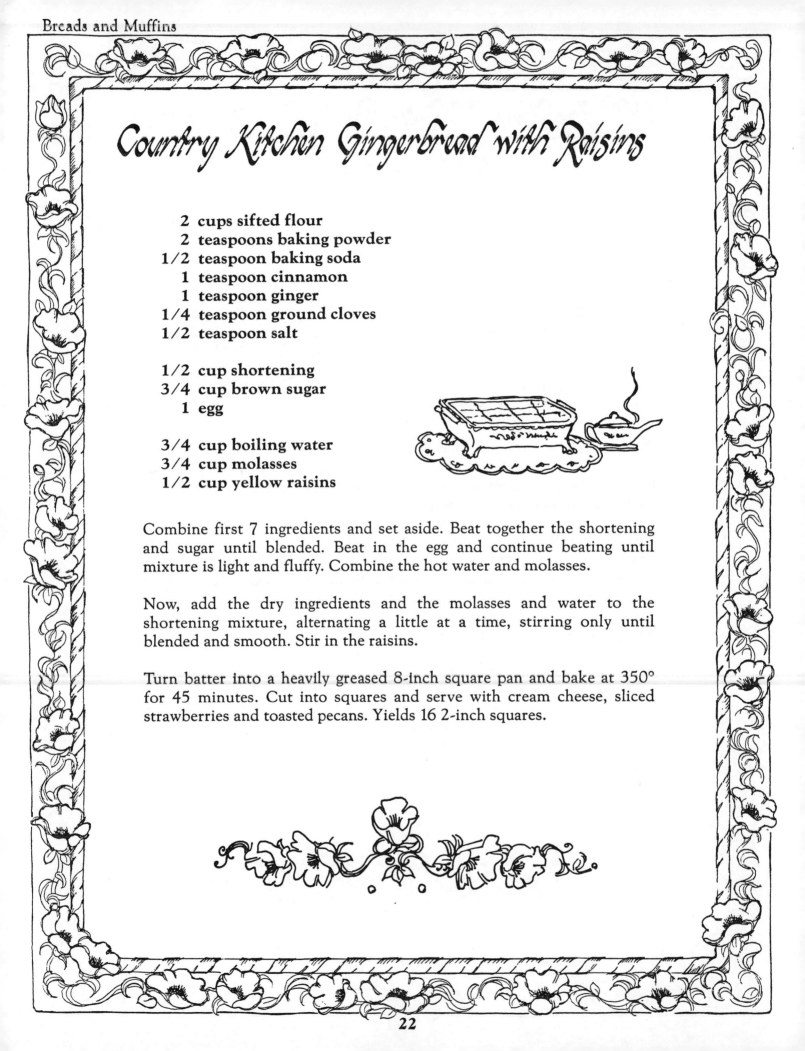

          2 cups sifted flour
          2 teaspoons baking powder
     1/2 teaspoon baking soda
          1 teaspoon cinnamon
          1 teaspoon ginger
     1/4 teaspoon ground cloves
     1/2 teaspoon salt

     1/2 cup shortening
     3/4 cup brown sugar
          1 egg

     3/4 cup boiling water
     3/4 cup molasses
     1/2 cup yellow raisins

Combine first 7 ingredients and set aside. Beat together the shortening and sugar until blended. Beat in the egg and continue beating until mixture is light and fluffy. Combine the hot water and molasses.

Now, add the dry ingredients and the molasses and water to the shortening mixture, alternating a little at a time, stirring only until blended and smooth. Stir in the raisins.

Turn batter into a heavily greased 8-inch square pan and bake at 350° for 45 minutes. Cut into squares and serve with cream cheese, sliced strawberries and toasted pecans. Yields 16 2-inch squares.

Casseroles

Chili Con Carne with Beans

3/4 pound onions, chopped
1 teaspoon garlic chips
2 pounds coarsely ground lean beef (using half pork
    is very good)
salt to taste

1 can (1 pound 12 ounces) crushed tomatoes. In
    absence of these, you can substitute whole
    tomatoes and chop them in a blender or food
    processor.
1 can (6 ounces) tomato paste
1 can (10 1/2 ounces) beef broth
3 to 4 tablespoons Spice Islands Chili Con Carne
    Seasoning*
1 teaspoon cumin
1 teaspoon sugar
1 can (1 pound) red kidney beans, drained
    and mashed

In a Dutch oven, saute onions, garlic and beef together until the meat loses its pinkness. Add the remaining ingredients, stir and simmer mixture uncovered for about 1 hour. Chili should be quite thick. If it seems too thick, add a little additional broth. Serve with rice and a sprinkling of chopped green onions. Serves 8.

Note: - *If you cannot find the Chili Con Carne Seasoning then use 3 tablespoons chili powder with 1/2 teaspoon oregano. Increase the cumin to 1 1/2 teaspoons.
- If you desire, you can use 2 cans of red kidney beans.
- As with most chilis, adjust seasonings about half way through cooking.

Chili of Champions

I like chili that is spicy, just a little hot and as thick as country gravy. When we were young, it was always served with beans and pink rice. The meat was usually chuck, cut into 1/2-inch cubes and cooked until it practically fell apart. One thing for certain, it sparkled my taste for chili, and I never tire of trying and tasting new and different styles of preparing this dish. This chili is very traditional and I hope you enjoy it.

- 2 **pounds coarsely ground beef**
- 2 **pounds coarsely ground pork**
- 2 **tablespoons oil**

- 3 **onions, chopped**
- 4 **cloves garlic, minced**

- 1 **can (28 ounces) crushed tomatoes in tomato puree**
- 1 **can (6 ounces) tomato paste**
- 1 **can (7 ounces) diced green chiles**
- 4 **to 6 tablespoons chili powder**
- 2 **teaspoons sugar**
- 1 **teaspoon oregano**
- 1 **teaspoon cumin**
  salt to taste

2 1/2 **cups grated Cheddar cheese**

In a skillet, saute beef and pork in oil until meat loses its pinkness. Place drained meat in a Dutch oven casserole. In same skillet, saute onions and garlic, until onions become transparent. Place onion mixture in Dutch oven, along with the tomatoes, tomato puree, chiles and seasonings.

Simmer mixture partially covered, for about 45 minutes. Mixture should be very thick. Place chili in a heated chafing dish and top with grated cheese. Wait till cheese melts and serve with corn chips or tortilla chips. Yields about 2 quarts chili.

Note: - You can add beans to this chili if that is your preference. You can add 1 or 2 cans (15 ounces, each) of either kidney beans or pinto beans or half of each. Rinse the beans and drain them. Add the drained beans to the Dutch oven at the same time with the canned tomatoes.
- This can be frozen.

Chicken & Wild Rice with Almonds

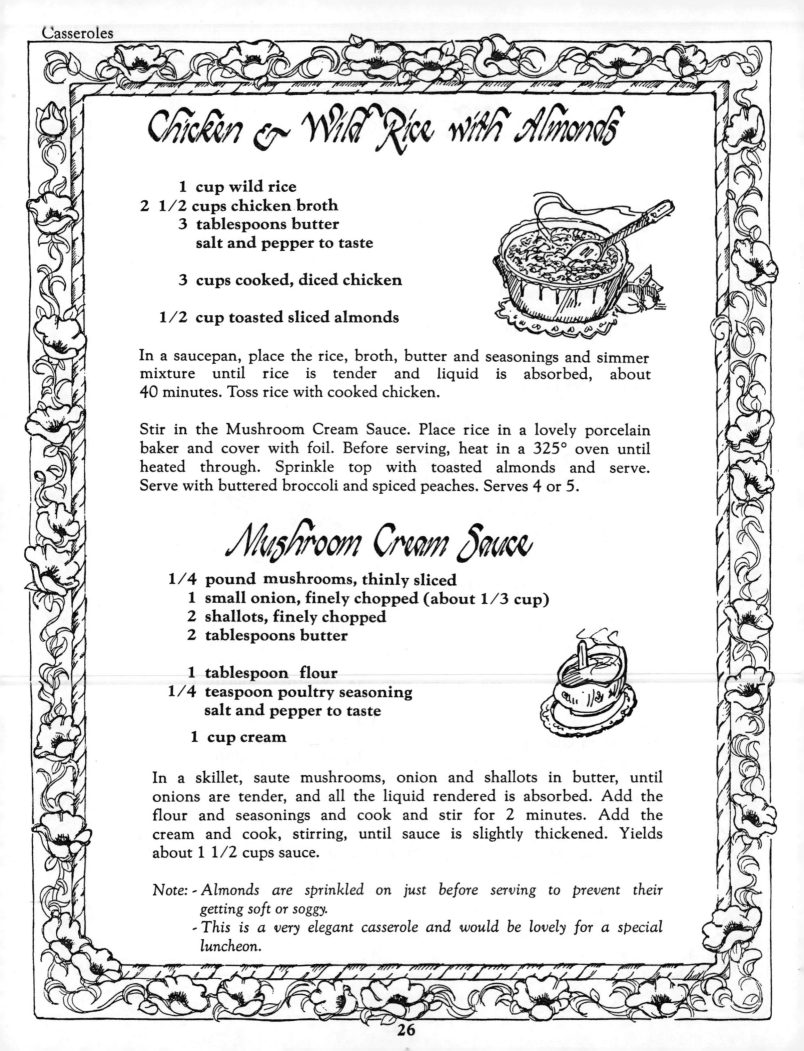

> 1 cup wild rice
> 2 1/2 cups chicken broth
> 3 tablespoons butter
> salt and pepper to taste
>
> 3 cups cooked, diced chicken
>
> 1/2 cup toasted sliced almonds

In a saucepan, place the rice, broth, butter and seasonings and simmer mixture until rice is tender and liquid is absorbed, about 40 minutes. Toss rice with cooked chicken.

Stir in the Mushroom Cream Sauce. Place rice in a lovely porcelain baker and cover with foil. Before serving, heat in a 325° oven until heated through. Sprinkle top with toasted almonds and serve. Serve with buttered broccoli and spiced peaches. Serves 4 or 5.

Mushroom Cream Sauce

> 1/4 pound mushrooms, thinly sliced
> 1 small onion, finely chopped (about 1/3 cup)
> 2 shallots, finely chopped
> 2 tablespoons butter
>
> 1 tablespoon flour
> 1/4 teaspoon poultry seasoning
> salt and pepper to taste
>
> 1 cup cream

In a skillet, saute mushrooms, onion and shallots in butter, until onions are tender, and all the liquid rendered is absorbed. Add the flour and seasonings and cook and stir for 2 minutes. Add the cream and cook, stirring, until sauce is slightly thickened. Yields about 1 1/2 cups sauce.

Note: - *Almonds are sprinkled on just before serving to prevent their getting soft or soggy.*
- *This is a very elegant casserole and would be lovely for a special luncheon.*

Pasta Primavera with Fresh Tomatoes & Mozzarella Cheese

1 pound thin spaghetti, cooked until just tender
1/2 cup (1 stick) butter, melted
salt and pepper to taste

6 tomatoes, peeled and finely chopped,
(about 2 pounds)
2 cups chopped green onions
4 cloves garlic, minced
4 tablespoons chopped parsley
1/4 teaspoon red pepper flakes
1/4 teaspoon oregano

4 cups grated Mozzarella cheese (1 pound)
1/2 cup grated Parmesan cheese

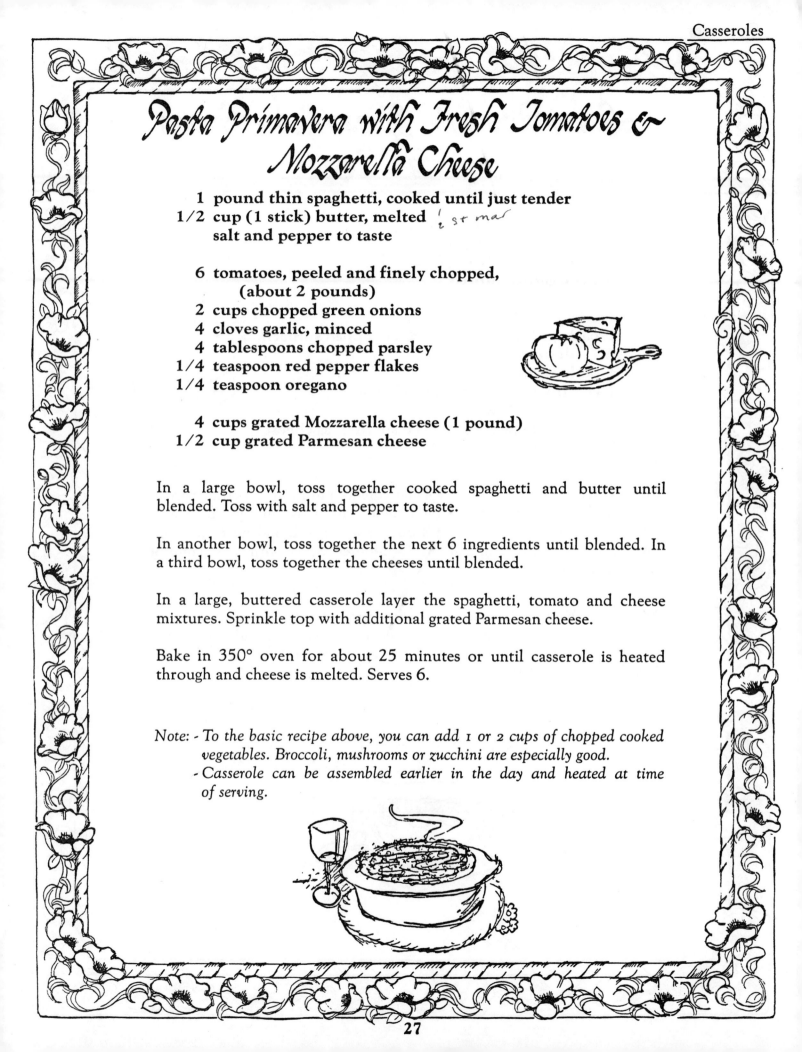

In a large bowl, toss together cooked spaghetti and butter until blended. Toss with salt and pepper to taste.

In another bowl, toss together the next 6 ingredients until blended. In a third bowl, toss together the cheeses until blended.

In a large, buttered casserole layer the spaghetti, tomato and cheese mixtures. Sprinkle top with additional grated Parmesan cheese.

Bake in 350° oven for about 25 minutes or until casserole is heated through and cheese is melted. Serves 6.

Note: - To the basic recipe above, you can add 1 or 2 cups of chopped cooked vegetables. Broccoli, mushrooms or zucchini are especially good.
- Casserole can be assembled earlier in the day and heated at time of serving.

Lemon Rice with Spinach, Mushrooms & Feta Cheese

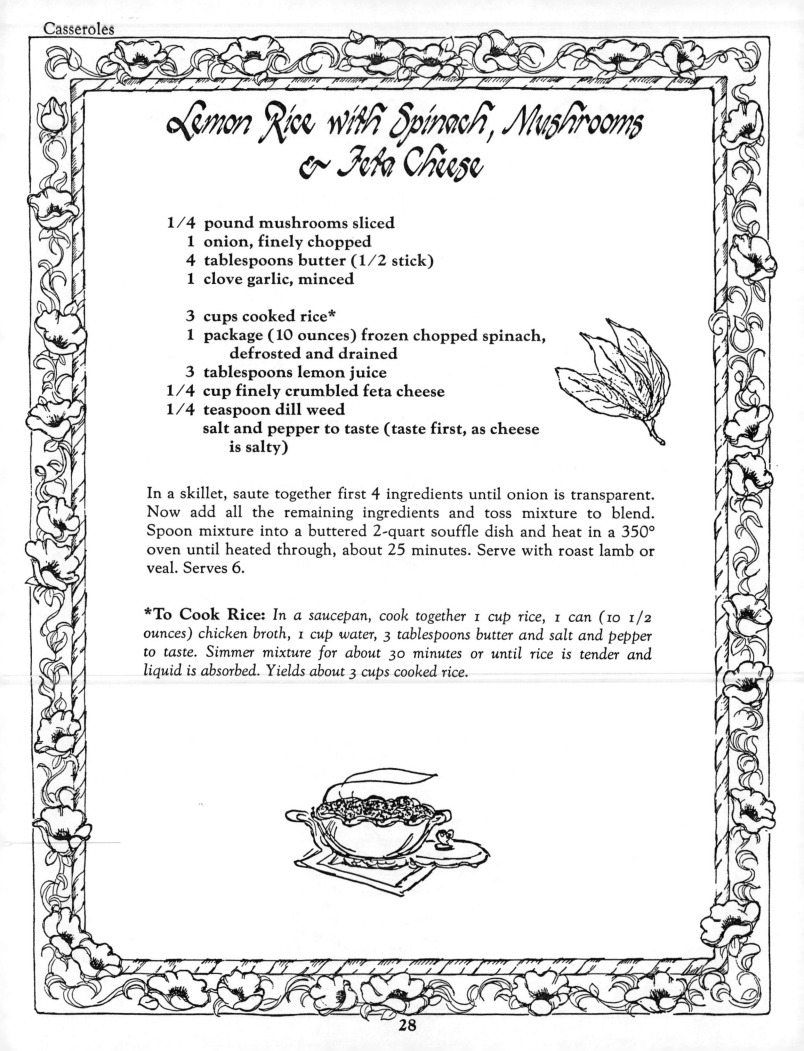

1/4 pound mushrooms sliced
1 onion, finely chopped
4 tablespoons butter (1/2 stick)
1 clove garlic, minced

3 cups cooked rice*
1 package (10 ounces) frozen chopped spinach,
   defrosted and drained
3 tablespoons lemon juice
1/4 cup finely crumbled feta cheese
1/4 teaspoon dill weed
   salt and pepper to taste (taste first, as cheese
      is salty)

In a skillet, saute together first 4 ingredients until onion is transparent. Now add all the remaining ingredients and toss mixture to blend. Spoon mixture into a buttered 2-quart souffle dish and heat in a 350° oven until heated through, about 25 minutes. Serve with roast lamb or veal. Serves 6.

*To Cook Rice: *In a saucepan, cook together 1 cup rice, 1 can (10 1/2 ounces) chicken broth, 1 cup water, 3 tablespoons butter and salt and pepper to taste. Simmer mixture for about 30 minutes or until rice is tender and liquid is absorbed. Yields about 3 cups cooked rice.*

Sweet & Sour Stuffed Cabbage with Raisin & Ginger Snap Sauce

This is a delicious family dish, full of flavor and deep solid character. Gravy is luscious and just right for dipping.

1 large head of cabbage (about 2 pounds)

1 pound ground beef
1 small onion, grated (about 1/2 cup)
1 cup raw rice
1 egg
1/3 cup beef broth
2 pinches garlic powder
salt and pepper to taste

2 ginger snap cookies, crushed into crumbs

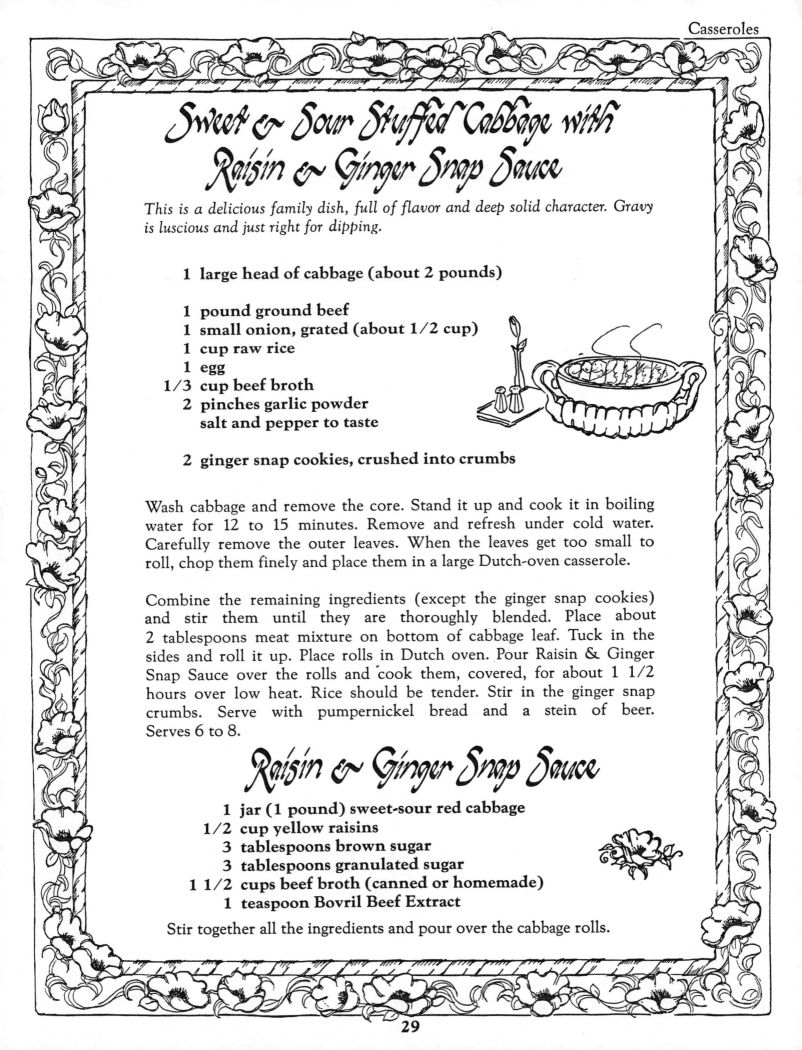

Wash cabbage and remove the core. Stand it up and cook it in boiling water for 12 to 15 minutes. Remove and refresh under cold water. Carefully remove the outer leaves. When the leaves get too small to roll, chop them finely and place them in a large Dutch-oven casserole.

Combine the remaining ingredients (except the ginger snap cookies) and stir them until they are thoroughly blended. Place about 2 tablespoons meat mixture on bottom of cabbage leaf. Tuck in the sides and roll it up. Place rolls in Dutch oven. Pour Raisin & Ginger Snap Sauce over the rolls and cook them, covered, for about 1 1/2 hours over low heat. Rice should be tender. Stir in the ginger snap crumbs. Serve with pumpernickel bread and a stein of beer. Serves 6 to 8.

Raisin & Ginger Snap Sauce

1 jar (1 pound) sweet-sour red cabbage
1/2 cup yellow raisins
3 tablespoons brown sugar
3 tablespoons granulated sugar
1 1/2 cups beef broth (canned or homemade)
1 teaspoon Bovril Beef Extract

Stir together all the ingredients and pour over the cabbage rolls.

Casserole of Fettuccine Verde with Chicken, Tomatoes & Chili

1/4 cup butter
  1 onion, chopped
  1 can (4 ounces) diced chiles
  1 can (1 pound) stewed tomatoes, drained and
     chopped

  3 cups diced, cooked chicken
    salt and pepper to taste

  8 ounces green noodles, cooked until tender
  2 tablespoons butter
1/4 cup cream
1/2 cup grated Parmesan cheese

In a skillet, saute onion in butter until onion is transparent. Add the chiles and tomatoes and simmer mixture for 10 minutes. Add the chicken and seasonings.

In a large bowl, toss the cooked noodles with the butter, cream and grated cheese. Combine noodles with the tomato mixture and toss until well mixed. Place mixture in a lovely heat and serve casserole and heat it in a 350° oven until piping hot. Sprinkle top with additional grated cheese if desired. Serves 6.

Note: - Casserole can be made earlier in the day and refrigerated. Bring to room temperature and reheat in a 350° oven.
    - Do not freeze.

We enjoyed the finest stuffed tomatoes at the Ristorante Panzeroni on the Piazza Navonna in Rome. They used the really large beefsteak tomatoes and filled them quite simply with rice, tomatoes, garlic and herbs. Oh, they were divine. I asked the chef, Sr. Pattanzi-Memmo if he would please share his recipe...which he did, in Italian and with much pleasure. He could not communicate the exact amounts of the ingredients, (I speak no Italian and he spoke no English) but with gestures and pointing, we managed quite well. Chef Pattanzi uses raw rice (riso crudo) for his recipe, garlic, basil, oil and parsley. The proportions I have worked out tasted very close to the original. So enjoy my adaptation of

Pomodōri Con Riso Panzerone
(Tomatoes Stuffed with Rice)

To Prepare the Tomatoes:
8 medium sized tomatoes (about 2 pounds), cut a 3/4-inch slice from the top and scoop out the centers with a grapefruit knife and a teaspoon. Reserve the tomato pulp. Sprinkle the tomatoes with salt and invert to drain. When ready to stuff, brush tomatoes, inside and out, lightly with oil.

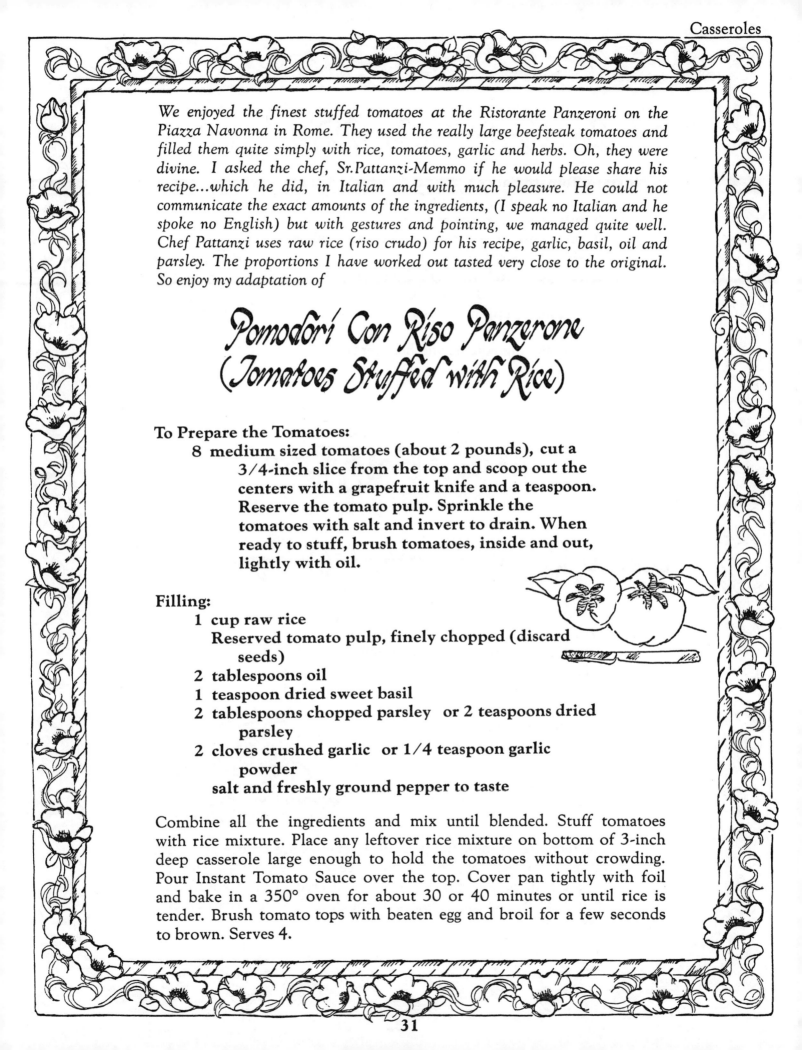

Filling:
1 cup raw rice
Reserved tomato pulp, finely chopped (discard seeds)
2 tablespoons oil
1 teaspoon dried sweet basil
2 tablespoons chopped parsley or 2 teaspoons dried parsley
2 cloves crushed garlic or 1/4 teaspoon garlic powder
salt and freshly ground pepper to taste

Combine all the ingredients and mix until blended. Stuff tomatoes with rice mixture. Place any leftover rice mixture on bottom of 3-inch deep casserole large enough to hold the tomatoes without crowding. Pour Instant Tomato Sauce over the top. Cover pan tightly with foil and bake in a 350° oven for about 30 or 40 minutes or until rice is tender. Brush tomato tops with beaten egg and broil for a few seconds to brown. Serves 4.

Tomatoes Stuffed with Rice (continued)

Instant Tomato Sauce:
- 1 can (1 pound) stewed tomatoes, chopped
- 3 tablespoons tomato paste
- 2 teaspoons instant minced onion flakes
- 2 teaspoons sugar
- 1/2 teaspoon Italian Herb Seasoning
- 1 teaspoon parsley flakes
- salt and pepper to taste

Combine all the ingredients and heat through.

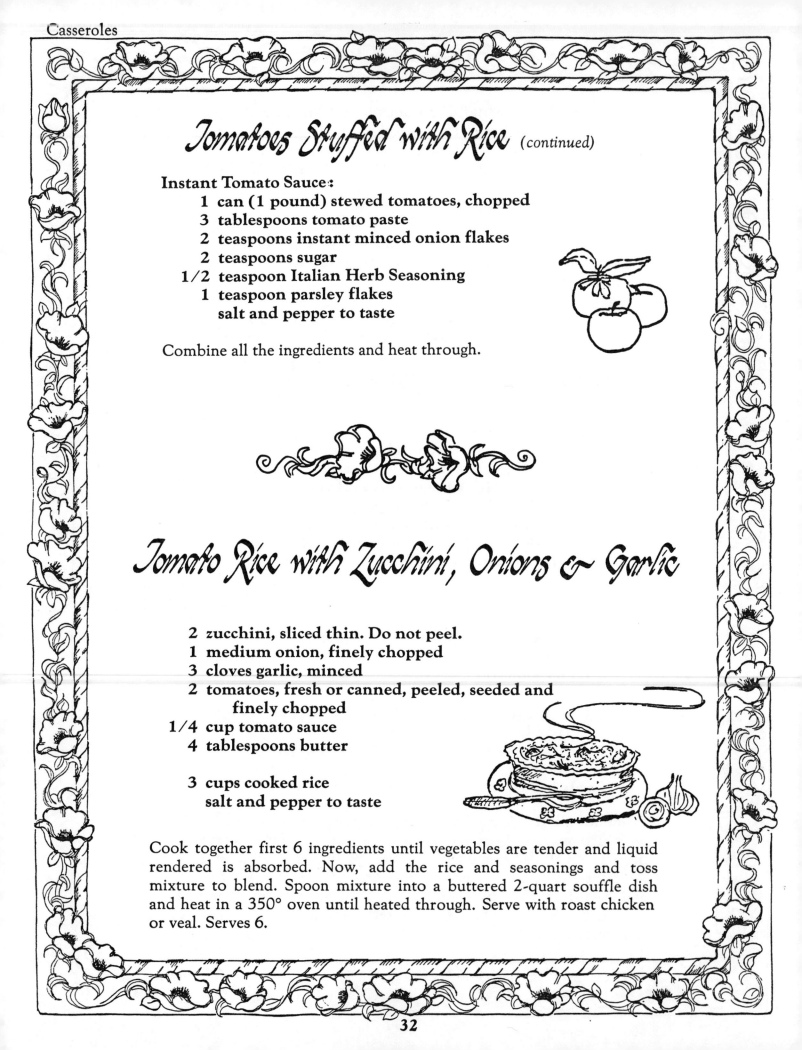

Tomato Rice with Zucchini, Onions & Garlic

- 2 zucchini, sliced thin. Do not peel.
- 1 medium onion, finely chopped
- 3 cloves garlic, minced
- 2 tomatoes, fresh or canned, peeled, seeded and finely chopped
- 1/4 cup tomato sauce
- 4 tablespoons butter

- 3 cups cooked rice
- salt and pepper to taste

Cook together first 6 ingredients until vegetables are tender and liquid rendered is absorbed. Now, add the rice and seasonings and toss mixture to blend. Spoon mixture into a buttered 2-quart souffle dish and heat in a 350° oven until heated through. Serve with roast chicken or veal. Serves 6.

Spinach & Beef Dumplings with Mushroom, Onion Cream Sauce

- 1 package (10 ounces) frozen chopped spinach, defrosted and drained
- 1 pound lean ground beef
- 1/2 cup fresh bread crumbs
- 1 small onion, grated (or very finely chopped in food processor)
- 2 eggs
- 4 tablespoons cracker crumbs
  salt and pepper to taste
  flour

Combine the first 7 ingredients together and stir until they are thoroughly blended. Shape mixture into 1-inch balls. Roll them in flour and flatten them gently to about 1/2-inch thickness.

Saute dumplings in butter until browned on both sides. Place dumplings in a porcelain casserole and pour Mushroom Onion Cream Sauce over the top. Heat in a 350° oven until heated through. Serve with brown rice. Serves 6.

Mushroom Onion Cream Sauce

- 1/2 pound mushrooms, thinly sliced
- 1 onion, finely chopped
- 2 shallots, finely chopped
- 1 clove garlic, minced
- 4 tablespoons butter

- 1/4 cup dry white wine

- 2 tablespoons flour
- 1 can (10 1/2 ounces) chicken broth
- 1 teaspoon Bovril, Beef Extract
- 3/4 cup cream
  salt and pepper to taste

Saute mushrooms, onion, shallots and garlic in butter until onions are soft. Add wine and cook until wine is almost evaporated. Add flour and cook for 2 minutes, stirring and turning. Add the remaining ingredients and cook, stirring, until sauce is thickened.

Rice Casserole with Shrimp, Tomatoes & Cheese

This is an excellent casserole to prepare some evening when you are running late. Add a green salad or some buttered vegetables and no one will ever know.

- 2 onions, chopped (can use the frozen onions)
- 2 cloves garlic, finely minced
- 3 tablespoons butter

- 1 cup rice

- 1 can (10 1/2 ounces) chicken broth, diluted
    with 1/4 cup water

- 2 tomatoes, peeled, seeded and chopped,
    (fresh or canned)

  salt and pepper to taste
  pinch of saffron threads

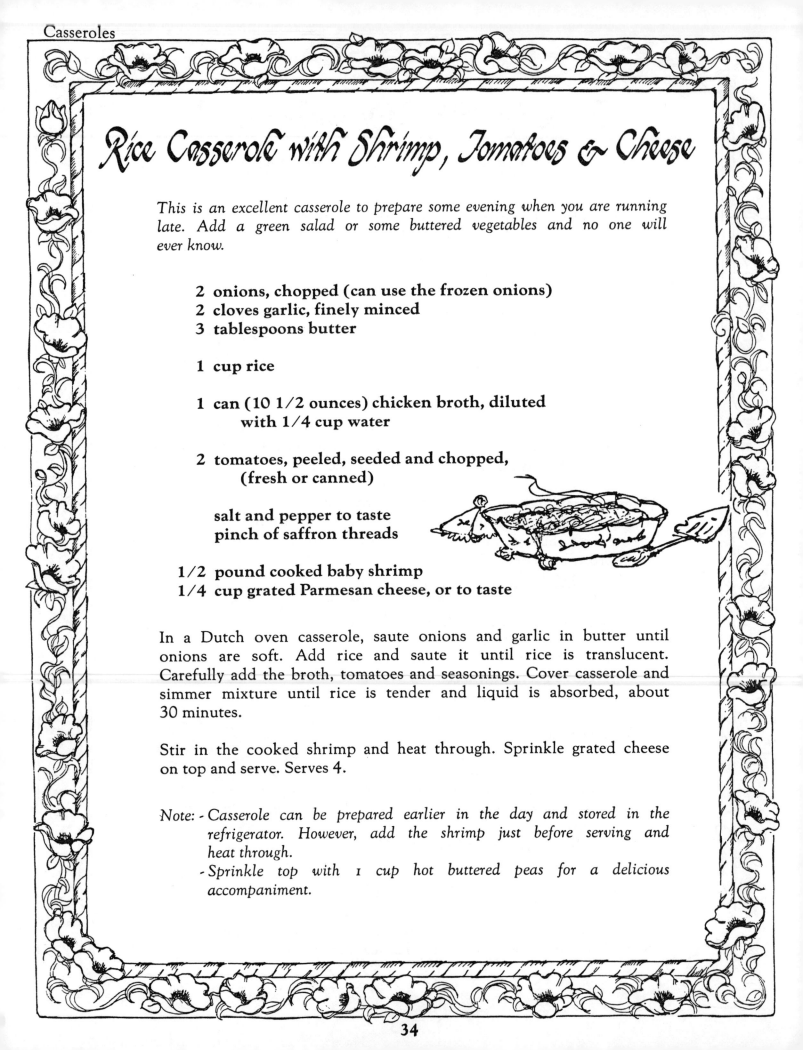

- 1/2 pound cooked baby shrimp
- 1/4 cup grated Parmesan cheese, or to taste

In a Dutch oven casserole, saute onions and garlic in butter until onions are soft. Add rice and saute it until rice is translucent. Carefully add the broth, tomatoes and seasonings. Cover casserole and simmer mixture until rice is tender and liquid is absorbed, about 30 minutes.

Stir in the cooked shrimp and heat through. Sprinkle grated cheese on top and serve. Serves 4.

Note: - Casserole can be prepared earlier in the day and stored in the refrigerator. However, add the shrimp just before serving and heat through.
- Sprinkle top with 1 cup hot buttered peas for a delicious accompaniment.

Easiest & Best New Orleans Jambalaya

This is not the traditional way to prepare this dish. It is usually made in one pan, but then the shrimp can over cook and the rice can get gummy. This process makes it totally foolproof.

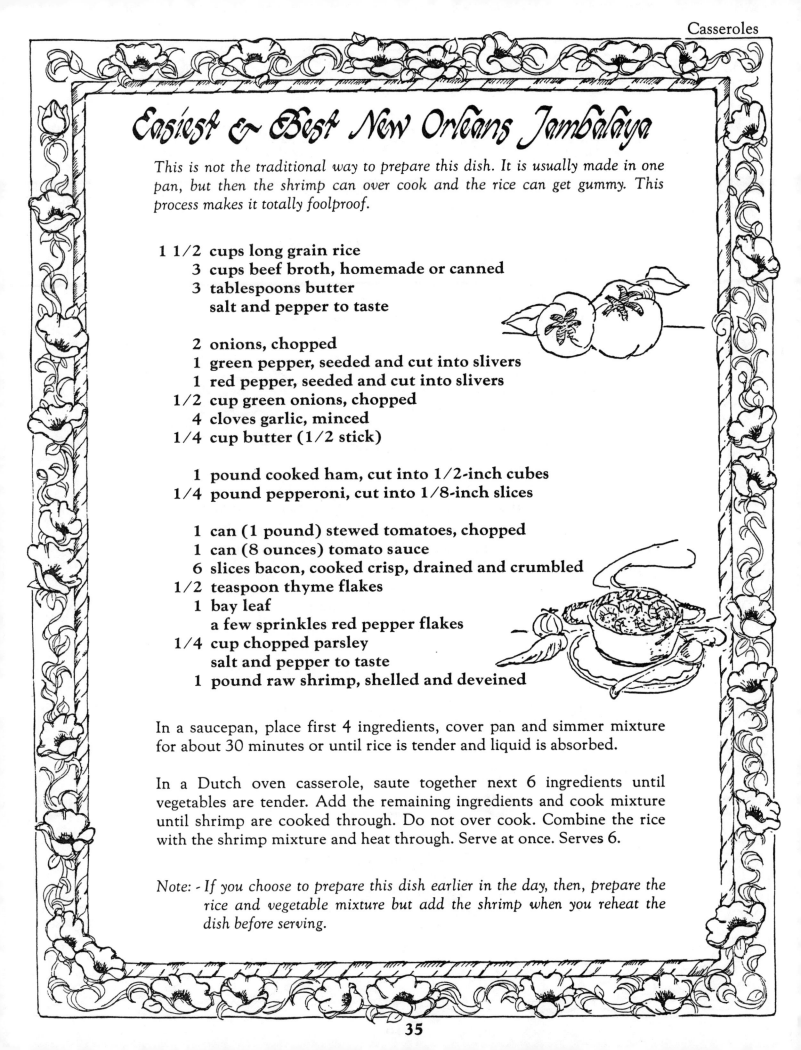

1 1/2 cups long grain rice
   3 cups beef broth, homemade or canned
   3 tablespoons butter
    salt and pepper to taste

   2 onions, chopped
   1 green pepper, seeded and cut into slivers
   1 red pepper, seeded and cut into slivers
1/2 cup green onions, chopped
   4 cloves garlic, minced
1/4 cup butter (1/2 stick)

   1 pound cooked ham, cut into 1/2-inch cubes
1/4 pound pepperoni, cut into 1/8-inch slices

   1 can (1 pound) stewed tomatoes, chopped
   1 can (8 ounces) tomato sauce
   6 slices bacon, cooked crisp, drained and crumbled
1/2 teaspoon thyme flakes
   1 bay leaf
    a few sprinkles red pepper flakes
1/4 cup chopped parsley
    salt and pepper to taste
   1 pound raw shrimp, shelled and deveined

In a saucepan, place first 4 ingredients, cover pan and simmer mixture for about 30 minutes or until rice is tender and liquid is absorbed.

In a Dutch oven casserole, saute together next 6 ingredients until vegetables are tender. Add the remaining ingredients and cook mixture until shrimp are cooked through. Do not over cook. Combine the rice with the shrimp mixture and heat through. Serve at once. Serves 6.

Note: - If you choose to prepare this dish earlier in the day, then, prepare the rice and vegetable mixture but add the shrimp when you reheat the dish before serving.

Green Noodles with Chicken, Tomatoes & Cheese

1/2 cup melted butter
1 package (8 ounces) green noodles, cooked
    and drained

1/2 cup green onions, chopped
1 can (1 pound) stewed tomatoes, drained
    and chopped
3 cups diced, cooked chicken
1 cup sour cream
1 cup grated Swiss cheese
1/2 cup grated Parmesan cheese
2 beaten eggs
1 clove garlic, put through a press
    salt and pepper to taste

Toss cooked noodles with melted butter in a 9x13-inch baking pan. Combine the remaining ingredients and toss until thoroughly blended. Combine chicken mixture with the noodles and toss until blended. Sprinkle top with extra Parmesan.

Bake casserole in a 350° oven for about 35 minutes or until piping hot and cheeses are melted. Serves 6.

Note: - This is a particularly beautiful casserole with the green noodles, red tomatoes, dark green onions and flecks of chicken and cheese.
- While entire dish can be assembled earlier in the day, bake it shortly before serving.

Zucchini Lasagna with Mushrooms, Tomatoes & Mozzarella Cheese

9 green lasagna noodles, cooked until tender and drained. Toss in 2 or 3 tablespoons oil.

1 1/2 cups ricotta cheese
1 package (8 ounces) cream cheese
3/4 pound Mozzarella cheese, grated
3 eggs
3 tablespoons chopped parsley
1/2 teaspoon Italian Herb Seasoning
1/4 teaspoon onion powder
1/2 cup grated Parmesan cheese
salt and pepper to taste

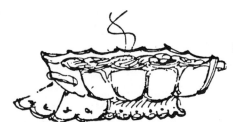

In a 9x13-inch pan, place 3 lasagna noodles. Beat together the remaining ingredients until blended. Place half the cheese over the noodles. Top the cheese with 1/3 of the Zucchini Tomato Sauce. Place another 3 noodles over the sauce and repeat 1st layer. Top with the remaining 3 noodles and remaining sauce. Bake in a 350° oven for about 40 to 50 minutes or until piping hot. Serves 8.

Zucchini Tomato Sauce

1 pound zucchini, cleaned and sliced. Do not peel.
1/2 pound mushrooms, thinly sliced
2 onions, finely chopped
2 cloves garlic, minced
3 tablespoons butter

1 can (1 pound 12 ounces) crushed tomatoes in tomato puree
2 tablespoons sugar
2 tablespoons chopped parsley
1 teaspoon Italian Herb Seasoning
1/4 teaspoon hot pepper flakes
salt and pepper to taste

In a Dutch oven, saute together zucchini, mushrooms, onions and garlic in butter until vegetables are tender. Add the remaining ingredients and simmer sauce for 10 minutes.

Cassoulet of Zucchini & Rice with Mushrooms, Onions & Cheese

    1 pound zucchini, cleaned and sliced. Do not peel.
1/2 cup green onions, finely chopped
1/2 pound mushrooms, thinly sliced
    2 cloves garlic, minced
    4 tablespoons butter

    2 tomatoes, peeled, seeded and chopped, fresh
        or canned
    2 cups grated Monterey Jack cheese
    3 eggs, beaten
    1 can (2 ounces) French Fried Onions
        salt and pepper to taste
    2 cups cooked rice

In a large skillet, saute together zucchini, green onions, mushrooms and garlic in butter until vegetables are tender. Spoon mixture into a large bowl and stir in the remaining ingredients until blended. Spread mixture evenly in a lovely oval baker and bake at 350° for about 40 minutes or until casserole is set and top is golden brown.

Serve with fresh fruit or a green salad. Serves 4 to 5.

Spinach & Potato Frittata with Cheese & Chives

1 package (10 ounces) frozen chopped spinach,
    defrosted and drained
1 can (1 pound) sliced boiled potatoes, drained and
    chopped
1/4 cup chopped chives
2 tablespoons chopped parsley
1/2 teaspoon oregano, or more to taste
1 cup grated Swiss cheese
1/2 cup grated Parmesan cheese
1 1/2 cups cottage cheese
1/2 cup Ritz cracker crumbs
3 eggs, beaten
1/2 cup cream
    salt and pepper to taste

Combine all the ingredients in a bowl and stir until thoroughly mixed. Place mixture into a very heavily buttered 9x13-inch pan (use about 3 tablespoons butter) and spread to even.

Bake in 350° oven for 50 minutes or until top is golden brown and eggs are set. Cut into squares and serve with spiced peaches or spiced apricots. Serves 8.

Spinach & Rice Casserole with Onions & Cheese

1 package (10 ounces) frozen chopped spinach,
  defrosted and drained
2 cups cooked rice
2 cups cottage cheese
3/4 cup grated Parmesan cheese
2 eggs
1/2 cup finely chopped green onions

2 cloves garlic, minced
4 tablespoons butter
  salt and pepper to taste

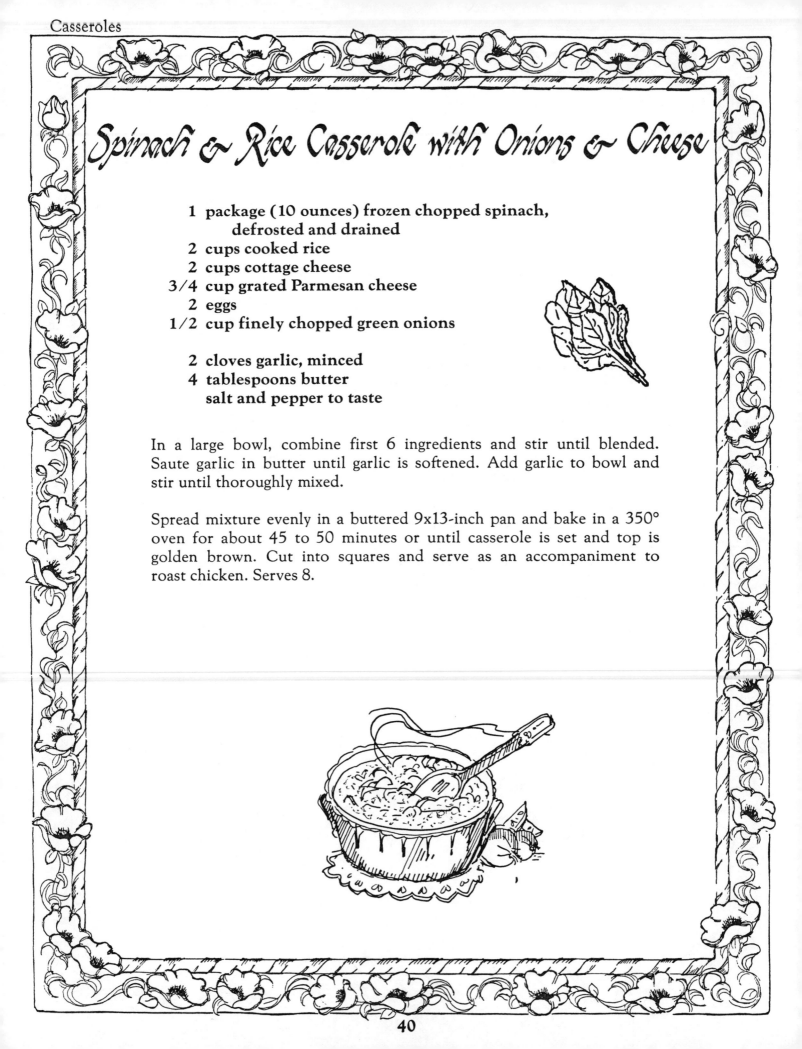

In a large bowl, combine first 6 ingredients and stir until blended. Saute garlic in butter until garlic is softened. Add garlic to bowl and stir until thoroughly mixed.

Spread mixture evenly in a buttered 9x13-inch pan and bake in a 350° oven for about 45 to 50 minutes or until casserole is set and top is golden brown. Cut into squares and serve as an accompaniment to roast chicken. Serves 8.

Noodle & Cottage Cheese Casserole with Onions & Parmesan

     1 package (8 ounces) medium noodles, cooked
        and drained
   1/4 cup melted butter
     1 pint cottage cheese
   1/2 cup grated onion
     4 tablespoons chopped parsley
     1 clove garlic, mashed or put through a press
     3 eggs, beaten
        salt and pepper to taste
   1/2 cup grated Parmesan cheese

Toss noodles in melted butter. Combine the remaining ingredients and stir until blended. Combine noodles and cheese mixture and toss until blended. Place mixture into a 9x13-inch porcelain baker and bake in a 350° oven for about 45 minutes or until top is a golden brown and casserole is nicely puffed. Serves 6.

Pink Rice Pilaf with Tomato & Herbs

 1 1/2 cups long grain rice
     3 tablespoons oil
     1 clove garlic, put through a press

     2 cans (10 1/2 ounces, each) chicken broth
   2/3 cup water
     3 tablespoons tomato sauce
     1 teaspoon parsley flakes
     1 teaspoon dried chives
        salt and pepper to taste

Saute rice in oil with garlic until rice is just beginning to color, stirring all the while. Carefully add the remaining ingredients, cover saucepan and simmer rice until liquid is absorbed and rice is tender, about 30 minutes. Excellent with Chili. Serves 8.

Mushroom, Onion & Tomato Strata with Cheese

1/2 pound mushrooms, thinly sliced
1/4 cup butter

6 slices bread, crusts removed and cubed
1/2 pound Swiss cheese, grated
3 tomatoes, chopped
3 tablespoons dried onion flakes
2 teaspoons chopped basil
6 eggs
2 cups half and half
1/2 cup grated Parmesan cheese
    salt and pepper to taste
6 slices bacon, cooked crisp, drained and crumbled

Saute mushrooms in butter until mushrooms are tender. Toss together the remaining ingredients with the mushrooms until the mixture is evenly mixed. Pour mixture into a buttered 9x13-inch pan and bake in a 350° oven for about 45 minutes or until the top is golden and eggs are set.

Cut into squares and serve with a green salad or stewed fruit. Serves 8.

Candied Yams with Apples, Carrots & Prunes

1 can (1 pound 13 ounces) yams, drained and
    sliced. Place yams in a buttered porcelain baker.

2 apples, peeled, cored and very thinly sliced
16 prunes, pitted
3 carrots, thinly sliced
1 cup orange juice
1/2 cup brown sugar
3 slices of lemon
1/2 cup chopped walnuts

In a saucepan, simmer together apples, prunes, carrots, orange juice, brown sugar and lemon until carrots are tender. Spoon mixture over and around yams. (Remove and discard lemon slices.) Sprinkle top with walnuts and heat in a 350° oven for about 20 minutes or until heated through. Serve warm as a side dish with the grand bird. Serves 8.

Nutcracker Sweet Potato Pudding with Orange & Pecans

1 can sweet potatoes (1 pound, 13 ounces) drained
  and mashed. Sprinkle lightly with salt.

3 eggs, beaten
1/2 cup orange juice concentrate
1/2 cup honey or brown sugar
1/2 cup canned crushed pineapple, drained
1 tablespoon grated orange peel
1 teaspoon grated lemon peel
1 cup vanilla wafer crumbs
2 teaspoons pumpkin pie spice

3/4 cup chopped pecans
6 tablespoons brown sugar
1/2 teaspoon cinnamon

In a bowl, stir together first 9 ingredients until blended. Place mixture into a buttered porcelain baker and sprinkle top with the mixture of pecans, brown sugar and cinnamon.

Bake in a 350° oven for about 40 minutes or until casserole is set. Serve with turkey or chicken. Serves 6 to 8.

Farmhouse Cinnamon Bread Pudding with Apples & Raisins

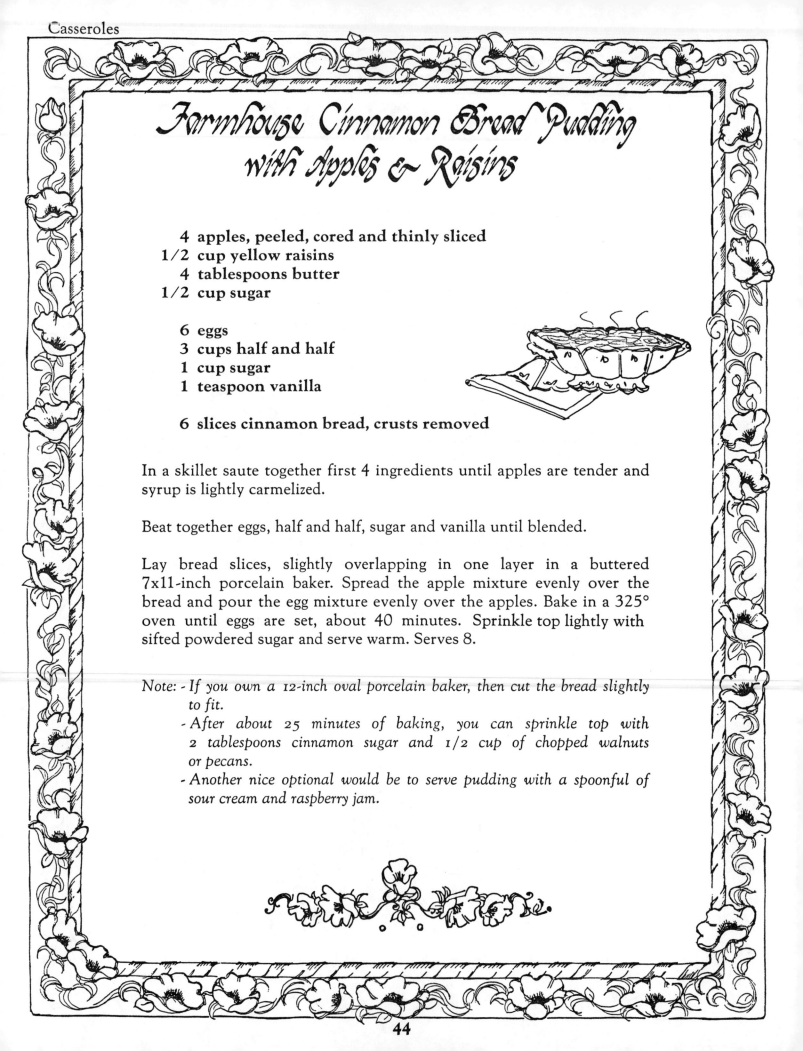

- 4 apples, peeled, cored and thinly sliced
- 1/2 cup yellow raisins
- 4 tablespoons butter
- 1/2 cup sugar

- 6 eggs
- 3 cups half and half
- 1 cup sugar
- 1 teaspoon vanilla

- 6 slices cinnamon bread, crusts removed

In a skillet saute together first 4 ingredients until apples are tender and syrup is lightly carmelized.

Beat together eggs, half and half, sugar and vanilla until blended.

Lay bread slices, slightly overlapping in one layer in a buttered 7x11-inch porcelain baker. Spread the apple mixture evenly over the bread and pour the egg mixture evenly over the apples. Bake in a 325° oven until eggs are set, about 40 minutes. Sprinkle top lightly with sifted powdered sugar and serve warm. Serves 8.

Note: - If you own a 12-inch oval porcelain baker, then cut the bread slightly to fit.
- After about 25 minutes of baking, you can sprinkle top with 2 tablespoons cinnamon sugar and 1/2 cup of chopped walnuts or pecans.
- Another nice optional would be to serve pudding with a spoonful of sour cream and raspberry jam.

Hors D'Oeuvres & Small Entrees

Royal Salmon Mousse with Lemon & Dill Sauce

1 1/2 packages (1 1/2 tablespoons) unflavored gelatin
1/2 cup water

1 pound fresh poached salmon fillets or
    2 cans (7 ounces, each) red salmon, drained
    and flaked
1/2 cup mayonnaise
1/2 cup sour cream
1/3 cup finely chopped green onions
  4 tablespoons lemon juice
1/2 teaspoon dried dill weed
    1 tablespoon prepared horseradish
    salt to taste
    1 cup cream, whipped

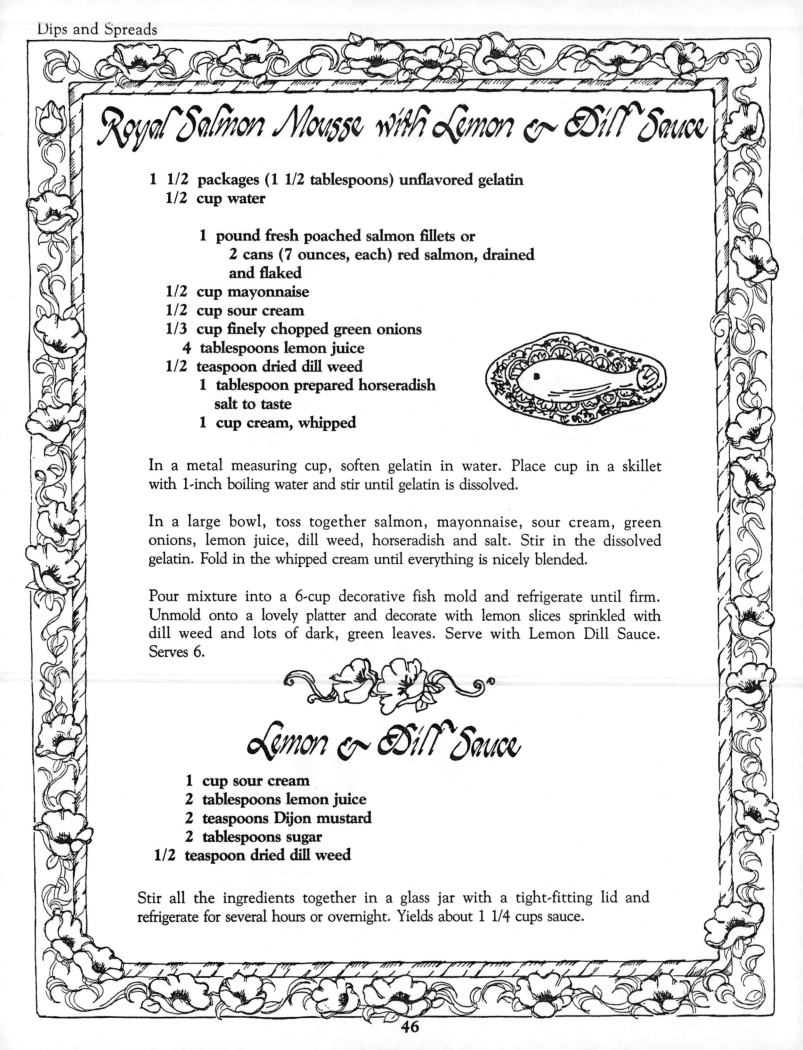

In a metal measuring cup, soften gelatin in water. Place cup in a skillet with 1-inch boiling water and stir until gelatin is dissolved.

In a large bowl, toss together salmon, mayonnaise, sour cream, green onions, lemon juice, dill weed, horseradish and salt. Stir in the dissolved gelatin. Fold in the whipped cream until everything is nicely blended.

Pour mixture into a 6-cup decorative fish mold and refrigerate until firm. Unmold onto a lovely platter and decorate with lemon slices sprinkled with dill weed and lots of dark, green leaves. Serve with Lemon Dill Sauce. Serves 6.

Lemon & Dill Sauce

1 cup sour cream
2 tablespoons lemon juice
2 teaspoons Dijon mustard
2 tablespoons sugar
1/2 teaspoon dried dill weed

Stir all the ingredients together in a glass jar with a tight-fitting lid and refrigerate for several hours or overnight. Yields about 1 1/4 cups sauce.

Gravad Lax with Sweet Mustard Dill Sauce

There are few hors d'oeuvres that one could make that are more exciting and satisfying than this one.

- 4 to 5 pound section of salmon, skinned and boned into 2 fillets
- 1/2 cup coarse (Kosher-style) salt
- 1/3 cup sugar
- 1/4 cup minced fresh dill

In a loaf-size glass pan, stir together salt, sugar and dill until blended. Rub this mixture on both sides of the fillets. Lay the fillets, one over the other, reversing ends. (Place thick end of one fillet over the thin end of the other.) Cover with wax paper and then foil and weigh down with heavy juice or fruit cans.

Refrigerate for 4 to 5 days, basting now and again with the salty juices that have formed. Remove salmon from the pan and scrape off dill. Brush lightly with salad oil to prevent drying. Slice thinly with a very sharp knife and serve with Sweet Mustard Dill Sauce on the side.

Sweet Mustard Dill Sauce:

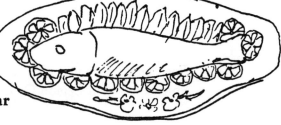

- 1/2 cup Dijon mustard
- 1/2 cup mayonnaise
- 1/4 cup sugar
- 4 tablespoons white wine vinegar
- 1/2 teaspoon dried dill weed

Combine all the ingredients until blended. Store sauce in the refrigerator for several hours to allow flavors to blend. Sauce will last for several weeks in the refrigerator.

Chicken Pate Mousse with Green Onions & Lemon Cream

1/2 **pound boned chicken breast, cut into**
   1-inch pieces
1 **egg**
1 **shallot**
1 **green onion**
1 **clove garlic**
2 **tablespoons butter**
1/2 **cup cream**
   salt and pepper to taste

Combine all the ingredients in a processor bowl and blend until chicken is a paste. Place mixture into an 8x4-inch loaf pan and cover it with foil.

Place pan in a large pan filled with 1-inch of water and bake in a 350° oven for about 40 minutes or until mousse is firm and a knife inserted in center comes out clean. Allow to cool and refrigerate, covered with plastic wrap.

Loosen sides, remove pate on a platter and spread top with Green Onions and Lemon Cream. Serve with delicate soda crackers.

Green Onions & Lemon Cream: Combine 1/4 cup sour cream, 1 teaspoon lemon juice and 1 teaspoon green onion, very finely chopped.

Note: - Pate can be prepared 1 day earlier and stored in the refrigerator. Spread top with Lemon Cream just before serving.

Mousse of Smoked Salmon with Green Onions & Cream

This is a lovely hors d'oeuvre and quite suitable for serving at dinner or brunch. It is delicate and attractive flecked with salmon and green onions.

- 1/4 pound smoked salmon (lox), finely chopped
- 1/3 cup chopped green onions
- 2 tablespoons chopped parsley
- 3 tablespoons lemon juice
- 2 cups sour cream

- 1 cup cream, whipped stiff

- 2 envelopes gelatin (2 tablespoons)
- 1/4 cup water

In a bowl, stir together salmon, green onions, parsley, lemon juice and sour cream. Stir in whipped cream.

Soften gelatin in water and dissolve it over hot water. Working quickly, stir gelatin into salmon mixture until blended.

Pour mousse into a 4-cup fish mold and refrigerate it until firm. Unmold on a lovely platter and decorate with slices of tomatoes and lemon sprinkled with parsley. Serve with crackers or thin slices of black bread.

Note: - This recipe is really very simple except for one consideration. When stirring gelatin into salmon mixture, work quickly so that the gelatin does not congeal too quickly giving the mousse a grainy texture.
- Mousse can be prepared 1 day earlier and stored in the refrigerator.

Shrimp Mold with Whipped Cheese, Garlic & Herbs

2 packages (5 ounces, each) Boursin or similar
French Creamed Cheese with Garlic and Herbs
2 tablespoons lemon juice
1 cup cream, whipped
1/4 pound cooked baby shrimp

1 tablespoon gelatin
1/4 cup milk

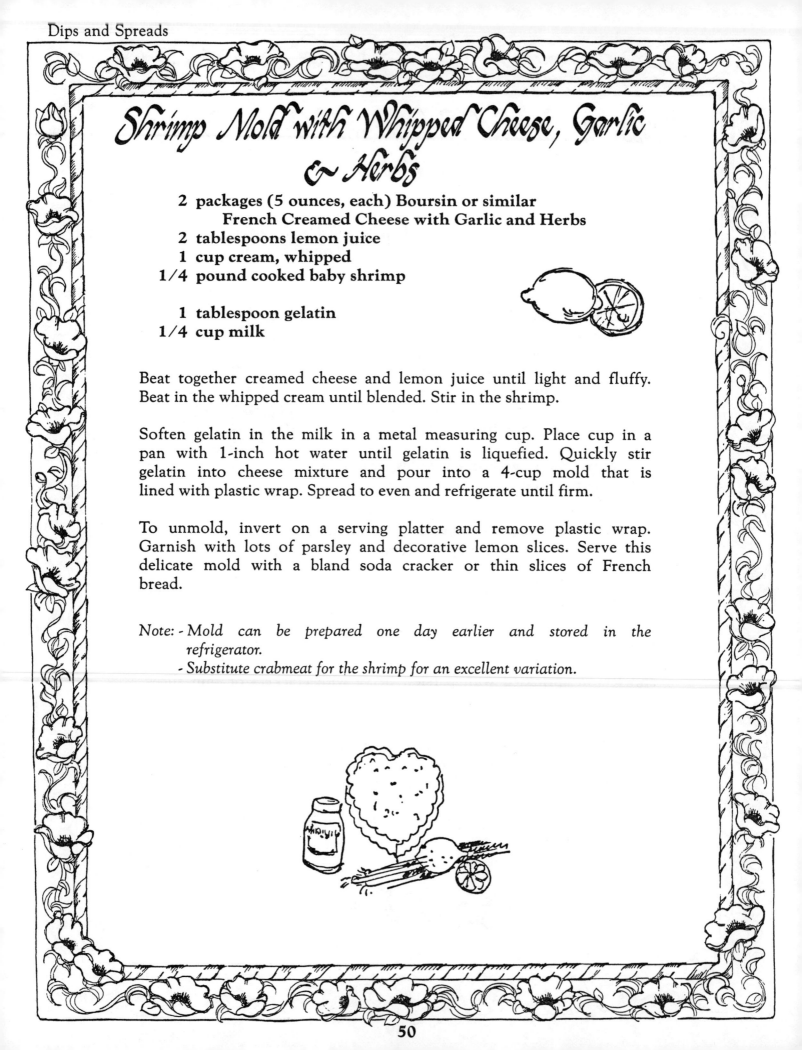

Beat together creamed cheese and lemon juice until light and fluffy. Beat in the whipped cream until blended. Stir in the shrimp.

Soften gelatin in the milk in a metal measuring cup. Place cup in a pan with 1-inch hot water until gelatin is liquefied. Quickly stir gelatin into cheese mixture and pour into a 4-cup mold that is lined with plastic wrap. Spread to even and refrigerate until firm.

To unmold, invert on a serving platter and remove plastic wrap. Garnish with lots of parsley and decorative lemon slices. Serve this delicate mold with a bland soda cracker or thin slices of French bread.

Note: - Mold can be prepared one day earlier and stored in the refrigerator.
- Substitute crabmeat for the shrimp for an excellent variation.

Mousseline Russe of Dilled Eggs & Caviar

   1 **package gelatin**
1/2 **cup water**

 10 **eggs, hard cooked, mashed. If you do this in the**
      processor, do not puree the eggs.
1/2 **cup mayonnaise**
1/2 **cup sour cream**
  2 **tablespoons lemon juice**
1/2 **cup finely chopped green onions**
1/2 **teaspoon dried dill weed**
      salt to taste
3/4 **cup sour cream**
  1 **jar (4 ounces) pink Salmon caviar**

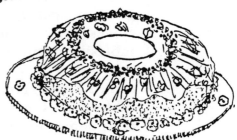

Place gelatin in a metal measuring cup. Add the water and stir until gelatin is softened. Place the cup in a pan with simmering water until gelatin is dissolved.

In a bowl, stir together eggs, mayonnaise, sour cream, lemon juice, green onions, dill weed and salt to taste. Stir in the dissolved gelatin. Pour mixture into an oiled 4-cup ring mold and refrigerate until firm.

Unmold onto a lovely footed platter and mask the top with sour cream. Just before serving spoon the caviar in a ring around the top and sprinkle with a little dill weed. Serve with chilled vodka or champagne. Serves 10 to 12.

Note: - The above dish can be served in another fashion for an entirely different effect. Instead of placing the egg salad in a ring mold, place it in a 10-inch glass pie plate and spread it evenly. Now spread the sour cream on top. Spoon the caviar in a ring, around the pie plate, just before serving. Sprinkle top with dill weed. This does not have to be unmolded, but do decorate with lots of parsley or green leaves.

- Serve the mousseline with black bread if you are using vodka as an accompaniment. If you are planning to serve it with champagne, then serve it with a bland soda cracker.

Hot & Spicy Eggplant Spread with Tomatoes & Onions

1 eggplant (about 1 1/2 pounds). Do not peel. Slice
   into 1/2-inch thick slices. Then cut each slice,
   roughly, into 1-inch squares.
2 large onions, chopped
1 green pepper, cut into 1/2-inch thick slices
2 cloves garlic, minced
4 tablespoons oil (use half olive oil)

1 can (8 ounces) tomato sauce
1 tablespoon sugar
1 teaspoon ground cumin
1/4 teaspoon cayenne pepper
1/4 cup lemon juice
2 tablespoons chopped parsley
   salt and pepper to taste

In a 9x13 roasting pan, place the first 5 ingredients and toss to mix. Cover pan tightly with foil and bake in a 400° oven for 20 minutes or until eggplant is soft.

In a Dutch oven casserole, stir together the remaining ingredients. Stir in the softened vegetables. Simmer mixture for about 30 to 40 minutes or until much of the liquid is absorbed and sauce is thickened. Stir it from time to time to prevent sticking. Place in a glass bowl, cover and refrigerate. Serve cold with cocktail sesame bread or crisped, toasted pita bread. Crackers, of course, are good, too. Yields about 3 cups.

Caponata Eggplant Spread with Tomato Vinaigrette

1 eggplant (about 1 1/2 pounds). Do not peel. Slice into 1/2-inch thick slices. Then cut each slice into, roughly, 1-inch squares.
2 large onions, chopped
4 tablespoons oil

1 can (1 pound) stewed tomatoes, chopped
1/4 cup tomato paste
1/3 cup small pimiento-stuffed green olives, sliced
1/3 cup red wine vinegar
3 tablespoons sugar
1 tablespoon capers, rinsed and drained
2 tablespoons chopped parsley
2 teaspoons sweet basil
   salt and pepper to taste

In a 9x13-inch roasting pan, place eggplant and onions and drizzle with oil. Cover pan tightly with foil and bake in a 400° oven for 20 minutes or until eggplant is soft.

In a Dutch oven casserole, stir together the remaining ingredients. Stir in the softened eggplant and onions.

Simmer mixture for 30 to 40 minutes or until much of the liquid is absorbed and sauce is thickened. Stir it from time to time to prevent scorching. Place in a glass bowl, cover and refrigerate. Serve cold with crackers or crusty French bread. Yields about 4 cups.

Note: - Steaming the eggplant in the oven, eliminates the use of 1 cup of oil.
      - To the above basic recipe, you can add 2 sliced, unpeeled zucchini and 1 green pepper, cut into 1/2-inch slices. Steam these with the eggplant and onions.

Hot Chile con Queso with Tomatoes & Onions

- 1 teaspoon butter
- 1 clove garlic, minced

- 1 can (1 pound) stewed tomatoes, very finely chopped
- 1 can (4 ounces) diced green chiles
- 3 green onions, minced

- 1 pound grated sharp Cheddar cheese
  pinch red pepper flakes
  salt and pepper to taste

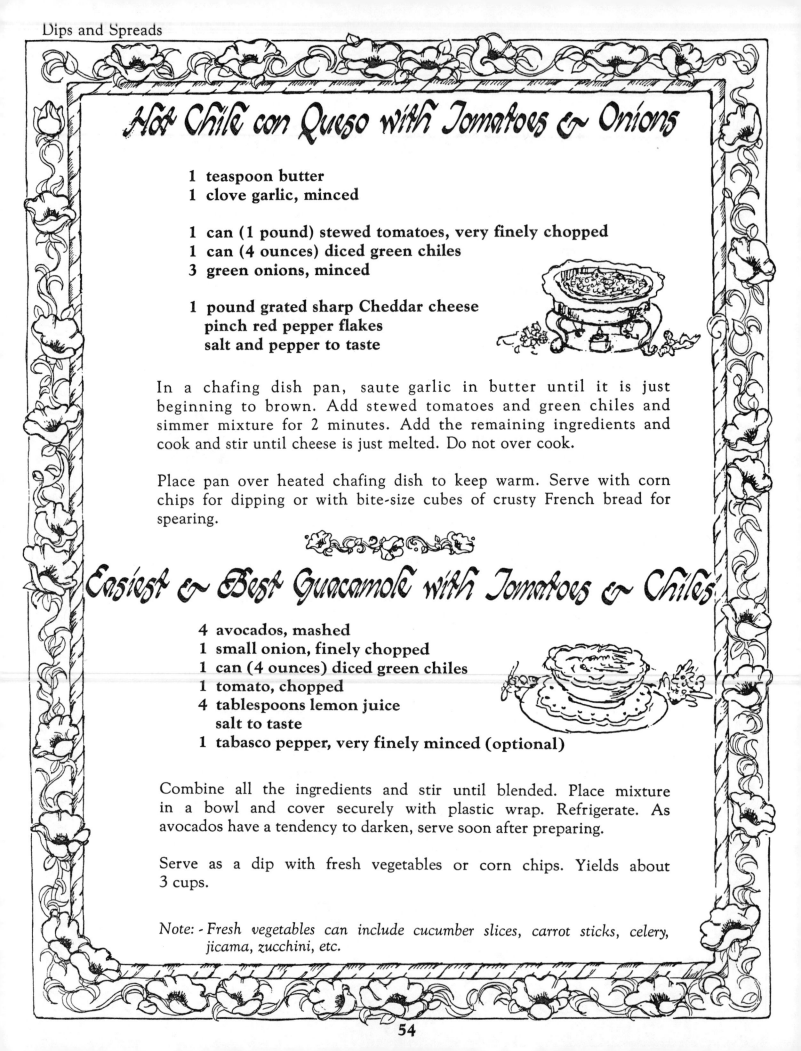

In a chafing dish pan, saute garlic in butter until it is just beginning to brown. Add stewed tomatoes and green chiles and simmer mixture for 2 minutes. Add the remaining ingredients and cook and stir until cheese is just melted. Do not over cook.

Place pan over heated chafing dish to keep warm. Serve with corn chips for dipping or with bite-size cubes of crusty French bread for spearing.

Easiest & Best Guacamole with Tomatoes & Chiles

- 4 avocados, mashed
- 1 small onion, finely chopped
- 1 can (4 ounces) diced green chiles
- 1 tomato, chopped
- 4 tablespoons lemon juice
  salt to taste
- 1 tabasco pepper, very finely minced (optional)

Combine all the ingredients and stir until blended. Place mixture in a bowl and cover securely with plastic wrap. Refrigerate. As avocados have a tendency to darken, serve soon after preparing.

Serve as a dip with fresh vegetables or corn chips. Yields about 3 cups.

Note: - Fresh vegetables can include cucumber slices, carrot sticks, celery, jicama, zucchini, etc.

Layered Mexican Casserole with Chiles, Tomatoes & Cheese

You'll enjoy serving this casserole as a small entree to precede a Mexican fiesta. Serve frosty Margaritas in large stemmed goblets.

1 onion, chopped
2 cloves garlic, minced
2 tablespoons butter

1 pound lean ground beef
1 envelope Taco Mix
 salt and pepper to taste

1 can (1 pound) refried beans
2 cups sharp Cheddar cheese, grated
1 can (4 ounces, diced green chiles)

1 cup sour cream
2 tomatoes, peeled, seeded and chopped
3 green onions, finely chopped

Saute onion and garlic in butter until onion is transparent. Add the beef, Taco Mix, and seasonings and saute until meat loses its pinkness. Drain beef and place in a 9x9-inch baking pan. Spread refried beans over the beef and sprinkle with cheese and chiles. Bake in a 350° oven for about 15 or 20 minutes or until cheese is melted and casserole is heated through.

Meanwhile, stir together sour cream, tomatoes and green onions until mixture is blended. When casserole is removed from the oven dot top with spoonfuls of sour cream mixture. Serve at once with corn chips for dipping.

Note: - Casserole can be assembled earlier in the day and stored in the refrigerator. However, this casserole must be baked before serving.
You might enjoy making your own tortilla chips for this casserole. Cut corn tortillas into 8 pie-shaped wedges and saute them in oil until they are crisp and golden. Drain on absorbent paper and store in plastic bags. These can be made earlier in the day.

Nachos Mejicanos with Chiles & Cheese

This is an exceedingly simple hors d'oeuvres that serves well with a Mexican dinner. Grownups and children love pulling a chip all laden with chiles and melted cheese.

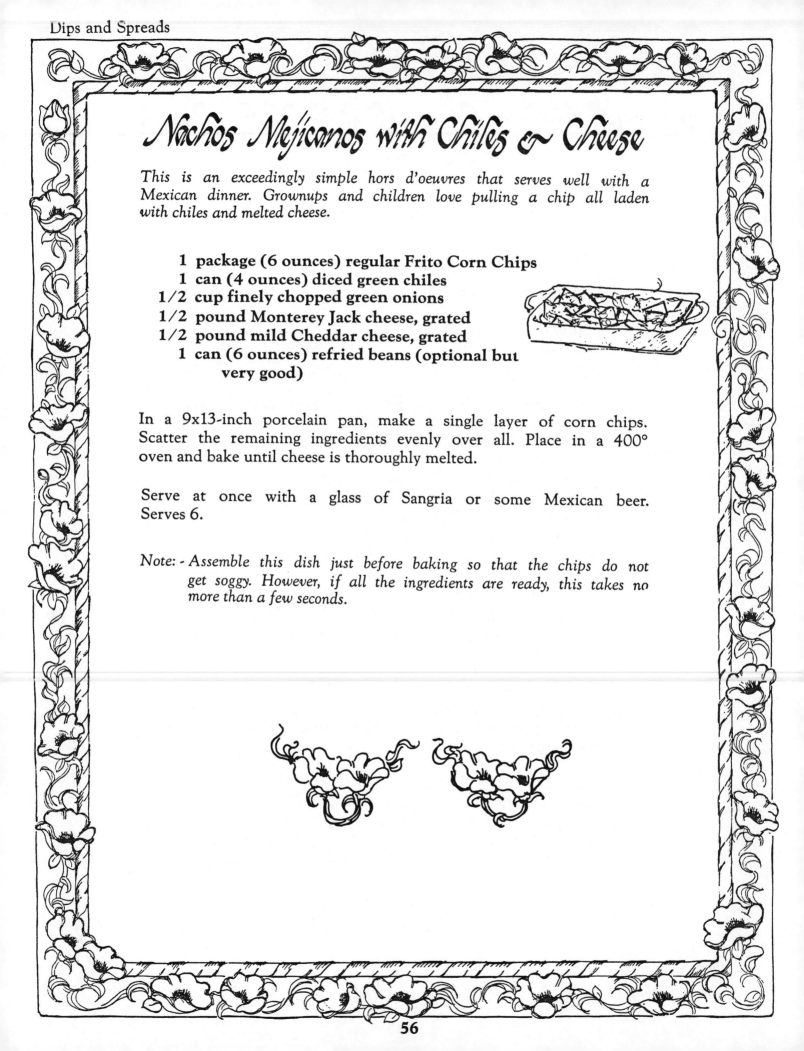

- 1 package (6 ounces) regular Frito Corn Chips
- 1 can (4 ounces) diced green chiles
- 1/2 cup finely chopped green onions
- 1/2 pound Monterey Jack cheese, grated
- 1/2 pound mild Cheddar cheese, grated
- 1 can (6 ounces) refried beans (optional but very good)

In a 9x13-inch porcelain pan, make a single layer of corn chips. Scatter the remaining ingredients evenly over all. Place in a 400° oven and bake until cheese is thoroughly melted.

Serve at once with a glass of Sangria or some Mexican beer. Serves 6.

Note: - Assemble this dish just before baking so that the chips do not get soggy. However, if all the ingredients are ready, this takes no more than a few seconds.

Fondue Swiss with Champagne, Bacon & Chives

This is not a traditional fondue, but the addition of bacon and chives adds a distinctive and interesting flavor to the basic fondue.

1 tablespoon butter
1 clove garlic, minced

1 cup champagne
1/4 cup finely chopped chives
2 teaspoons Dijon mustard
    salt and pepper to taste

3/4 cup grated Swiss cheese, tossed with 1 tablespoon flour
6 strips bacon, cooked crisp, drained and crumbled

In the skillet that sits over the water in a chafing dish, saute garlic in butter until it is starting to brown. Add champagne, chives, mustard and seasonings and heat until wine starts to bubble. Add the cheese and bacon and continue cooking and stirring until cheese is melted.

Place pan over heated chafing dish to keep warm, and serve immediately. To serve, spear bite-size cubes of crusty French bread, with long-handled forks to dip into the melted cheese.

Note: - This dish cannot be prepared earlier in the day.
    - Traditionally, anyone, whose bread drops off the fork and into the fondue, must pay a forfeit . . . like sing a song or tell a funny story.
    - If you are a purist, then omit the bacon for the more traditional fondue.

Royal Crabmeat Spread with Tomatoes & Onions

1/4   **pound crabmeat, picked over for bones**
1   **package (8 ounces) cream cheese, at room temperature**
2   **tablespoons lemon juice**
1/4   **cup sour cream**
1/3   **cup finely chopped green onions**

1   **tomato, peeled, seeded and chopped**

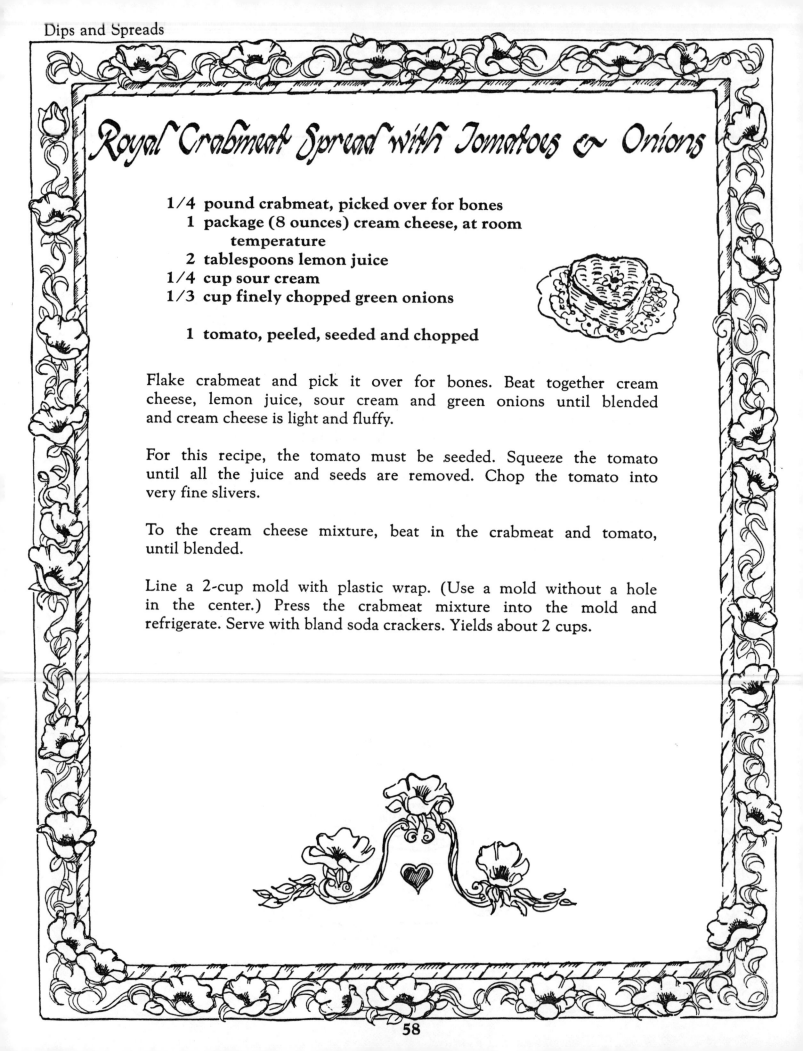

Flake crabmeat and pick it over for bones. Beat together cream cheese, lemon juice, sour cream and green onions until blended and cream cheese is light and fluffy.

For this recipe, the tomato must be seeded. Squeeze the tomato until all the juice and seeds are removed. Chop the tomato into very fine slivers.

To the cream cheese mixture, beat in the crabmeat and tomato, until blended.

Line a 2-cup mold with plastic wrap. (Use a mold without a hole in the center.) Press the crabmeat mixture into the mold and refrigerate. Serve with bland soda crackers. Yields about 2 cups.

Crabmeat Butter with Cream Cheese & Chives

  1/2 pound cooked crabmeat (picked over
        for bones and flaked.)
  1/2 pound cream cheese and chives
        (at room temperature.)
  2 tablespoons sour cream
  6 tablespoons butter (at room temperature.)
  4 tablespoons lemon juice
  1 or 2 tablespoons prepared horseradish
  1/8 teaspoon dried dill weed

In a food processor or blender, blend together all the ingredients, until the crabmeat is very finely chopped, but not pureed. Place crabmeat butter in a pretty mold, lined with plastic wrap and press it to take the shape of the mold. This makes it easier to unmold. Refrigerate until firm.

Unmold and remove plastic wrap. Decorate platter with green onion frills and lemon slices. Serve with a lovely soda cracker or thin slices of black pumpernickel bread.

Creamed Mousseline of Pink Caviar

  1 jar (3 ounces) pink salmon caviar
  3 tablespoons finely minced parsley
  3/4 cup finely minced chives
  4 tablespoons lemon juice
  2 cups sour cream

  2 packages (2 tablespoons) unflavored gelatin
  1/2 cup water
  2 cups cream, whipped

In a bowl, stir together the first five ingredients until blended. In a metal cup, soften gelatin in water and place cup in pan with simmering water until gelatin is dissolved. Stir into sour cream mixture. Fold in whipped cream. Place mousse into an 8-cup decorative mold that has been lightly oiled and refrigerate until firm.

Unmold onto a lovely platter and decorate with green leaves and lemon slices sprinkled with parsley. Serve with champagne or vodka. Serves 12.

Seafood Cocktail with Tomato & Lemon Vinaigrette

This is a rather interesting cocktail sauce, filled with all good things. It is an excellent hors d'oeuvre or small entree.

3/4 **cup ketchup**
3/4 **cup chili sauce**
3 **green onions, finely minced**
1/4 **teaspoon minced garlic**
3/4 **cup grated cucumber, peeled and seeded**
3/4 **cup finely chopped tomato**
1/4 **cup finely chopped green pepper**
2 **tablespoons lemon juice**
2 **tablespoons vinegar**
1 **tablespoon oil**
1/4 **teaspoon red pepper flakes**

2 **pounds cooked shellfish, combination of shrimp, crabmeat and lobster**

Combine all of the ingredients, except the shellfish, and stir until blended. Refrigerate sauce until ready to use. At serving time place the seafood in individual clam shells and top with the sauce. Serve with cocktail forks. Yields about 3 1/2 cups sauce and about 16 servings.

Note: - Sauce can be made 1 day earlier and refrigerated.

- This can also be served on a large platter. Seafood can be arranged around the sauce and served with picks or cocktail forks.

Crabmeat with Royal Louis Dressing

1 pound cooked crabmeat, picked over for bones

Royal Louis Dressing:

- 3/4 cup mayonnaise
- 3/4 cup sour cream
- 1/4 cup chopped chives or green onions
- 2 tablespoons chopped parsley
- 2 tablespoons prepared horseradish
- 2 tablespoons lemon juice
- salt and pepper to taste

Place crabmeat along the edge of an attractive platter. Place the remaining ingredients in a blender container and blend until mixture is pureed.

Place dressing in a bowl and set in the center of the platter. Serve with picks or cocktail forks. Serves 6 as an hors d'oeuvre.

Note: - Dressing can be made several days earlier and refrigerated.

Shrimp with Mustard Dill Sauce

1 pound medium cooked shrimp

Mustard Dill Sauce:

- 1/2 cup oil
- 2 tablespoons white vinegar
- 2 tablespoons sugar
- 1 tablespoon Dijon mustard
- 1/2 teaspoon dried dill weed
- salt and pepper to taste
- 1/4 cup green onions

Place cooked shrimp along the edge of an attractive platter. Place the remaining ingredients in a blender container and blend until mixture is pureed.

Place dressing in a bowl and set in the center of the platter. Serve with picks or cocktail forks. Serves 6 as an hors d'oeuvre.

Note: - Dressing can be prepared several days earlier and stored in the refrigerator.

Pink Mayonnaise for Fish & Shellfish

- 1 cup mayonnaise
- 1/4 cup chili sauce
- 1/4 cup chopped chives
- 2 tablespoons prepared horseradish
- 2 tablespoons lemon juice
- 1/4 cup cream, whipped
- 1 tablespoon chopped parsley

Combine all the ingredients in a glass bowl and stir until blended. Refrigerate sauce until ready to use. Place sauce in a lovely bowl and surround with cooked fish or shellfish. Yields about 2 cups sauce.

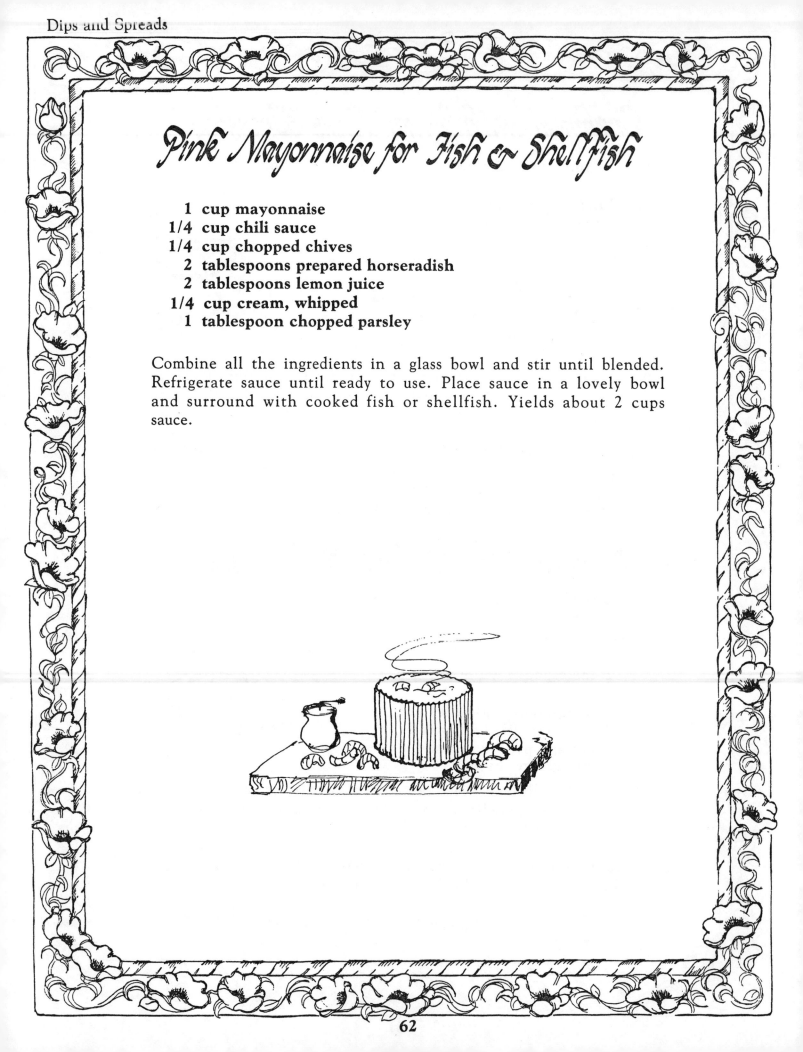

Emerald Cocktail Sauce for Fish & Shellfish

- 1/2 cup mayonnaise
- 1/2 cup sour cream
- 2 green onions (remove the whiskers and use the whole onion)
- 6 sprigs of parsley (remove stems and use only the leaves)
- 1/2 teaspoon garlic powder
- 2 tablespoons lemon juice
- 1/4 teaspoon dried dill weed

Combine all the ingredients in a blender container and blend until mixture is pureed. Place sauce in a pretty server and surround with cooked shrimp, crabmeat or lobster pieces. Sauce can be made earlier in the day and stored in the refrigerator until ready to use.

Red Cocktail Sauce for Fish & Shellfish

- 1/2 cup chili sauce
- 1/2 cup ketchup
- 2 tablespoons prepared horseradish
- 2 tablespoons lemon juice
- 2 tablespoons finely minced green onions

Combine all the ingredients and stir until blended. Refrigerate sauce until ready to use. Place sauce in a pretty server and surround with cooked shrimp, crabmeat or lobster pieces. Yields about 1 1/4 cups sauce.

Mushrooms with Beef & Pork, Onions & Garlic

1 pound large mushrooms, about 1 1/2-inches in diameter. Clean and remove the stems. Brush the caps with melted butter.

1/4 pound lean ground beef
1/4 pound lean ground pork
1/4 cup finely chopped green onions
1 clove garlic, finely minced
1/4 cup fresh bread crumbs
1/4 cup cream
1 egg
1/4 teaspoon thyme
salt and pepper to taste
2 tablespoons Ritz cracker crumbs

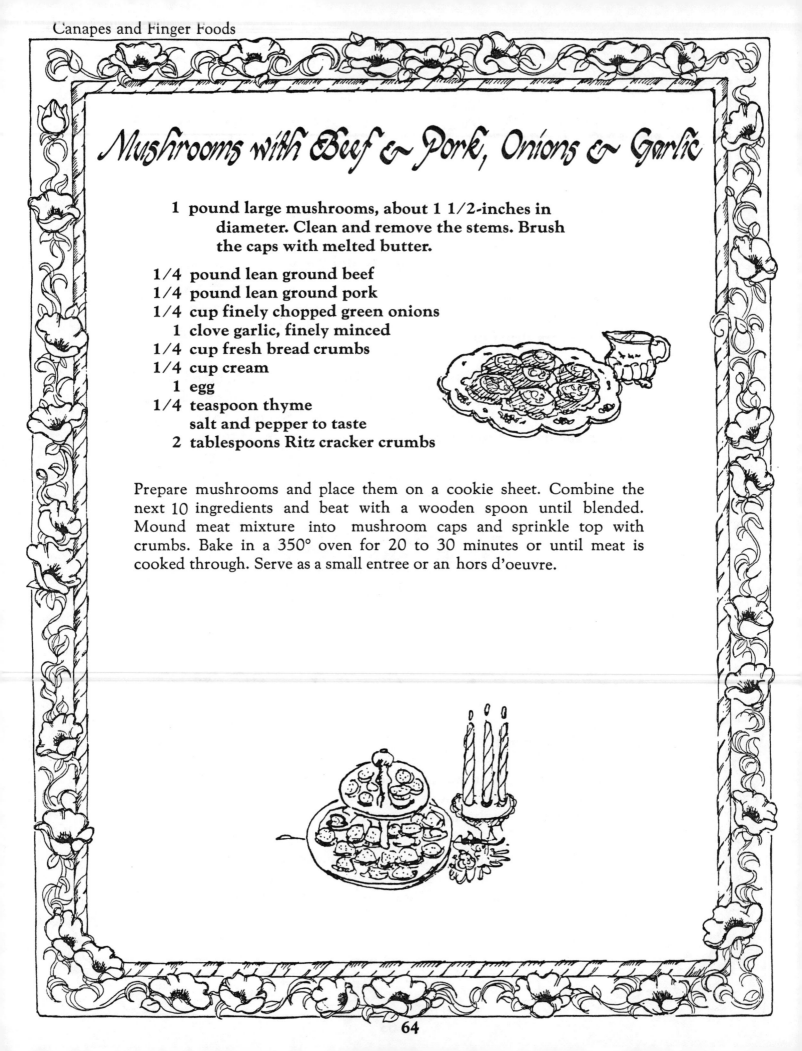

Prepare mushrooms and place them on a cookie sheet. Combine the next 10 ingredients and beat with a wooden spoon until blended. Mound meat mixture into mushroom caps and sprinkle top with crumbs. Bake in a 350° oven for 20 to 30 minutes or until meat is cooked through. Serve as a small entree or an hors d'oeuvre.

Mushrooms Filled with Cheese, Garlic & Lemon

1 pound large mushrooms, about 1 1/2 to 2-inches
in diameter. Remove the stems. Brush the caps
with melted butter.

3 packages (3 ounces, each) cream cheese and chives
1/2 cup grated Swiss cheese
1/4 cup grated Parmesan cheese
1/2 cup garlic croutons, rolled into crumbs
1 tablespoon parsley, finely chopped
2 tablespoons lemon juice
1 clove garlic, finely minced

5 tablespoons grated Swiss cheese
3 tablespoons grated Parmesan cheese
paprika

Prepare mushrooms and place them on a cookie sheet. Combine the next 7 ingredients until blended. Fill the mushrooms with the cheese mixture. Combine the Swiss and Parmesan cheeses and sprinkle them on top of the mushrooms. Sprinkle tops with a little paprika.

Bake in a 350° oven until heated through, about 20 minutes. Serve as an hors d'oeuvre or small entree.

Note: - *Reserve stems for a soup or stew.*
- *To prevent mushrooms from tipping, here is a little technique that will help them stay upright. On a cookie sheet, place a length or two of crumpled foil. Place the mushrooms on the foil, nestled between the creases that will support their standing upright. It is important for this dish, because you do not want the melted cheese to run out of the caps.*

Mushrooms Filled with Cream Cheese & Chives

1 pound large mushrooms, about 1 1/2-inches in
    diameter. Clean and remove the stems. Brush
    tops with melted butter.

1/2 cup fresh bread crumbs
1/2 cup grated Swiss cheese
1/2 cup grated Parmesan cheese
  1 package (3 ounces) cream cheese and chives
  1 tablespoon minced parsley
    salt and pepper to taste
1/4 cup cream (about)
    paprika
    grated Parmesan cheese

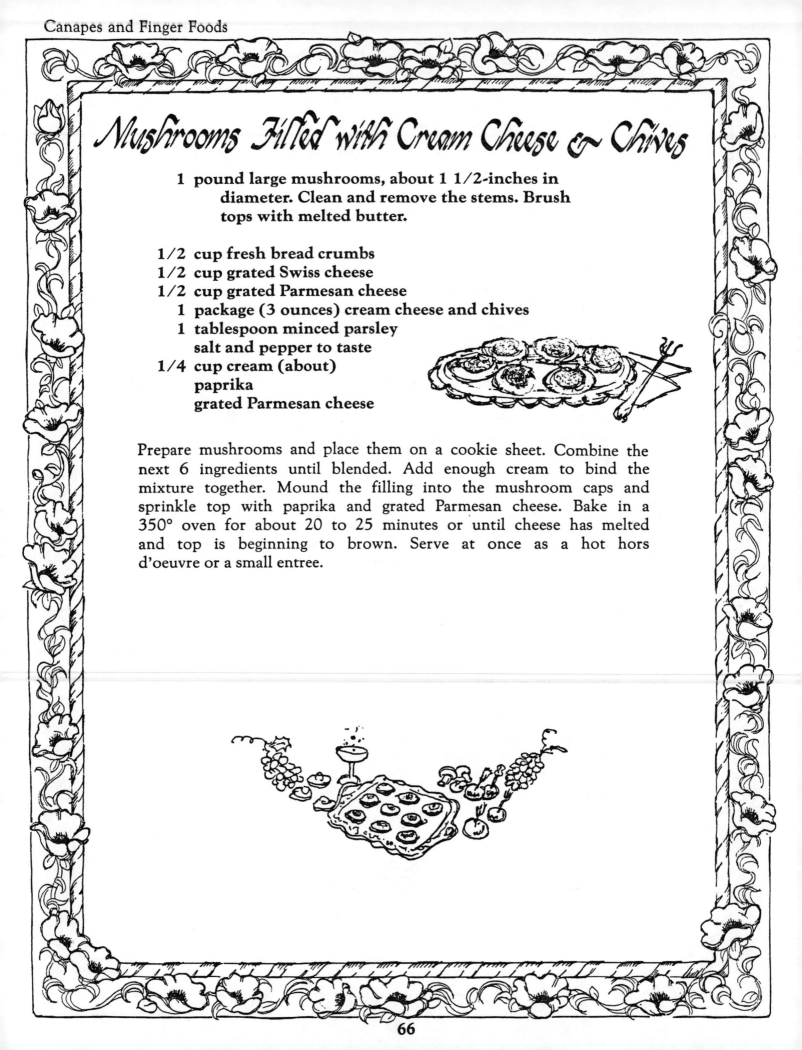

Prepare mushrooms and place them on a cookie sheet. Combine the next 6 ingredients until blended. Add enough cream to bind the mixture together. Mound the filling into the mushroom caps and sprinkle top with paprika and grated Parmesan cheese. Bake in a 350° oven for about 20 to 25 minutes or until cheese has melted and top is beginning to brown. Serve at once as a hot hors d'oeuvre or a small entree.

Petite Muffins with Smoked Salmon & Sour Cream

- 1 cup small curd cottage cheese
- 2 tablespoons sour cream
- 1 tablespoon chopped chives
- 2 eggs
- 1 tablespoon melted butter
- 1/2 cup Bisquick
- 1/4 teaspoon dried dill weed

Combine all the ingredients in a large mixer bowl and heat until blended. Grease hors d'oeuvre size teflon-lined muffin pans and fill 1/2 full with batter. Bake in a 350° oven for about 25 minutes or until muffins are puffed and very lightly browned.

To serve, cut muffins in half and place 1/2 teaspoonful of Smoked Salmon and Sour Cream Filling in center. Cover with top of muffin. Yields about 30 muffins.

Salmon and Sour Cream Filling:
- 1/2 cup sour cream
- 2 ounces smoked salmon
- 1 tablespoon chopped green onions
- 1 tablespoon lemon juice

Combine all the ingredients in a blender container and blend until salmon and onions are pureed. Will fill 30 muffins.

Note: - Muffins can be prepared earlier in the day. Salmon and Sour Cream Filling can be prepared earlier in the day. Before serving, heat muffins and fill with salmon filling.

Perhaps the simplest canape base you can prepare, is made when you separate Flaky Rolls or Flaky Biscuits. Each roll separates easily into 3 layers and is then ready for topping.

Place separated layers on an ungreased cookie sheet and cover with any number of fillings. Wrap pan securely with plastic wrap and refrigerate. When ready to serve, remove plastic wrap and bake in a 400° oven for 8 minutes. Serve at once.

Petite Pizzas with Pepperoni & Mozzarella

30 (1-inch squares) sliced Mozzarella cheese
 1 can (6 ounces) Pizza Sauce
30 thin slices Pepperoni

 1 package (10 rolls) Flaky Biscuits. Separate each roll into
    3 layers, producing 30 canape bases.

On each canape base, place 1 slice of cheese, 1 teaspoon of Pizza Sauce and 1 slice of pepperoni. Place canapes on an ungreased cookie sheet and bake in a 400° oven for 8 minutes, or until cheese is melted and edges of canapes are beginning to color. Serve hot and serve at once. Yields 30 canapes.

Caponata & Mozzarella Canapes

 1 can (4 ounces) caponata (eggplant spread)
30 (1-inch squares) sliced Mozzarella cheese

 1 package (10 rolls) Flaky Biscuits. Separate each biscuit
    into 3 layers, producing 30 canape bases.

On each flaky layer, place 1/2 teaspoon caponata and top with 1 slice Mozzarella cheese. Place layers on an ungreased cookie sheet and bake in a 400° oven for 8 minutes or until cheese is melted and edges of canapes are beginning to color. Serve hot and serve at once. Yields 30 canapes.

Curried Crabmeat with Cream Cheese & Chives

1/4 pound cream cheese and chives
1/4 teaspoon curry powder
       pinch of garlic powder
1/4 pound crabmeat, picked over for bones and flaked

1 package (10 rolls) Flaky Biscuits. Separate each roll
       into 3 layers, producing 30 canape bases.

Beat together cream cheese and chives, curry powder and garlic powder until blended. Stir in the crabmeat. Spread mixture on flaky layers and place them on an ungreased cookie sheet. Bake in a 400° oven for 8 minutes or until canapes are piping hot and the edges are beginning to color. Serve hot and serve at once. Yields 30 canapes.

Miniature Cheeseburgers

1/2 pound ground beef, seasoned with salt, pepper, garlic
         powder and 1 tablespoon grated onion
  5 tablespoons ketchup
30 (1 inch squares) sliced Cheddar cheese

1 package (10 rolls) Flaky Biscuits. Separate each roll
       into 3 layers, producing 30 canape bases.

Mix ground beef with seasonings and shape into thin 3/4-inch patties. Place 1 patty on each flaky biscuit. Spread meat with a dot of ketchup and place a slice of Cheddar cheese over all. Place canapes on an ungreased cookie sheet and bake in a 400° oven for about 8 minutes or until meat is still a little pink and edges are beginning to color. Serve hot and serve at once. Yields 30 canapes.

Miniature Tacos with Cheddar & Green Onions

- 1/2 pound ground beef
-   1 teaspoon dried onion flakes
- 1/2 envelope taco seasoning

-   1 cup grated Cheddar cheese
- 1/2 cup finely chopped green onions
- 1/2 cup sour cream

-   1 package (10 rolls) Flaky Biscuits. Separate each roll into 3 layers, producing 30 canape bases.

Saute beef with onion and taco seasoning until meat loses its pinkness. Place canape bases on an ungreased cookie sheet and top with 1 teaspoon ground beef mixture. Sprinkle tops with Cheddar cheese and minced green onions. Bake in a 400° oven for 8 minutes or until cheese is melted and edges of canapes are beginning to color. Serve with a small dot of sour cream on top. Serve at once. Yields 30 canapes.

Crabmeat with Cream Cheese & Chives

- 1/2 cup (4 ounces) cream cheese and chives
-   4 ounces cooked crabmeat, picked over for bones and flaked
-   grated Parmesan cheese

-   1 package (10 rolls) Flaky Biscuits. Separate each biscuit into 3 layers, producing 30 canape bases.

Spread cream cheese and chives over each flaky layer and place on an ungreased cookie sheet. Top with a small piece of crabmeat and sprinkle lightly with grated Parmesan cheese. Bake in a 400° oven for 8 minutes or until cheese is melted and edges of canapes are beginning to color. Serve hot and serve at once. Yields 30 canapes.

Savory Cheese Puffs with Dill & Chives

1/2 **cup milk**
  3 **tablespoons butter**

1/2 **cup flour**
    pinch salt

  2 **eggs**

1/2 **cup grated Swiss cheese**
  2 **tablespoons grated Parmesan cheese**
  2 **tablespoons chopped chives**
1/4 **teaspoon dried dill weed**

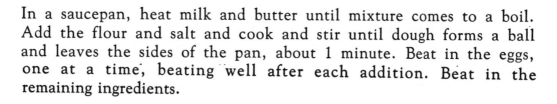

In a saucepan, heat milk and butter until mixture comes to a boil. Add the flour and salt and cook and stir until dough forms a ball and leaves the sides of the pan, about 1 minute. Beat in the eggs, one at a time, beating well after each addition. Beat in the remaining ingredients.

Drop dough by the tablespoonful on a greased cookie sheet leaving a 1 1/2-inch space between the mounds so that the puffs don't touch. Bake in a 400° oven for 20 minutes or until puffs are golden brown. Serve with cheese or pate and a glass of wine. Yields about 24 puffs.

Note: - Batter can be made earlier in the day and spooned onto the cookie sheet. Refrigerate until ready to bake. Bake as described above, but add a few minutes to baking time.

- Puffs can be baked earlier in the day and reheated before serving. Take care that they do not get too dry.

Shrimp Puffs with Lemon, Cheese & Chives

6 slices egg bread, crusts removed. Cut each slice into
4 squares or 4 triangles. Toast lightly in a 350° oven.

1/4 pound cooked baby shrimp (about 48 to 72 little shrimp)

1/4 cup mayonnaise
4 tablespoons cream cheese and chives (at room
temperature)
2 tablespoons ketchup
1 tablespoon lemon juice
1 tablespoon prepared horseradish
salt to taste

1 egg white, beaten stiff

Place toasted bread slices, in 1 layer, on an ungreased cookie sheet.
Place 2 or 3 small shrimp on each piece of bread.

Beat together mayonnaise, cream cheese, ketchup, lemon juice,
horseradish and salt until blended. Stir in egg white until blended.
Place 1 teaspoon of mayonnaise mixture over the shrimp and
sprinkle top with a pinch of chives.

Broil about 3 or 4 minutes or until puffs are bubbling and lightly
browned. Yields 24 puffs.

Clam & Swiss Puffs with Lemon, Cream Cheese & Chives

1 can (8 ounces) chopped clams, drained. Reserve
juice for another use.
1 package (3 ounces) cream cheese and chives
1 teaspoon lemon juice
1/4 cup grated Swiss cheese
5 slices egg bread, crusts removed and cut into
fourths. Saute bread slices in butter to crisp
both sides.
paprika

Beat together clams, cream cheese, lemon juice and Swiss cheese
until blended. Spread mixture on bread squares and sprinkle
lightly with paprika. Broil until bubbly, just before serving.

Royal Crab Puffs
with Sour Cream Horseradish Sauce

1 cup flour

1 cup milk
6 tablespoons butter (3/4 stick)

4 eggs, at room temperature
1/4 teaspoon salt

1/4 pound crabmeat, picked over for bones and finely
    flaked
1 cup grated Swiss cheese
1/4 cup finely minced green onions

Place flour in the large bowl of an electric mixer.

In a saucepan, heat milk and butter until mixture comes to a boil. Pour boiling milk mixture into the bowl with the flour and beat until the dough is smooth, about 2 minutes. Beat in the eggs, one at a time, beating well after each addition. Beat in the remaining ingredients.

By the teaspoonful, drop crab mixture into the hot oil and fry the puffs until golden on both sides. Drain on paper towels.

At serving time, brush puffs with a little mayonnaise and sprinkle with grated Parmesan cheese. Heat in a 350° oven until crisp. Serve with Sour Cream Horseradish Sauce on the side for dipping. Yields about 48 bite-sized puffs.

Sour Cream Horseradish Sauce (continued)

1 **cup sour cream**
2 **tablespoons lemon juice**
1 to 2 **tablespoons prepared Horseradish Sauce**
1/3 **cup chopped chives**
salt to taste

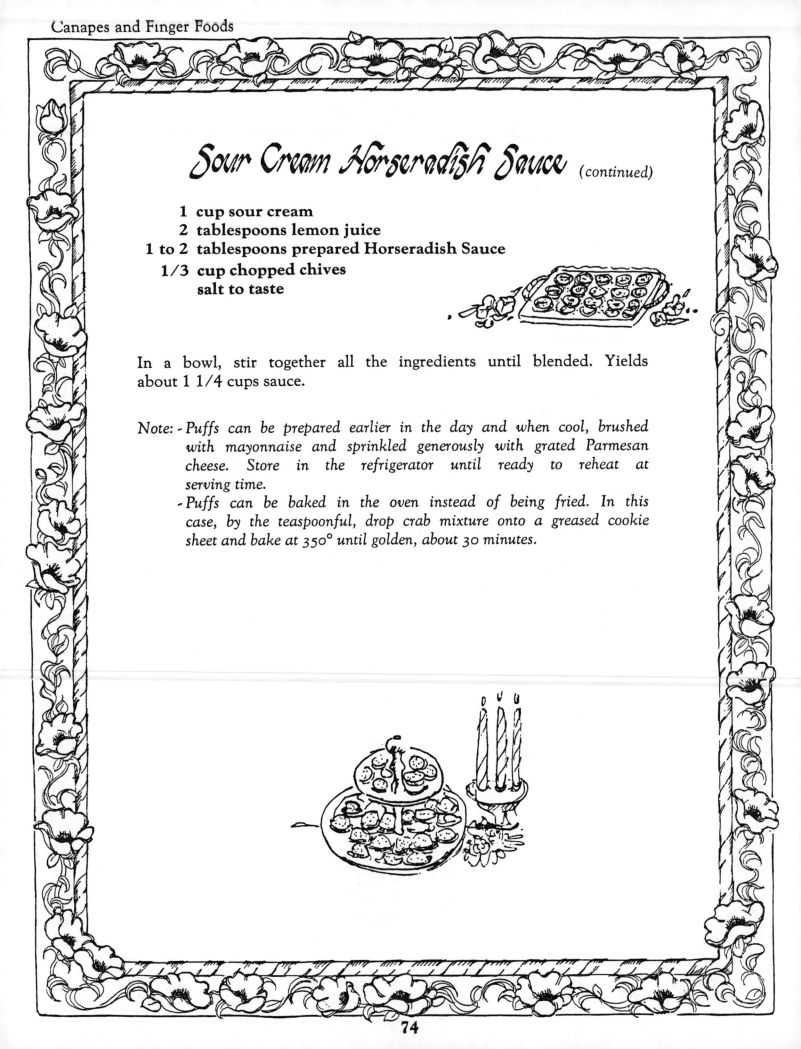

In a bowl, stir together all the ingredients until blended. Yields about 1 1/4 cups sauce.

Note: - *Puffs can be prepared earlier in the day and when cool, brushed with mayonnaise and sprinkled generously with grated Parmesan cheese. Store in the refrigerator until ready to reheat at serving time.*
 - *Puffs can be baked in the oven instead of being fried. In this case, by the teaspoonful, drop crab mixture onto a greased cookie sheet and bake at 350° until golden, about 30 minutes.*

Sesame Chicken with Peanut Apricot Sauce

2 chicken breasts, boned, skinned and cut into
   1-inch pieces. Sprinkle with salt and pepper.

1/2 cup bread crumbs
1/2 cup flour
   1 tablespoon paprika
1/2 teaspoon garlic powder

In a glass jar with a tight-fitting lid, place crumbs, flour, paprika and garlic powder and shake until blended. Roll chicken pieces in crumb mixture and saute them in butter until golden on all sides.

Place cooked chicken pieces in a chafing dish pan and place over a heated chafing dish. Pour Peanut Apricot Sauce over the top and keep warm to serve. Serve with toothpicks or cocktail forks.

Peanut Apricot Sauce:
   1 cup apricot jam, sieved
1/4 cup peanut butter
   2 tablespoons lemon juice
   2 tablespoons ketchup
   2 tablespoons toasted sesame seeds

Combine all the ingredients in a small saucepan and heat until mixture is blended.

Sesame Chicken Wings with Honey Barbecue Glaze

This is probably one of the easiest barbecue sauces. It is uncommonly good, in spite of its simplicity.

3 pounds chicken wings, remove wing tips.
Sprinkle with salt, garlic powder and optional pepper. Brush with Teriyaki Marinade.

Honey Barbecue Glaze

sesame seeds

Place chicken in a 9x13-inch roasting pan and bake in a 350° oven for 20 minutes. Now, start basting with Honey Barbecue Glaze and continue baking for 25 minutes. Chicken will be a beautiful golden brown. Sprinkle with sesame seeds and continue baking for 10 minutes.

Honey Barbecue Glaze

1 cup prepared barbecue sauce
1 cup honey

Cook together the barbecue sauce and honey until the mixture is blended. Store any unused sauce in the refrigerator.

Teriyaki Marinade

1 cup soy sauce
1 cup brown sugar
1/4 cup butter (1/2 stick)

Cook together all the ingredients until the sugar is dissolved.

Hot & Spicy Crusty Chicken Wings with Hot Apricot Sauce

The highly spiced coating adds an uncommon, but interesting, touch to this delectable hors d'oeuvre. The Hot Apricot Sauce is sparkled with nutmeg and cloves and is an especially good accompaniment.

4 pounds chicken wings. (Remove and discard wing tips, leaving the 2 wing bones attached.)
Hot and Spicy Seasoned Coating

2 eggs
2 tablespoons water

Dust the chicken wings with Hot and Spicy Seasoned Coating until they are thoroughly coated. In a large skillet, heat about 1/2-inch of oil until it is very hot, but not brown. Beat together the eggs with the water until blended.

Dip the coated chicken wings in the egg mixture and fry them until they are golden brown on both sides. Drain chicken wings on absorbent paper and place them in a 12x16-inch roasting pan. Heat in a 350° oven for about 20 minutes before serving. Serve with Hot Apricot Sauce for dipping. Yields about 20 to 24 wings.

Hot and Spicy Seasoned Coating:
  1/2 cup flour
  1/2 cup grated Parmesan cheese
1 1/2 teaspoons garlic powder
    1 teaspoon onion powder
    1 tablespoon paprika
  1/2 teaspoon cayenne pepper
  1/2 teaspoon salt

In a plastic container with a tight-fitting lid, combine all the ingredients and shake to blend. Unused coating mix can be stored in the freezer.

Hot & Spicy Crusty Chicken Wings (continued)

Hot Apricot Sauce:
- 1 cup apricot jam, sieved
- 1 tablespoon grated orange peel
- 1/4 teaspoon nutmeg
- 1/4 teaspoon ground cloves
- 1 teaspoon Dijon mustard
- 1/3 cup apricot nectar

Combine all the ingredients in a saucepan and simmer mixture for 10 minutes. Serve sauce warm. Unused sauce can be stored in the refrigerator and can be used for glazing chicken or pork.

Rumaki with Dates, Water Chestnuts & Honey

If chicken livers are a no-no for your family or friends, this a lovely variation. There is usually a lot of guessing as to the dates and very few (if any) ever discover the magic substitute.

- 20 pitted dates
- 10 water chestnuts, cut into halves
- 10 slices bacon, cut into halves, partially cooked and drained

- 4 tablespoons soy sauce
- 2 tablespoons honey
- 1 tablespoon brown sugar
- pinch of ground ginger

Place 1 date and 1 piece of water chestnut on each 1/2 slice of bacon. Roll these up and fasten them securely with a toothpick.

In a shallow glass pan, place the rolled rumaki. Combine the remaining ingredients and pour it over the rumaki to coat them evenly. Broil the rumaki about 5 minutes on each side or until bacon is crisped. Yields 20 hors d'oeuvres.

Rumaki with Chicken Livers, Water Chestnuts & Honey Glaze

5 chicken livers, remove all the connective tissues
  and cut into fourths. You will have 20 pieces.
10 slices bacon, cut into halves, partially cooked and
  drained
10 water chestnuts, cut into halves
4 tablespoons teriyaki marinade
2 tablespoons honey
 pinch of ground ginger

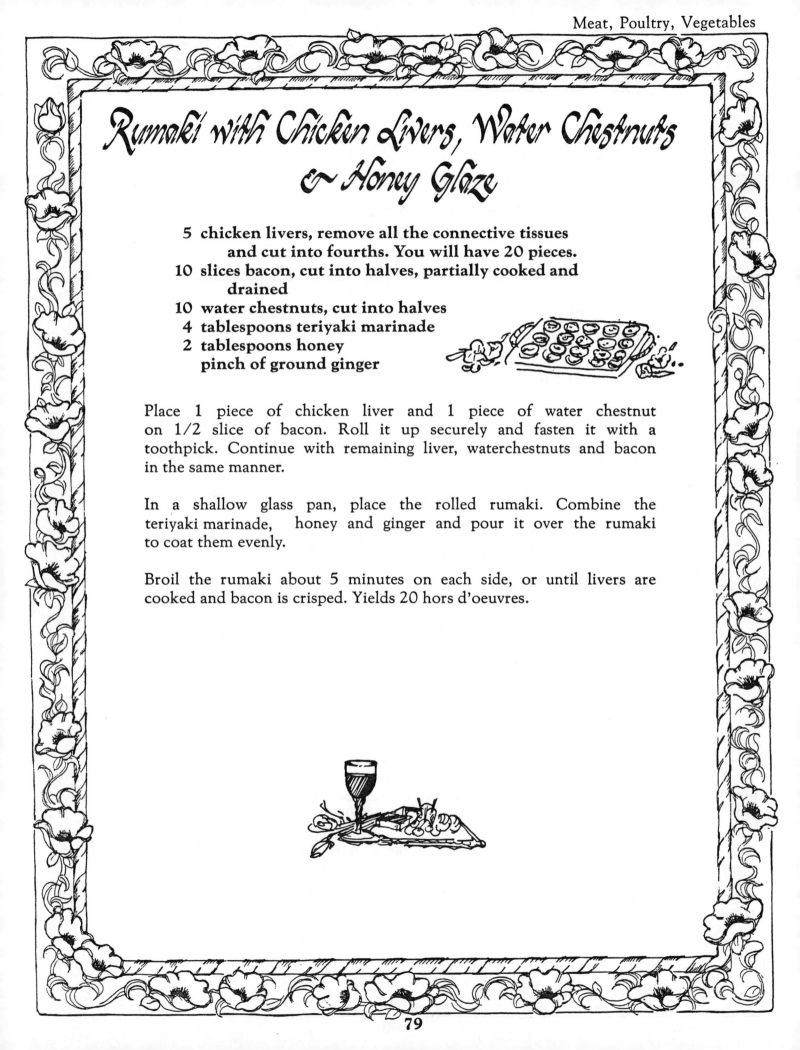

Place 1 piece of chicken liver and 1 piece of water chestnut on 1/2 slice of bacon. Roll it up securely and fasten it with a toothpick. Continue with remaining liver, waterchestnuts and bacon in the same manner.

In a shallow glass pan, place the rolled rumaki. Combine the teriyaki marinade, honey and ginger and pour it over the rumaki to coat them evenly.

Broil the rumaki about 5 minutes on each side, or until livers are cooked and bacon is crisped. Yields 20 hors d'oeuvres.

Spicy Oven~Fried Chicken with Garlic & Herbs

This highly seasoned chicken is a grand choice for a picnic in a rolling meadow. It is also delectable for an informal dinner with family and friends.

3 pounds chicken wings, remove and discard wing tips

Milk

Garlic and Herb Coating

Dip chicken pieces in milk and then in Garlic and Herb Coating. Place chicken pieces in one layer in a 12x16-inch teflon-coated pan and bake in a 350° oven for 1 hour 15 minutes. Serve with a vegetable salad and fresh biscuits with honey. Serves 6 to 8.

Garlic & Herb Coating

- 1 **cup bread crumbs**
- 1/2 **cup flour**
- 1/2 **cup grated Parmesan cheese**
- 2 **tablespoons paprika**
- 1 **teaspoon Italian Herb Seasoning**
- 1/2 **teaspoon garlic powder**
- 1/4 **teaspoon onion powder**
- 1 **teaspoon salt**
- 1/2 **teaspoon pepper**

Combine all the ingredients in a glass jar with a tight-fitting lid and shake to blend. Use to coat chicken or fish. Yields about 2 cups coating. Store unused coating in the refrigerator.

Note: - If you are not counting calories, it would be very nice to drizzle 1/2 cup melted butter over the chicken, after it has been coated
- If you do not own a teflon-coated pan, then lightly grease the pan.

spray00

Sesame Winglets in Sweet & Sour Honey Sauce

24 chicken wings, remove wing tip and then separate
   each into 2 pieces at the joint. Sprinkle with
   salt, pepper and garlic powder. Brush wings
   with soy sauce.

Basting Marinade:
   3/4 cup pineapple juice
   3/4 cup honey
      3 tablespoons lemon juice
      3 tablespoons ketchup

   sesame seeds

In a 12x16-inch pan, place chicken wings in one layer and bake in
a 350° oven for 25 minutes.

Meanwhile, heat together pineapple juice, honey, lemon juice and
ketchup until mixture is thoroughly blended. Baste chicken wings
with honey mixture and continue baking and basting for 15
minutes. Sprinkle sesame seeds over the chicken and bake for
another 10 minutes or until seeds are just beginning to color. Serve
hot. Can also be served as a main course, in which case, it will
serve 4.

Note: - Entire dish can be prepared one day earlier and refrigerated.
   - Store unused sauce in the refrigerator. Sauce will keep for 1 week.

Cocktail Franks in Sweet & Sour Currant Sauce

   1 pound cocktail-size frankfurters, cooked in
      boiling water for 3 minutes and drained
1/2 cup chili sauce
   1 cup currant jelly
   4 tablespoons brown sugar
   2 tablespoons lemon juice

Heat together the chili sauce, currant jelly, brown sugar and lemon
juice and simmer for 2 minutes. Add the franks and simmer for
another 5 minutes. Place the mixture in a chafing dish. Serve with
picks or spears.

Spinach & Cheese Dumplings with Lemon Herb Creme Fraiche

What an unusual and delicious hors d'oeuvre. Make extras because their clean, fresh taste makes them irresistible.

- **1 package (10 ounces) frozen chopped spinach, defrosted and drained**
- **1 cup Ricotta cheese**
- **3/4 cup grated Parmesan cheese**
- **1/2 cup fresh bread crumbs**
- **1/4 cup finely chopped green onions**
- **2 eggs**
- **1/2 teaspoon Italian Herb Seasoning**
  salt and pepper to taste

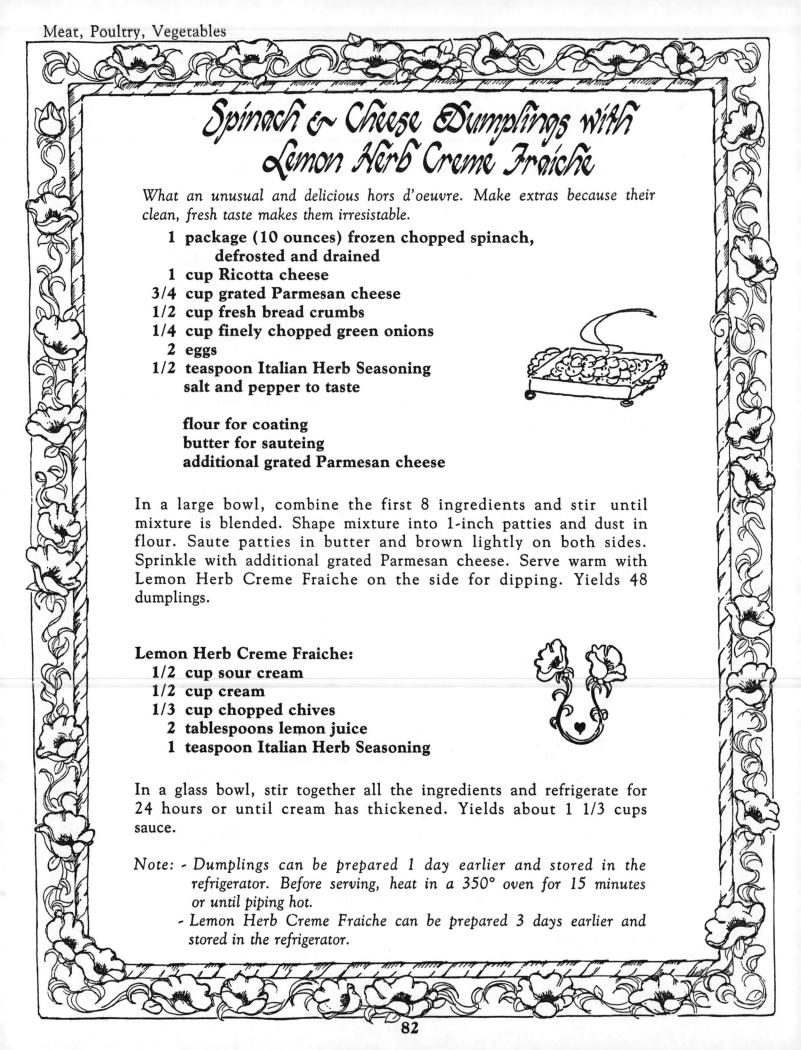

flour for coating
butter for sauteing
additional grated Parmesan cheese

In a large bowl, combine the first 8 ingredients and stir until mixture is blended. Shape mixture into 1-inch patties and dust in flour. Saute patties in butter and brown lightly on both sides. Sprinkle with additional grated Parmesan cheese. Serve warm with Lemon Herb Creme Fraiche on the side for dipping. Yields 48 dumplings.

Lemon Herb Creme Fraiche:
- **1/2 cup sour cream**
- **1/2 cup cream**
- **1/3 cup chopped chives**
- **2 tablespoons lemon juice**
- **1 teaspoon Italian Herb Seasoning**

In a glass bowl, stir together all the ingredients and refrigerate for 24 hours or until cream has thickened. Yields about 1 1/3 cups sauce.

Note: - Dumplings can be prepared 1 day earlier and stored in the refrigerator. Before serving, heat in a 350° oven for 15 minutes or until piping hot.

- Lemon Herb Creme Fraiche can be prepared 3 days earlier and stored in the refrigerator.

Teriyaki Spareribs with Ginger Honey Plum Glaze

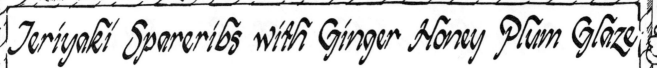

These are a great hors d'oeuvre, so make extras. Have the butcher cut the ribs in half, so that they are easier to handle.

3 pounds pork spareribs. Ask the butcher to cut these in half, crosswise, and then cut through and separate each rib. Sprinkle with salt and pepper to taste.

1/2 cup teriyaki sauce
2 tablespoons brown sugar
2 tablespoons lemon juice
1 clove garlic, finely minced
salt and pepper to taste

Place ribs in a 12x16-inch pan. Stir together teriyaki sauce, sugar, lemon juice, garlic and seasonings until blended. Brush ribs, on both sides, with teriyaki mixture. Tent pan with foil (loosely cover) and bake in a 350° oven for 50 minutes, basting now and again, with the teriyaki mixture.

Now, baste heavily with Ginger Honey Plum Glaze and continue basting, and baking for 20 minutes, uncovered, or until ribs are deeply glazed. Serve hot and have lots of napkins close by.

Ginger Honey Plum Glaze:
   1/2 cup plum jam
   1/2 cup honey
     2 tablespoons ketchup
     2 tablespoons lemon juice
   1/2 teaspoon ground ginger

Combine all the ingredients in a saucepan and heat until mixture is blended. Store unused glaze in the refrigerator. It will last for weeks.

Note: - Spareribs can be prepared earlier in the day with the following considerations. You can bake them with the teriyaki marinade for about 50 minutes, and then store them in the refrigerator. About 30 minutes before serving, glaze them with the Ginger Honey Plum Glaze and continue baking and basting for about 20 minutes.

Spareribs with Honey Barbecue Sauce

**4 pounds spareribs, cut into separate ribs, sprinkle lightly
with salt, pepper, garlic powder, paprika and flour**

Honey Barbecue Sauce:
- 1 cup chili sauce
- 1 cup ketchup
- 1/4 cup honey
- 1 medium onion, grated
- 2 tablespoons vinegar
- 2 tablespoons brown sugar
- 2 teaspoons prepared mustard
- 1/4 teaspoon hot pepper sauce

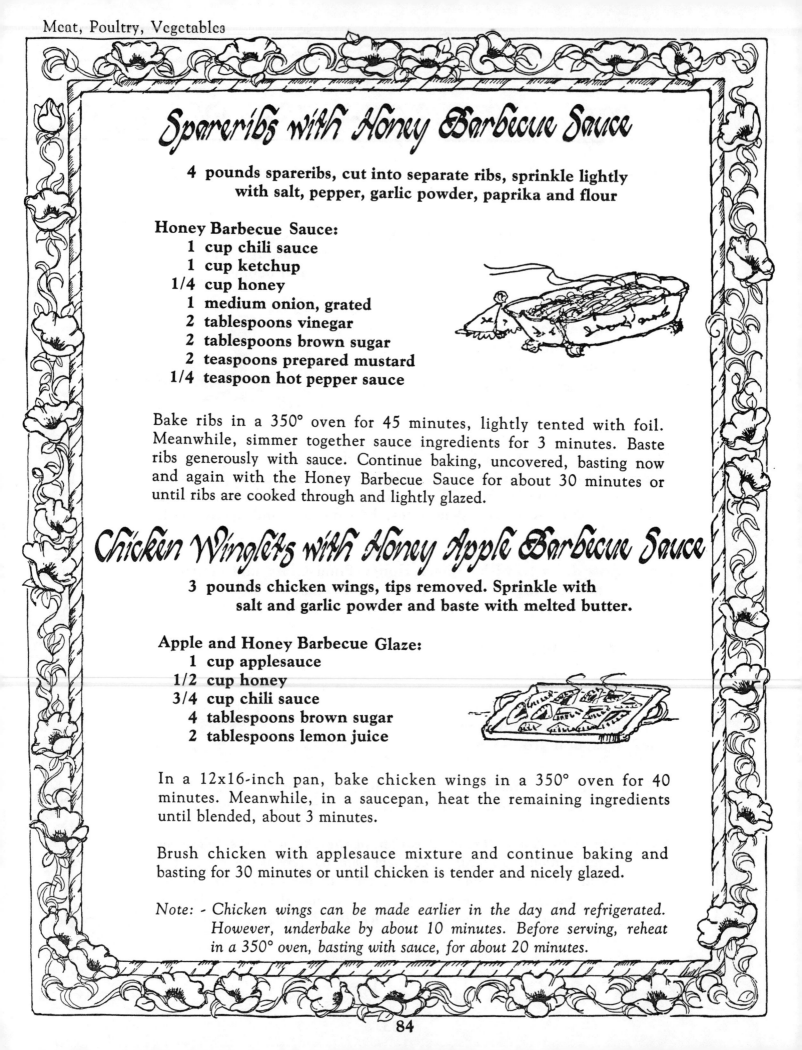

Bake ribs in a 350° oven for 45 minutes, lightly tented with foil.
Meanwhile, simmer together sauce ingredients for 3 minutes. Baste
ribs generously with sauce. Continue baking, uncovered, basting now
and again with the Honey Barbecue Sauce for about 30 minutes or
until ribs are cooked through and lightly glazed.

Chicken Winglets with Honey Apple Barbecue Sauce

**3 pounds chicken wings, tips removed. Sprinkle with
salt and garlic powder and baste with melted butter.**

Apple and Honey Barbecue Glaze:
- 1 cup applesauce
- 1/2 cup honey
- 3/4 cup chili sauce
- 4 tablespoons brown sugar
- 2 tablespoons lemon juice

In a 12x16-inch pan, bake chicken wings in a 350° oven for 40
minutes. Meanwhile, in a saucepan, heat the remaining ingredients
until blended, about 3 minutes.

Brush chicken with applesauce mixture and continue baking and
basting for 30 minutes or until chicken is tender and nicely glazed.

*Note: - Chicken wings can be made earlier in the day and refrigerated.
However, underbake by about 10 minutes. Before serving, reheat
in a 350° oven, basting with sauce, for about 20 minutes.*

Teriyaki Meatballs with Chinese Hot Plum Sauce

You will find that you cannot make enough of these succulent meatballs. Serving these will make an informal dinner seem like a party. And how delicious they are and so simple to prepare.

1/2 pound ground beef
1/2 pound lean ground pork
1/3 cup chopped green onions
1/3 cup mushrooms, finely chopped
1 tablespoon teriyaki marinade
   salt and pepper to taste

   flour
1 egg, beaten

Combine first 6 ingredients and mix until thoroughly blended. Shape meat mixture into small meatballs.

Roll meatballs in flour until coated evenly and dip them into the beaten egg. Fry them in 1/2-inch of hot oil until browned on 1 side. Turn and brown other side. Drain on paper towels.

Spear with a toothpick and serve with Chinese Hot Plum Sauce on the side for dipping. Yields about 4 dozen cocktail-size meatballs.

Chinese Hot Plum Sauce

1/2 cup plum preserves
2 tablespoons lemon juice
2 tablespoons ketchup
2 tablespoons brown sugar
1/4 teaspoon dry mustard

Combine all the ingredients in a saucepan and cook for 3 minutes or until sugar has dissolved and mixture is blended. Allow to cool for a few minutes and serve warm. Yields about 3/4 cup sauce.

Note: - Meatballs and sauce can be prepared earlier in the day and heated before serving. Do not overcook the meatballs, but simply heat through.

Chicken Meatballs in Sweet & Sour Cranberry Sauce

3 **cups cooked chicken**
2 **green onions**
1 **egg**
   salt and pepper to taste

Place all the ingredients in a food processor bowl and blend until mixture is finely chopped. Shape mixture into 1-inch balls and bake in a 350° oven for about 15 minutes or until meat balls are set. Place chicken in a heated chafing dish and pour Sweet and Sour Cranberry Sauce over the top. Keep warm while serving. Yields about 4 dozen chicken meatballs.

Sweet & Sour Cranberry Sauce:
   1 **cup whole cranberry sauce**
1/2 **cup ketchup**
   2 **tablespoons lemon juice**
   2 **tablespoons brown sugar**

In a small saucepan, place all the ingredients and heat until blended. Yields about 1 1/2 cups sauce.

Pork Meatballs with Peanut Plum Sauce

1   pound lean ground pork
1   clove garlic, finely minced
1/4 cup finely chopped green onions
1   tablespoon teriyaki marinade
1/4 teaspoon ground ginger
1   teaspoon sugar
    salt and pepper to taste
1   egg, beaten
1/2 cup fresh bread crumbs

Combine all the ingredients and blend thoroughly. Shape into 1/2-inch balls and brown in a large skillet, shaking the pan frequently so that the meatballs will brown on all sides. Spear with toothpicks and serve warm with Peanut Plum Sauce on the side for dipping. Yields about 40 meatballs.

Peanut Plum Sauce

1/2 cup plum preserves
2   tablespoons brown sugar
2   tablespoons lemon juice
4   tablespoons very finely chopped peanuts

Combine all the ingredients in a small saucepan and heat until mixture is blended. Serve sauce warm, not hot. Yields about 3/4 cup sauce.

Note: - Meatballs can be made earlier in the day and stored in the refrigerator. Heat in a 350° oven until warmed through.

Company Meatballs in Sweet & Sour Honey Sauce

- 1 pound ground beef
- 1/2 cup bread crumbs
- 1/2 cup finely chopped green onions
- 1 clove garlic, put through a press
- 1/4 cup cream
- 1 egg, beaten
  salt and pepper to taste

Combine all the ingredients and shape into cocktail-size meatballs. Roll meatballs in Coating Mixture and place in one layer on a greased cookie-sheet. Bake at 325° until cooked through (time will depend on size of meatballs), and turn them once or twice during the cooking time.

Serve with Sweet and Sour Honey Sauce on the side for dipping. Yields about 4 dozen cocktail-size meatballs.

Coating Mixture:
- 1/4 cup flour
- 1/4 cup cracker crumbs
- 1/4 cup sesame seeds
- 1/4 cup grated Parmesan cheese
- 1 teaspoon paprika
- 1/2 teaspoon garlic powder
  salt and pepper to taste

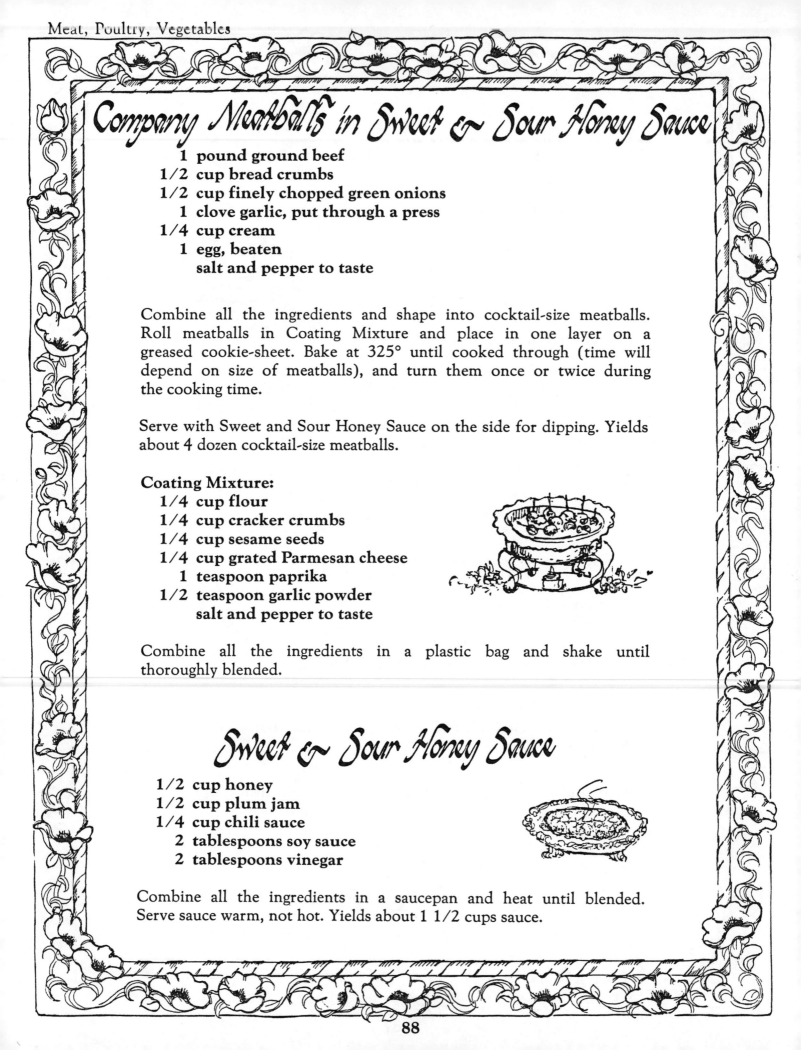

Combine all the ingredients in a plastic bag and shake until thoroughly blended.

Sweet & Sour Honey Sauce

- 1/2 cup honey
- 1/2 cup plum jam
- 1/4 cup chili sauce
- 2 tablespoons soy sauce
- 2 tablespoons vinegar

Combine all the ingredients in a saucepan and heat until blended. Serve sauce warm, not hot. Yields about 1 1/2 cups sauce.

Beer~Batter Fried Vegetables with Garlic Lemon Wine Sauce

Zuchini, unpeeled and cut into 1/4-inch thick slices
Mushrooms, cleaned, stemmed and left whole. Use
    stems for another use
Carrots, peeled and cut on the diagonal into 1/4-inch
    thick slices
Eggplant, peeled and sliced into 3x1/2-inch thick
    matchsticks
Green Pepper, cut into slices.

Dip vegetables in Beer Batter and fry in hot oil until golden on all sides. Keep warm in a 250° oven. Drain and serve with Garlic, Lemon Wine Sauce on the side for dipping.

Beer Batter:
    2 eggs
    1 cup beer
    1 cup flour
    1/2 teaspoon paprika
    1/4 teaspoon garlic powder
    1/4 teaspoon salt

Beat all ingredients together until blended.

Garlic Lemon Wine Sauce:
    4 tablespoons butter
    2 cloves garlic, minced

    1/4 cup white wine
    3 tablespoons lemon juice

Saute garlic in butter until softened. Add the remaining ingredients and simmer sauce for 2 minutes. Place in a bowl and serve warm. Yields about 2/3 cup sauce.

Batter-Fried Shrimp with Tartar Sauce

2 pounds shrimp, shelled and deveined. Dust
    lightly with flour.

1 cup flour
1 cup beer
1 egg
1/8 teaspoon garlic powder
1/8 teaspoon salt

Beat together flour, beer, egg, garlic powder and salt until mixture
is blended. Dip shrimp in batter and fry in hot oil until browned on
both sides. Remove from oil and drain. Keep warm in a 250° oven.
Serve with Tartar Sauce or Lemon Butter Garlic Sauce, on the side
for dipping.

Tartar Sauce

1/2 cup mayonnaise
1/2 cup sour cream
2 green onions, finely minced
2 tablespoons parsley, finely minced
2 tablespoons lemon juice
3 tablespoons sweet relish

Place all the ingredients in a glass jar with a tight-fitting lid and
stir until blended. Refrigerate sauce until ready to use. Yields about
1 1/4 cups sauce.

Lemon Butter Garlic Sauce

1/2 cup butter
2 cloves garlic, minced
2 tablespoons lemon juice
1 tablespoon chopped parsley
1 tablespoon chopped chives
1 tablespoon rinsed capers
1 teaspoon finely grated lemon peel
1 teaspoon Dijon mustard
1/8 teaspoon salt

Saute garlic in butter until softened. Add the remaining ingredients
and simmer sauce for 5 minutes. Drizzle sauce over fried fish and
shellfish, or use on the side for dipping. Yields about 3/4 cup sauce.

Shrimp Provencal in Red Hot Clam Sauce

1 large onion, chopped
3 cloves garlic, minced
2 tablespoons oil
1 can (1 pound) stewed tomatoes, minced and drained.
    Reserve juice for another use.
1 can (8 ounces) tomato sauce
1 can (7 ounces) minced clams
2 tablespoons lemon juice
2 tablespoons chopped parsley
1/4 teaspoon sweet basil
1/2 teaspoon thyme flakes
1 teaspoon sugar
1/4 teaspoon tumeric
    pinch of red pepper flakes
    salt and pepper to taste

3/4 pound uncooked shrimp, shelled and deveined
3/4 pound scallops, cut into 1/2-inch slices

In a Dutch oven, combine all the ingredients except the shellfish, and simmer mixture, uncovered, for 20 minutes. Bring sauce to a boil and add the shrimp and scallops. Simmer for about 5 minutes or until fish becomes opaque. Place in a heated chafing dish and serve with long picks or cocktail forks. Some crusty French bread can be held close by for dunking.

Note: - Sauce can be made earlier in the day and refrigerated. Remove from the refrigerator about 30 minutes before serving. Bring sauce to a boil and add the shellfish. Cook as directed above.
- If you are serving these in small ramekins as a small entree, then a sprinkling of grated Parmesan cheese on top of each, is a lovely addition. Serves 5 or 6.

Easiest & Best Bacon & Cheese Custard Pie
(Quiche Lorraine)

This is a new way to prepare an old favorite. The cream cheese imparts an interesting and delicious touch which gives this dish a completely different character.

**1 9-inch deep dish pie shell, baked in a 400°
        oven for about 10 minutes or until shell is just
        beginning to brown.**

**1/2 pound bacon, cooked crisp, drained and crumbled
1 cup grated Swiss cheese
1 package (3 ounces) cream cheese and chives**

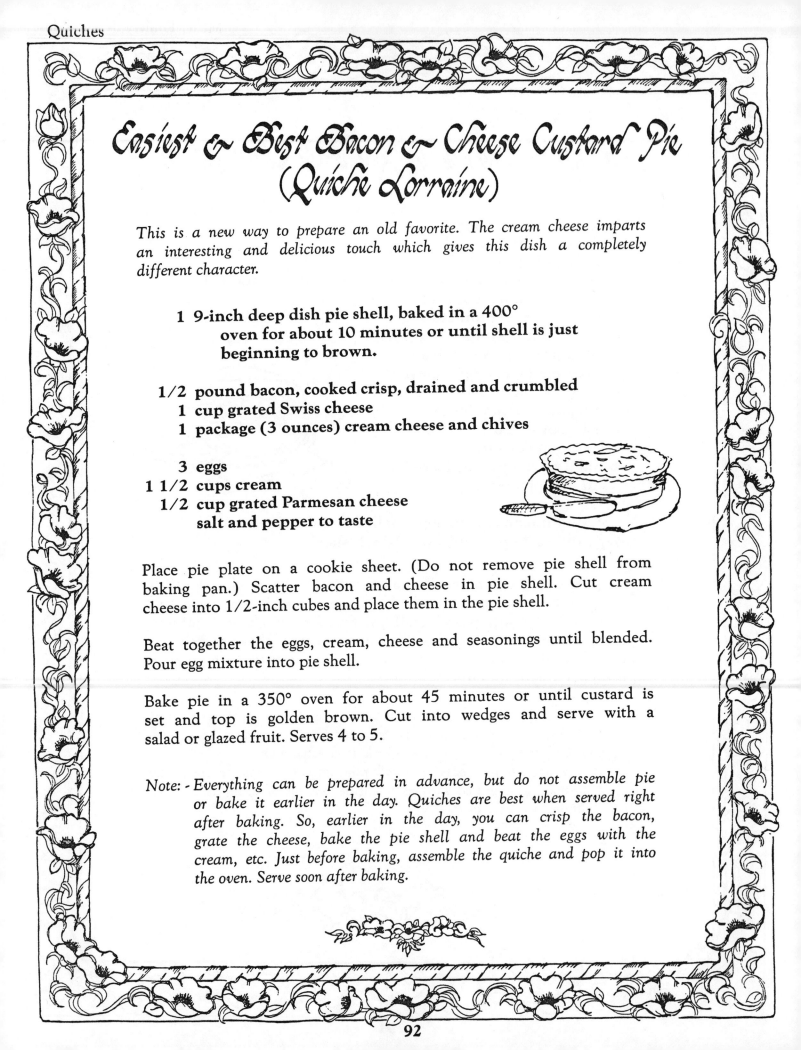

**3 eggs
1 1/2 cups cream
1/2 cup grated Parmesan cheese
        salt and pepper to taste**

Place pie plate on a cookie sheet. (Do not remove pie shell from baking pan.) Scatter bacon and cheese in pie shell. Cut cream cheese into 1/2-inch cubes and place them in the pie shell.

Beat together the eggs, cream, cheese and seasonings until blended. Pour egg mixture into pie shell.

Bake pie in a 350° oven for about 45 minutes or until custard is set and top is golden brown. Cut into wedges and serve with a salad or glazed fruit. Serves 4 to 5.

Note: - Everything can be prepared in advance, but do not assemble pie or bake it earlier in the day. Quiches are best when served right after baking. So, earlier in the day, you can crisp the bacon, grate the cheese, bake the pie shell and beat the eggs with the cream, etc. Just before baking, assemble the quiche and pop it into the oven. Serve soon after baking.

Greek Cheese Pie with Tomatoes & Onions

This is not a traditional quiche, but very satisfying in taste and texture. While it is Greek in feeling (because of the use of Feta cheese) it is just an old-fashioned American Cheese Pie.

    1   9-inch deep dish frozen pie shell, baked unfilled
            in a 400° oven for about 10 minutes or until
            golden brown.

  3/4   pound feta cheese, crumbled and mashed
    4   eggs
    1   cup cream (can substitute half and half)
  1/4   cup grated Parmesan cheese

  3/4   cup finely chopped stewed tomatoes, drained.
            (About 3/4 of a 1-pound can.)
  1/2   cup chopped green onions
        salt and pepper to taste (Please keep in mind that
            the cheese is salty.)

Prepare pie shell and set aside. Beat together the feta cheese, eggs, cream and grated Parmesan until the mixture is nicely blended. Place pie shell on a cookie tin. (Leave pie in pan.)

Scatter tomatoes and green onions evenly over baked pie shell. Pour egg mixture over. Place in a 350° oven and bake for 40 to 45 minutes or until custard is set and top is golden. Serves 6.

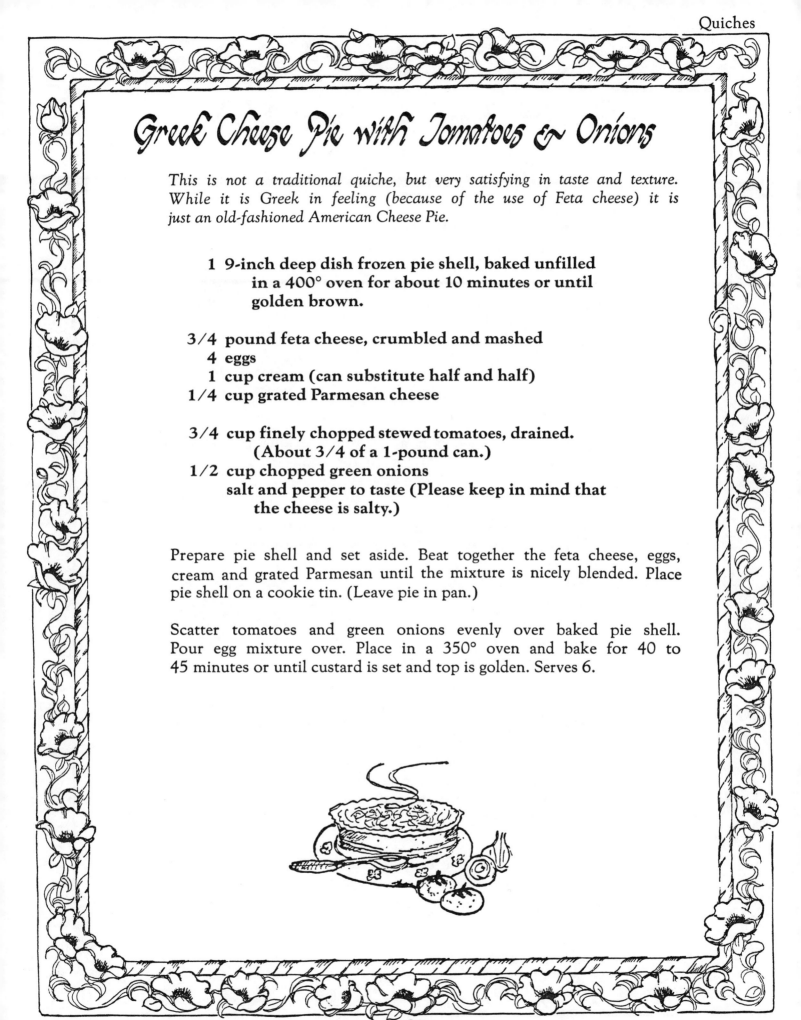

Eggplant, Tomato & Onion Quiche with Herbs & Cheese

Vegetable Mixture:
- 1/2 eggplant, peeled and sliced
- 2 zucchini, sliced
- 1 small onion, chopped
- 1 tomato, peeled, seeded and chopped
- 1/2 green bell pepper, chopped
- 1 clove garlic, minced
- 1/4 cup melted butter (1/2 stick)
- 1/2 teaspoon basil
- 1/4 teaspoon thyme
  - salt and pepper to taste

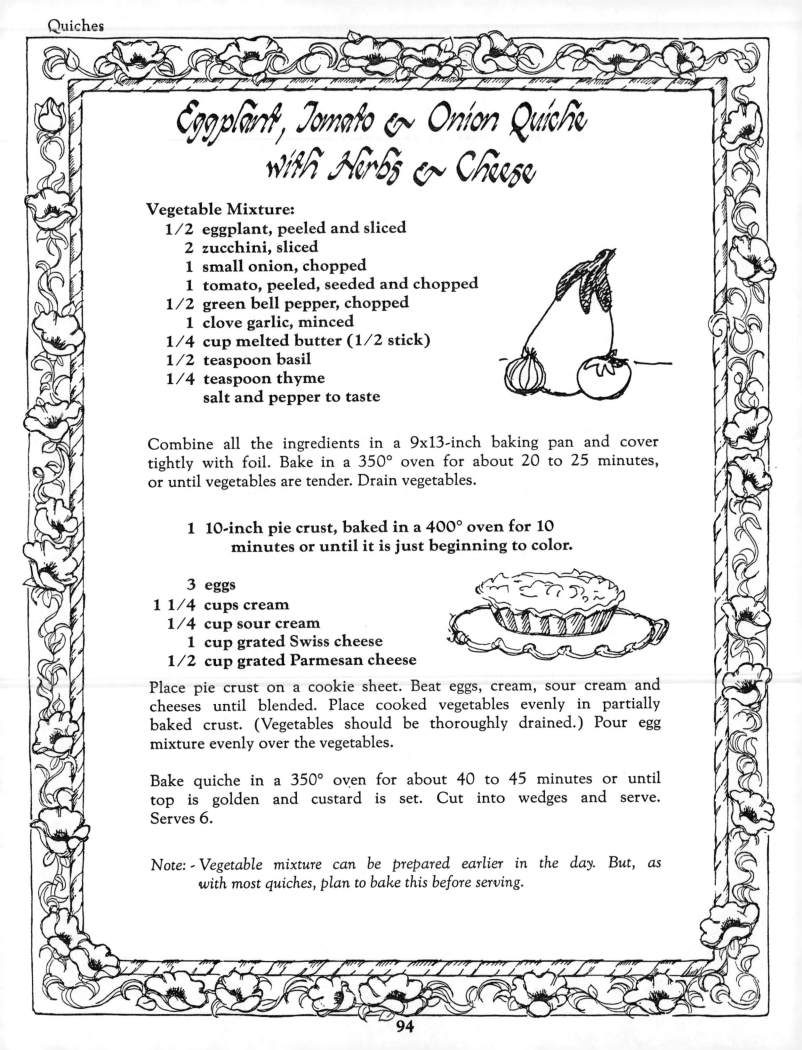

Combine all the ingredients in a 9x13-inch baking pan and cover tightly with foil. Bake in a 350° oven for about 20 to 25 minutes, or until vegetables are tender. Drain vegetables.

- 1 10-inch pie crust, baked in a 400° oven for 10 minutes or until it is just beginning to color.

- 3 eggs
- 1 1/4 cups cream
- 1/4 cup sour cream
- 1 cup grated Swiss cheese
- 1/2 cup grated Parmesan cheese

Place pie crust on a cookie sheet. Beat eggs, cream, sour cream and cheeses until blended. Place cooked vegetables evenly in partially baked crust. (Vegetables should be thoroughly drained.) Pour egg mixture evenly over the vegetables.

Bake quiche in a 350° oven for about 40 to 45 minutes or until top is golden and custard is set. Cut into wedges and serve. Serves 6.

Note: - Vegetable mixture can be prepared earlier in the day. But, as with most quiches, plan to bake this before serving.

Torta Rustica ~~ A Country Ham & Cheese Pie

1 9-inch deep dish pie shell, baked in a 400° oven
    for 10 minutes

1/2 pound baked ham, (leftover ham is perfect for this
    dish), chopped
1/2 pound Mozzarella cheese, grated
4 eggs
1 1/2 cups cream or half and half
1/2 teaspoon Italian Herb Seasoning
1 tablespoon chopped parsley
1/3 cup grated Parmesan cheese
    salt and pepper to taste

Place ham and Mozzarella in prepared pie shell. Beat together the remaining ingredients until blended and pour this over the ham and cheese. Sprinkle top with a little additional grated cheese.

Place quiche on a cookie sheet and bake in a 350° oven for 45 minutes or until custard is set. Cut into wedges and serve 6.

Quiche with Salami & Cheese Italienne

1 9-inch deep dish pie shell, baked in a 400°
    oven for 10 minutes

1/2 pound hard Italian salami, sliced and
    then chopped
1 pound Ricotta cheese
3/4 cup grated Parmesan cheese
4 eggs
2 tablespoons lemon juice
1/2 cup cream
1/8 teaspoon nutmeg

Prepare pie shell. Combine the remaining ingredients and beat until blended. Pour mixture into prepared shell and bake in a 350° oven for about 45 minutes to 1 hour or until quiche is set and top is golden brown. Cut into wedges and serve 6.

Note: - Quiches are best when served shortly after baking. Both of these quiches can be served hot or warm.

Quiche Florentine with Spinach, Tomatoes & Cheese

You will have to go far and wide to find a more delectable quiche. The little dots of cream cheese add a wonderful character to this dish. The creamy filling is delicious with a hint of nutmeg.

- 1 9-inch deep dish frozen pie shell. Bake in a 400° oven for 10 minutes or until crust is very lightly browned

- 1 package (10 ounces) frozen chopped spinach, defrosted and drained
- 1/3 cup minced green onions
- 3 eggs
- 1 1/2 cups cream
- 1 cup grated Swiss cheese
- 1/2 cup grated Parmesan cheese
- 1/4 teaspoon nutmeg
  salt and pepper to taste

- 8 tablespoons cream cheese

- 6 thin slices tomato
- 1/2 cup grated Swiss cheese

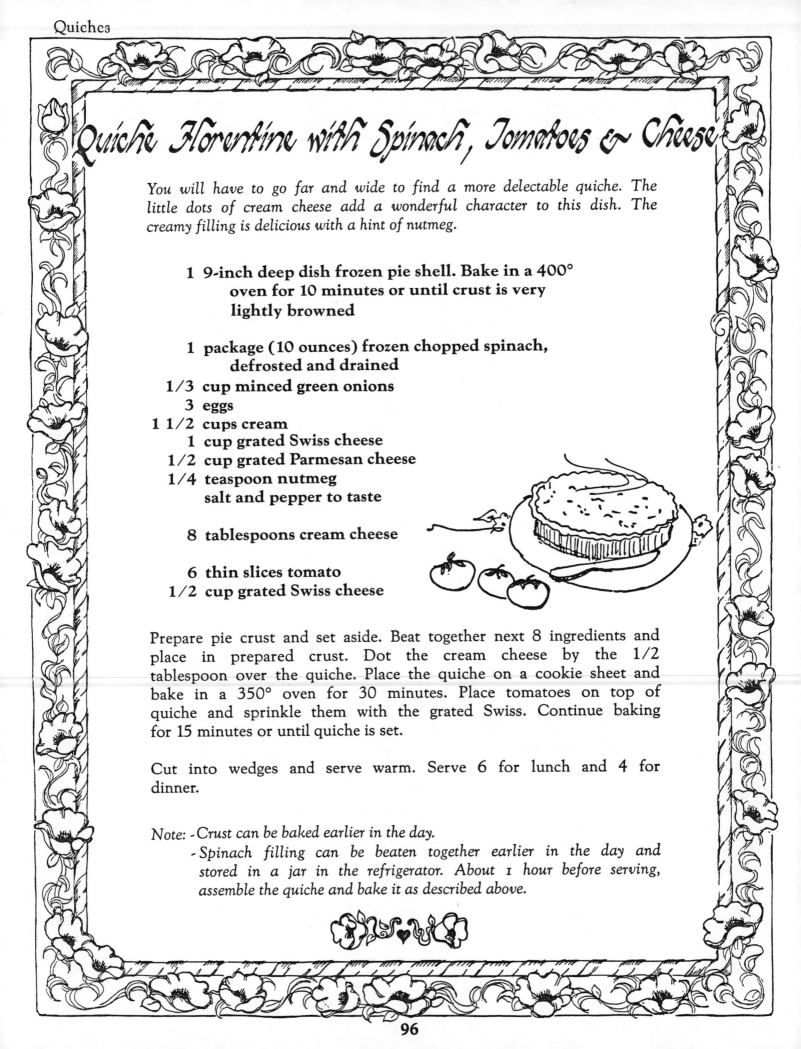

Prepare pie crust and set aside. Beat together next 8 ingredients and place in prepared crust. Dot the cream cheese by the 1/2 tablespoon over the quiche. Place the quiche on a cookie sheet and bake in a 350° oven for 30 minutes. Place tomatoes on top of quiche and sprinkle them with the grated Swiss. Continue baking for 15 minutes or until quiche is set.

Cut into wedges and serve warm. Serve 6 for lunch and 4 for dinner.

Note: - Crust can be baked earlier in the day.
- Spinach filling can be beaten together earlier in the day and stored in a jar in the refrigerator. About 1 hour before serving, assemble the quiche and bake it as described above.

Mexican Meat Pie with Tomatoes, Chiles & Cheese

Meat pies are so versatile. They are an excellent hors d'oeuvre, a satisfying lunch and do very well as a light supper. Serve them with a salad and a refreshing fruit dessert for a hearty, stimulating meal.

1 **9-inch deep dish frozen pie shell, baked unfilled in a 400° oven for about 10 minutes or until golden brown.**

1 **pound lean ground beef**
1 **tablespoon dried onion flakes***
1 **teaspoon beef seasoned stock base***
1 **tablespoon Spice Islands Chili con Carne Seasoning (or more to taste)***
1/8 **teaspoon garlic powder**
 salt and pepper to taste

2 **ounces diced green chiles (1/2 of a 4-ounce can)**
3/4 **cup finely chopped stewed tomatoes, drained, (about 3/4 of a 1-pound can)**
1 **egg, beaten**

1 **cup sour cream**
1 **cup grated Cheddar cheese**
1/4 **cup finely chopped green onions**

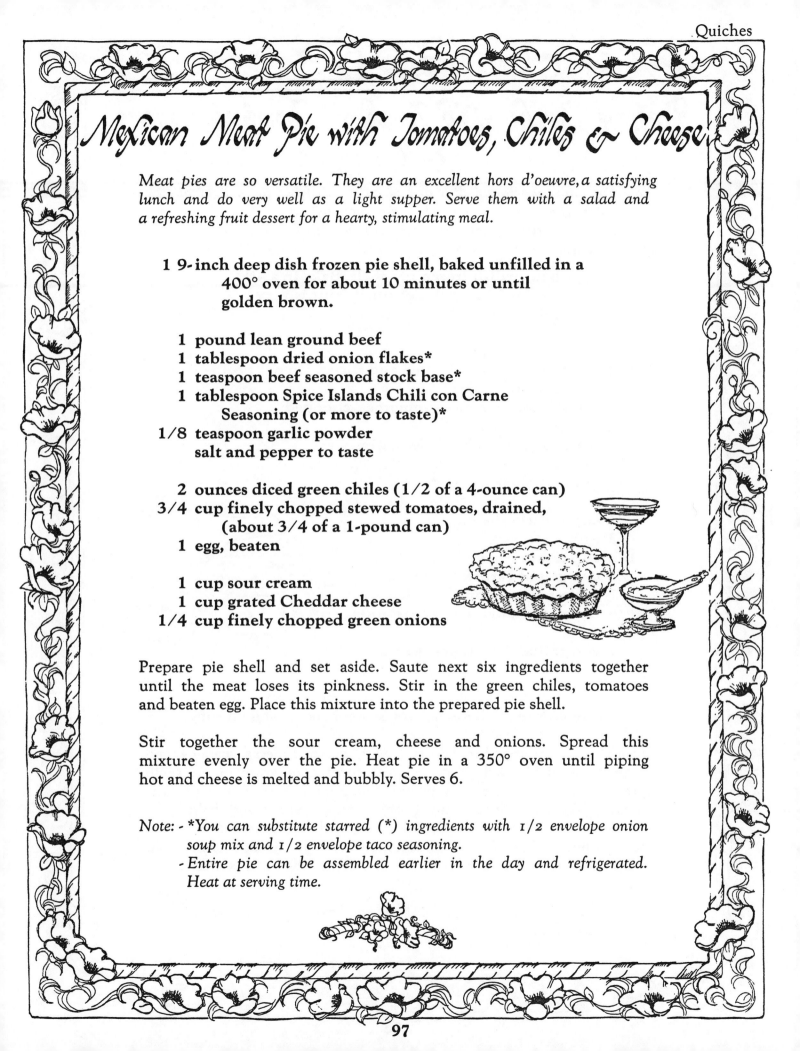

Prepare pie shell and set aside. Saute next six ingredients together until the meat loses its pinkness. Stir in the green chiles, tomatoes and beaten egg. Place this mixture into the prepared pie shell.

Stir together the sour cream, cheese and onions. Spread this mixture evenly over the pie. Heat pie in a 350° oven until piping hot and cheese is melted and bubbly. Serves 6.

*Note: - *You can substitute starred (*) ingredients with 1/2 envelope onion soup mix and 1/2 envelope taco seasoning.*
- Entire pie can be assembled earlier in the day and refrigerated. Heat at serving time.

Peasant Quiche with Zucchini, Tomatoes, Onions & Cheese

This is a hardy vegetarian dish and is quite satisfying for a light dinner. It is filled with "good things" that are supposed to be "good" for you, too. Serve it with pink rice and some fresh fruit as a nice accompaniment.

1 9-inch deep dish frozen pie shell. Bake in a 400°
   oven for 10 minutes or until crust is very
   lightly browned

1 onion, chopped
1/2 pound zucchini, scrubbed and sliced. Do not peel.
2 cloves garlic, minced
1 can (1 pound) stewed tomatoes, chopped
   and drained
1/2 teaspoon Italian Herb Seasoning
2 tablespoons oil
   salt and pepper to taste

1 cup Ricotta cheese
3 eggs
1/2 cup cream
1/2 cup grated Parmesan cheese
1 tablespoon chopped parsley
1/4 teaspoon Italian Herb Seasoning

1 cup grated Mozzarella cheese

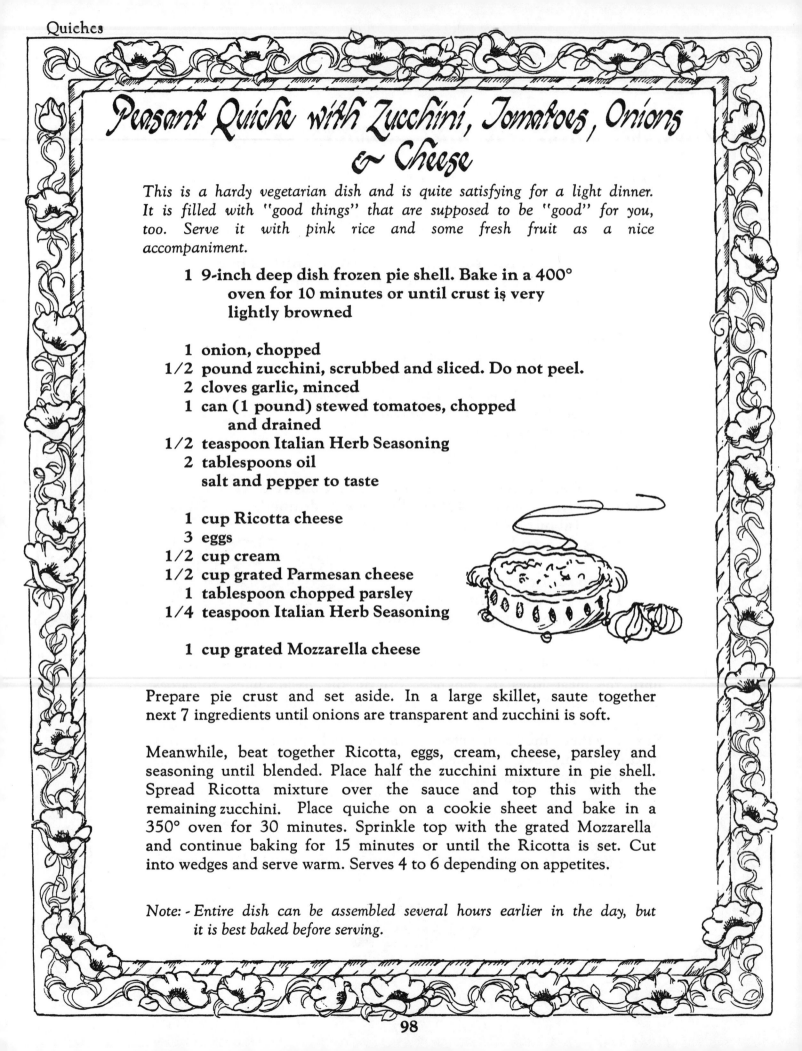

Prepare pie crust and set aside. In a large skillet, saute together next 7 ingredients until onions are transparent and zucchini is soft.

Meanwhile, beat together Ricotta, eggs, cream, cheese, parsley and seasoning until blended. Place half the zucchini mixture in pie shell. Spread Ricotta mixture over the sauce and top this with the remaining zucchini. Place quiche on a cookie sheet and bake in a 350° oven for 30 minutes. Sprinkle top with the grated Mozzarella and continue baking for 15 minutes or until the Ricotta is set. Cut into wedges and serve warm. Serves 4 to 6 depending on appetites.

Note: - Entire dish can be assembled several hours earlier in the day, but it is best baked before serving.

Eggplant Crustless Quiche with Onions & Cheese

1 eggplant (about 1 pound), peeled and cut into
    1/4-inch slices

3 eggs
2 packages (3 ounces, each) cream cheese and chives
1 1/2 cups cottage cheese
3/4 cup grated Parmesan cheese
1/2 cup fresh bread crumbs
3 green onions, finely chopped
    salt to taste

Place eggplant slices in a 9x13-inch roasting pan and cover tightly with foil. Bake eggplant in a 400° oven for about 20 minutes or until eggplant is soft.

Place eggplant and remaining ingredients in the large bowl of an electric mixer and beat until blended. Place eggplant mixture in a 9x13-inch roasting pan that has been heavily oiled, and bake in a 350° oven for 45 minutes or until top is crusty; and golden brown.

To serve, cut into squares and serve warm. Serve with picks or cocktail forks.

Note: - *Entire dish can be prepared earlier in the day and stored in the refrigerator. Heat in a 350° oven for about 20 minutes or until piping hot. Serve warm.*
    - Zucchini can be substituted for the eggplant.

Crustless Quiche with Zucchini, Onions, Tomatoes & Cheese

6 small zucchini, unpeeled and thinly sliced
1/2 pound mushrooms, sliced
1 large onion, chopped
3 cloves garlic, minced
4 tablespoons butter

6 eggs, beaten
6 slices bacon, cooked crisp, drained and crumbled
2 cups grated Swiss cheese
1/2 cup grated Parmesan cheese
1/2 teaspoon sweet basil
salt and pepper to taste

8 thin slices tomato

In a skillet, saute zucchini, mushrooms, garlic and onion in butter until onions are soft and liquid rendered is evaporated. In a bowl, beat eggs and add bacon, cheeses, seasonings and zucchini mixture.

Pour mixture into a greased 9x13-inch baking pan and top with tomato slices. Bake in a 350° oven until eggs are puffed and set, about 45 minutes.

Cut into squares and serve at once. Yields about 24 (2-inch) square servings.

Note: - Entire casserole can be assembled earlier in the day and stored in the refrigerator. However, bake before serving.
- This is an excellent small entree or luncheon dish.

Salmon Poached in Wine with Dijon Dill Sauce

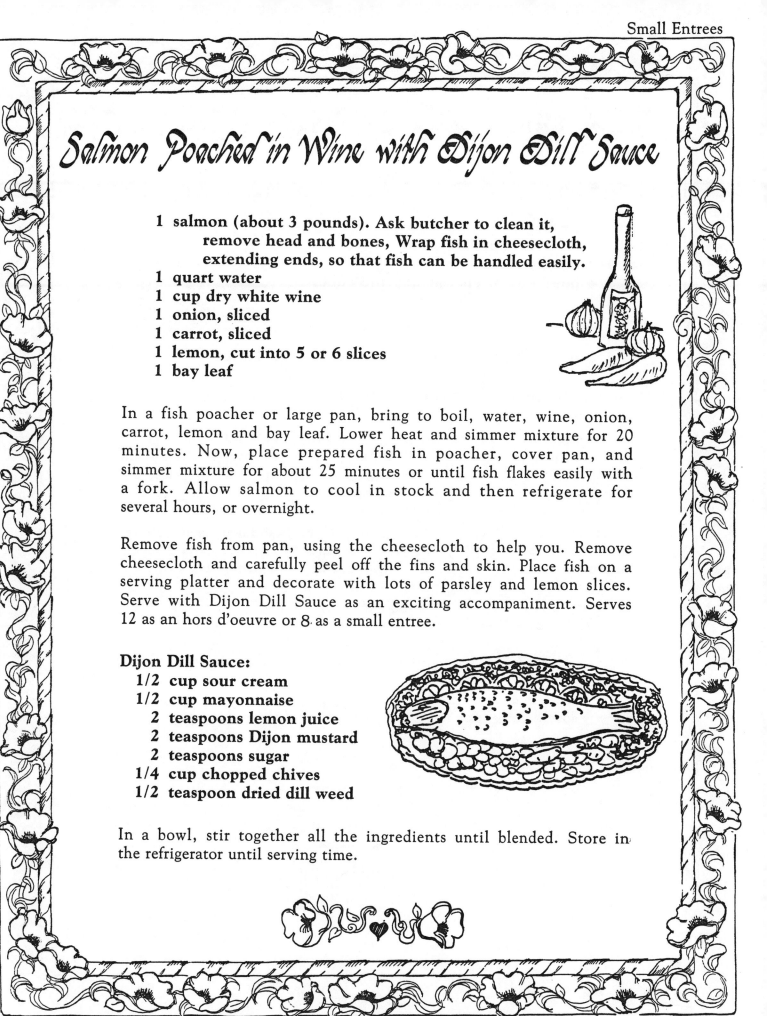

1 salmon (about 3 pounds). Ask butcher to clean it,
   remove head and bones, Wrap fish in cheesecloth,
   extending ends, so that fish can be handled easily.
1 quart water
1 cup dry white wine
1 onion, sliced
1 carrot, sliced
1 lemon, cut into 5 or 6 slices
1 bay leaf

In a fish poacher or large pan, bring to boil, water, wine, onion, carrot, lemon and bay leaf. Lower heat and simmer mixture for 20 minutes. Now, place prepared fish in poacher, cover pan, and simmer mixture for about 25 minutes or until fish flakes easily with a fork. Allow salmon to cool in stock and then refrigerate for several hours, or overnight.

Remove fish from pan, using the cheesecloth to help you. Remove cheesecloth and carefully peel off the fins and skin. Place fish on a serving platter and decorate with lots of parsley and lemon slices. Serve with Dijon Dill Sauce as an exciting accompaniment. Serves 12 as an hors d'oeuvre or 8 as a small entree.

Dijon Dill Sauce:
   1/2 cup sour cream
   1/2 cup mayonnaise
     2 teaspoons lemon juice
     2 teaspoons Dijon mustard
     2 teaspoons sugar
   1/4 cup chopped chives
   1/2 teaspoon dried dill weed

In a bowl, stir together all the ingredients until blended. Store in the refrigerator until serving time.

Crabmeat Mini-Souffles with Swiss Cheese & Chives

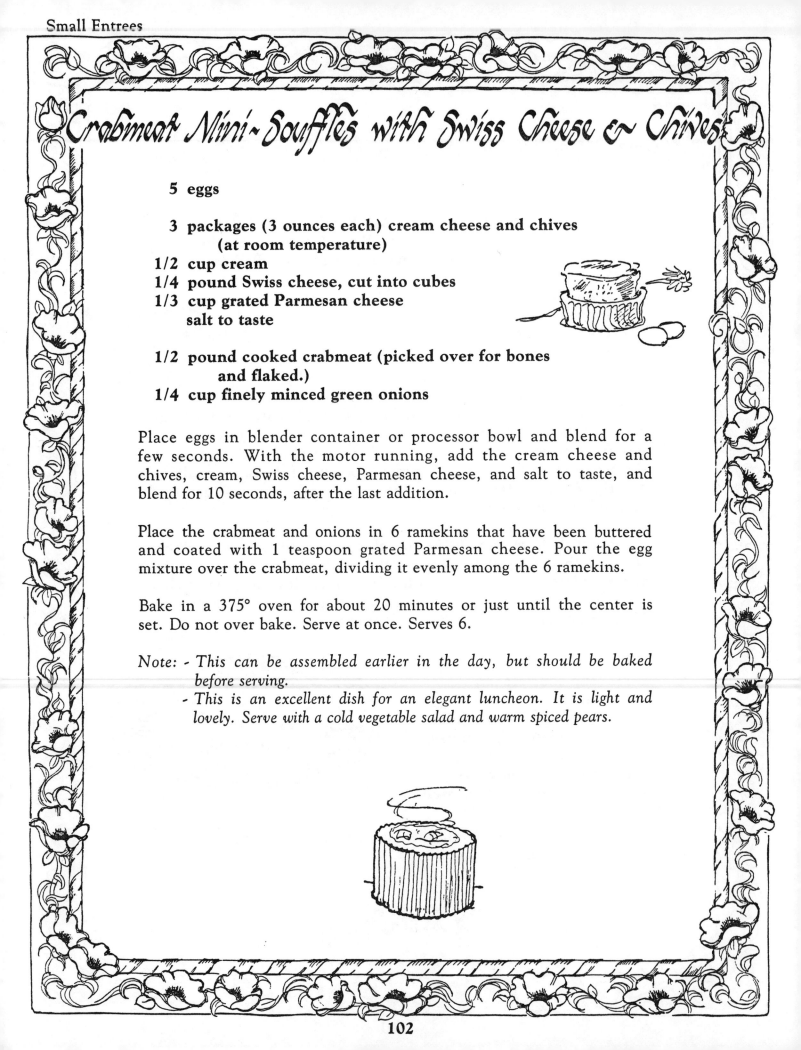

    5 **eggs**

    3 **packages (3 ounces each) cream cheese and chives**
          (at room temperature)
1/2 **cup cream**
1/4 **pound Swiss cheese, cut into cubes**
1/3 **cup grated Parmesan cheese**
      salt to taste

1/2 **pound cooked crabmeat (picked over for bones**
        and flaked.)
1/4 **cup finely minced green onions**

Place eggs in blender container or processor bowl and blend for a few seconds. With the motor running, add the cream cheese and chives, cream, Swiss cheese, Parmesan cheese, and salt to taste, and blend for 10 seconds, after the last addition.

Place the crabmeat and onions in 6 ramekins that have been buttered and coated with 1 teaspoon grated Parmesan cheese. Pour the egg mixture over the crabmeat, dividing it evenly among the 6 ramekins.

Bake in a 375° oven for about 20 minutes or just until the center is set. Do not over bake. Serve at once. Serves 6.

Note: - This can be assembled earlier in the day, but should be baked
before serving.
    - This is an excellent dish for an elegant luncheon. It is light and
lovely. Serve with a cold vegetable salad and warm spiced pears.

Mousselines of Sole in Mushroom & Cream Sauce

With the help of the food processor, this truly majestic dish is easy enough for even the most novice cook to prepare. The mousselines are actually ethereal, light as clouds, sole dumplings, simmered in wine and served in a delightful Mushroom Cream Sauce. Normally, mousselines (also called "quenelles") can be a little tricky to prepare, for they can disintegrate in the poaching liquid. To avoid this, I added the extra egg whites and the cream cheese, making them totally foolproof.

Poaching Liquid:
- 1/2 cup dry white wine
- 1/2 cup clam juice
- 1 small onion, chopped
- 2 or 3 slices of lemon

Mousselines:
- 1/2 pound fillets of sole
- 4 egg whites (or 2 whole eggs)
- 1 package (3 ounces) cream cheese with chives
- 1 cup cream
- salt and pepper to taste
- 1/8 teaspoon nutmeg

In a 10-inch skillet, heat together the white wine, clam juice, onion and lemon. Keep the mixture hot, but do not let it boil.

In the processor bowl, fitted with the steel blade, blend together the sole and eggs until fish is pureed. Add the cream cheese and process until blended. With the machine running, drizzle in the cream until it is incorporated. Beat in the seasonings.

Gently scoop the mousseline, 1 heaping tablespoon at a time, into the wine mixture. (If you are using a smaller pan, poach only 1 layer at a time.) Allow the dumplings to poach gently in the hot liquid for about 15 to 20 minutes, turning them, so that they poach evenly on both sides.

Remove mousselines from poaching liquid with a slotted spoon and drain them on a towel. Place them in a lovely porcelain baker, spoon the Mushroom Sauce on top and place in a 350° oven until heated through. Serve 4 with majesty and pride.

Mousselines of Sole (continued)

Mushroom Sauce: Saute 1/4 pound sliced mushrooms in 3 tablespoons butter until tender. Add 2 tablespoons flour and cook for 2 minutes. Add 3/4 cup cream, 3/4 cup sour cream and 1/4 cup white wine. Cook and stir until blended. Stir in salt and pepper to taste and 2 tablespoons chopped chives. Heat through, but do not boil.

Giant Cheese Pastelles Greek Style

1 package (10 ounces) frozen patty shells (6 shells)
1 cup crumbled feta cheese (about 6 ounces), mashed
2 eggs
6 ounces cream cheese
1 tablespoon parsley (or 1 teaspoon dried flakes)
2 tablespoons, each, bread crumbs and grated Parmesan cheese

Thaw patty shells in refrigerator. Beat together the remaining ingredients until blended. Roll out each patty shell to measure a 6-inch circle. Place 1/6 of the filling in center. Moisten the edges with water and fold dough over. Trim the edges and press them down with the tines of a fork. Scallop them, if you have the time.

Brush tops with beaten egg and pierce with the tines of a fork. Sprinkle the tops with additional grated Parmesan cheese. Place Pastelles on a greased pan and bake at 400° for about 20 to 25 minutes or until pastry is puffed and tops are golden brown. Serve with fresh fruit. Serves 6.

Stuffed Clam Shells with Cheese, Garlic & Herbs

6 cloves garlic, finely minced
1 large onion, finely chopped
3 shallots, minced
1/2 cup butter (1 stick)

1/4 cup dry white wine
1/2 teaspoon paprika
1/2 teaspoon thyme
1/4 teaspoon oregano
    salt and pepper to taste

3 cups fresh egg bread crumbs (about 6 slices)
2 cups grated Swiss cheese
1/2 cup grated Parmesan cheese
2 cans (7 ounces, each) minced clams, drained.
    Reserve clam juice.

4 tablespoons grated Parmesan cheese
2 tablespoons finely minced parsley

Saute garlic, onion and shallots in butter until onion is soft. Add the wine and seasonings and simmer mixture until wine is almost evaporated. Stir in bread crumbs, grated cheeses and minced clams and toss until mixture is blended. Add a few drops of clam juice if the mixture appears dry.

Divide mixture between 12 clam shells. Sprinkle top with grated Parmesan cheese and parsley. Place clams on a cookie sheet and bake in a 350° oven until heated through. Broil for a few seconds to lightly brown top. Serves 12 as an hors d'oeuvre or serves 6 as a small entree.

Scallop Shells with Crabmeat, Mushroom, Swiss Cheese & Wine Sauce

1/2 pound mushrooms, sliced
1 onion, chopped
2 shallots, minced
2 cloves garlic, minced
4 tablespoons butter

1/4 cup dry white wine
   salt and pepper to taste

1/2 teaspoon poultry seasoning
2 tablespoons flour

1 cup cream

1/2 pound crabmeat (picked over for bones and flaked).
2 cups grated Swiss cheese
2 tablespoons lemon juice

In a skillet saute mushrooms, onions, garlic, and shallots until onion is soft. Add the wine, salt and pepper and simmer mixture until wine is evaporated. Add poultry seasoning and flour and cook and stir for 2 minutes. Add cream and cook and stir until sauce has thickened. Stir in the crabmeat, grated Swiss cheese, and lemon juice.

Divide mixture between 6 scallop shells. Sprinkle tops of scallop shells with 1 tablespoon of Cheese Crumbs.

Place scallop shells on a cookie sheet and bake in a 350° oven until heated through, about 20 minutes.

Broil tops for a few seconds to lightly brown. Serves 6 as an hors d'oeuvre.

Cheese Crumbs:
1/4 cup grated Parmesan cheese
1/4 cup toasted bread crumbs
2 tablespoons melted butter

Combine and toss until blended.

Crusty Shrimp in Lemon, Garlic & Wine Sauce

This dish is a grand choice for an hors d'oeuvre or small entree. The sauce is incredibly delicious. Serve with crisp French bread to dip in the delectable gravy.

1 1/2 pounds, large raw shrimp, shelled and deveined

1/2 cup flour
1/4 cup grated Parmesan cheese
1/2 teaspoon garlic powder
1/2 teaspoon paprika
1/4 teaspoon salt

1 cup cream
4 tablespoons butter

Combine flour, grated cheese, garlic powder, paprika and salt in a glass jar and shake until mixture is blended. Dust shrimp with this mixture. Dip the shrimp in the cream and dust them again in the flour mixture. Set on waxed paper and let them rest for about 20 minutes.

In a large skillet, heat the butter and cook the shrimp for a few minutes on each side until golden brown.

Place shrimp in a porcelain baker and drizzle with Lemon, Garlic and Wine Sauce.

Serve at once with a crusty bread. Serves 6 to 8 as an hors d'oeuvre.

Lemon, Garlic & Wine Sauce (continued)

1/2 **cup butter (1 stick)**
  2 **cloves garlic, minced**

1/2 **cup white wine**
  3 **tablespoons lemon juice**
1/4 **cup chopped chives**
  2 **tablespoons chopped parsley**

Saute garlic in butter for 2 minutes. Add the wine and cook until wine is reduced by 1/2. Add the remaining ingredients and cook an additional 2 minutes. Drizzle over cooked fish or shellfish.

Note: - Entire dish can be kept warm in a 300° oven for about 15 minutes.

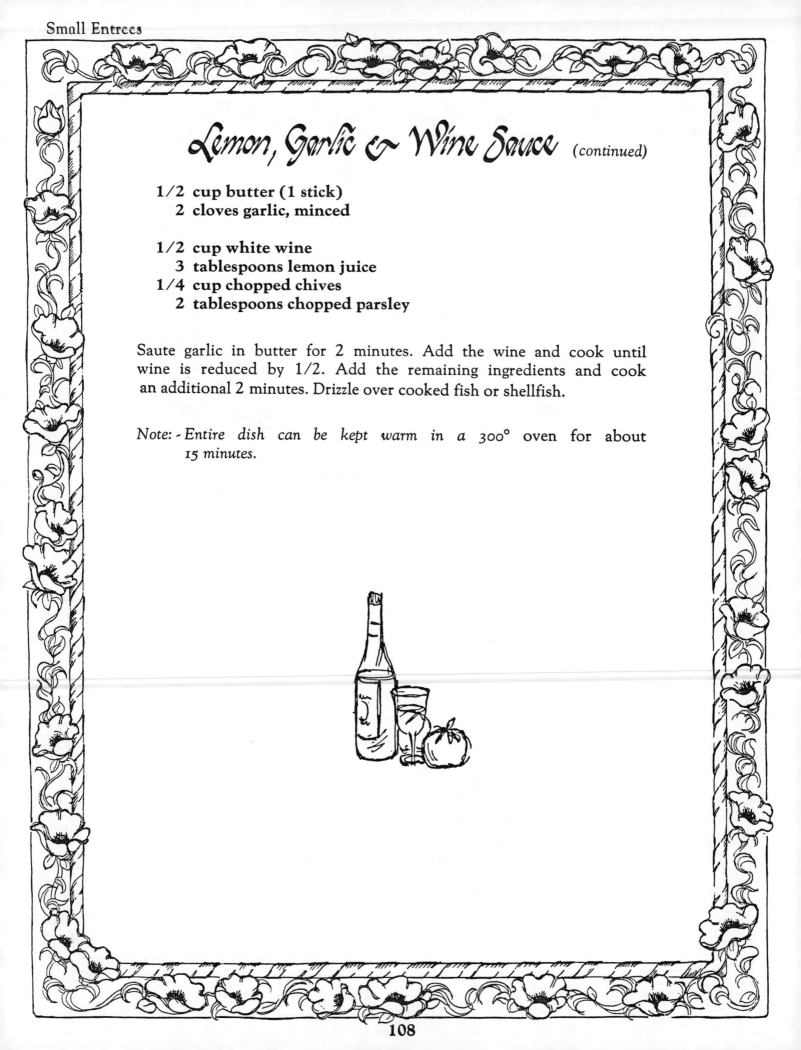

Zucchini Stuffed with Meat, Cheese & Tomatoes

- 4 medium zucchini, cooked in boiling water for 12 minutes and cut in half lengthwise. With a spoon scoop out the pulp and mince it.
- 1/2 pound ground beef
- 1/2 cup frozen chopped spinach, drained
- 1/2 cup tomato sauce
- 4 tablespoons grated onion
- 3/4 cup fresh bread crumbs
- 1 egg
- 1/4 cup grated Parmesan cheese
  salt and pepper to taste

- 8 slices, 1 ounce each Swiss cheese
- 1 can (16 ounces) stewed tomatoes, drained and finely chopped

In a bowl, combine minced pulp with ground beef, spinach, tomato sauce, onion, bread crumbs, egg, Parmesan cheese and seasonings. Divide mixture between the prepared zucchini shells. Place shells in a 9x13-inch roasting pan.

Place a slice of Swiss cheese over each shell, and scatter chopped tomatoes over all. Bake in a 350° oven for 20 to 30 minutes or until meat mixture is cooked through. Serve warm with a spoonful of tomato on top. Serves 4 to 8.

Note: - Entire dish can be assembled earlier in the day and stored in the refrigerator. Bake before serving.
- A nice touch (and for easier serving) would be to place zucchini in individual porcelain servers. In this manner, you could cook and serve in the same dish.

Garlic Shrimp in Lemon Wine Sauce & Cheese Crumb Topping

This is a sumptuous dish to serve as an hors d'oeuvre or small entree. If you own a copper au gratin pan, cook and serve it right in the pan. The shrimp can be speared with cocktail forks, or served on individual small plates. Any way you serve it, it is a very delicious dish...plump shrimp, sparkled with wine and flavored with lemon and garlic.

4 tablespoons butter (1/2 stick)
2 shallots, finely chopped
4 cloves garlic

1/4 cup dry white wine

2 tablespoons lemon juice
1 tablespoon chopped chives
1 tablespoon chopped parsley

1 pound raw shrimp, shelled and deveined.
1/2 teaspoon paprika
1/4 teaspoon thyme flakes

3 tablespoons fresh bread crumbs
3 tablespoons grated Parmesan cheese

In a skillet, saute shallots and garlic in butter until shallots are softened. Add the wine and cook until wine is reduced and almost evaporated. Add lemon juice, chives, parsley, shrimp, paprika and thyme flakes. Saute shrimp, tossing and turning, over medium high heat, until shrimp are opaque and cooked through. Do not overcook.

Sprinkle with bread crumbs and grated cheese and cook and toss for another minute. Serve with cocktail forks or in individual little plates. Serves 6.

Artichokes Filled with Creamed Mushrooms in Wine Sauce

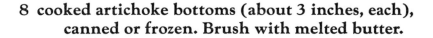

1/2 pound mushrooms, thinly sliced
1/4 cup chopped onions
1/4 cup chopped shallots
  2 cloves garlic, minced
  4 tablespoons butter
    salt and pepper to taste

1/4 cup dry white wine
  2 tablespoons flour
1/4 teaspoon poultry seasoning
3/4 cup cream

  8 cooked artichoke bottoms (about 3 inches, each),
    canned or frozen. Brush with melted butter.

1/2 cup sour cream
  1 cup grated Swiss cheese

In a skillet, saute together first 6 ingredients until onions are tender and the liquid rendered is evaporated. Add the wine and continue cooking until wine has evaporated. Add the flour and poultry seasoning and cook and stir for 3 minutes. Stir in the cream and cook and stir until sauce has thickened.

In a 6x12-inch baking dish, arrange artichoke bottoms in one layer. Fill centers with mushroom mixture. Combine sour cream and Swiss cheese and spoon over the mushrooms. Sprinkle top with a little paprika. Bake in a 350° oven for about 20 to 25 minutes or until heated through and cheese is melted. Serves 4 as a small entree or 8 as an hors d'oeuvre.

Note: - Entire dish can be assembled earlier in the day and stored in the refrigerator. Bake just before serving.
- Artichokes should lay side by side in the pan. If the artichoke bottoms are smaller, then you will need extras, or use a smaller pan.

Puff Pastry Piroshkis with Beef & Pork Filling

Beef and Pork Filling:
- 1 large onion, finely minced
- 2 shallots, finely minced
- 2 cloves garlic, finely minced
- 4 tablespoons butter

- 1/2 pound lean ground beef
- 1/2 pound lean ground pork
- 1/2 teaspoon thyme flakes
- salt and pepper to taste

- 4 tablespoons fresh bread crumbs
- 1/2 cup sour cream

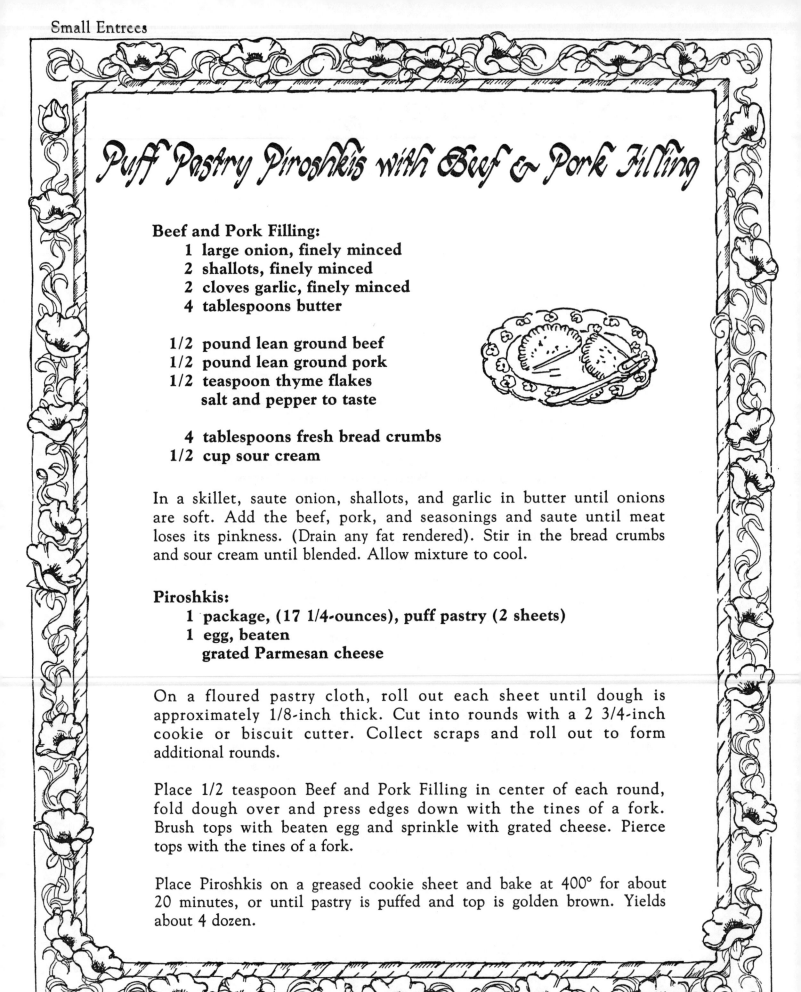

In a skillet, saute onion, shallots, and garlic in butter until onions are soft. Add the beef, pork, and seasonings and saute until meat loses its pinkness. (Drain any fat rendered). Stir in the bread crumbs and sour cream until blended. Allow mixture to cool.

Piroshkis:
- 1 package, (17 1/4-ounces), puff pastry (2 sheets)
- 1 egg, beaten
- grated Parmesan cheese

On a floured pastry cloth, roll out each sheet until dough is approximately 1/8-inch thick. Cut into rounds with a 2 3/4-inch cookie or biscuit cutter. Collect scraps and roll out to form additional rounds.

Place 1/2 teaspoon Beef and Pork Filling in center of each round, fold dough over and press edges down with the tines of a fork. Brush tops with beaten egg and sprinkle with grated cheese. Pierce tops with the tines of a fork.

Place Piroshkis on a greased cookie sheet and bake at 400° for about 20 minutes, or until pastry is puffed and top is golden brown. Yields about 4 dozen.

Coulibiac of Salmon with Salad Cucumber

A coulibiac of salmon is probably one of the true delights of the culinary experience. Making it in the traditional manner requires the preparation of brioche dough, crepes, salmon and mushroom filling, and rice or barley with egg filling. While it is not beyond the average capabilities, it is a labor of much love and adoration. This is an abbreviated version but so delicious, it is worth the extra effort.

1 package frozen patty shells (6 shells), thawed
1 egg, beaten
2 tablespoons grated Parmesan cheese

On a flour surface, stack 3 patty shells and roll them out to measure about 9-inches round. Place on a lightly greased cookie sheet and brush edges with beaten egg. Place Salmon Mushroom Filling in center of pastry, leaving a 1-inch border without filling.

Stack and roll remaining shells in the same manner. Place pastry over the first shell. Press the edges down with the tines of a fork to seal. With your fingers, scallop the edges for a decorative effect. Brush top with beaten egg and sprinkle with grated Parmesan cheese. Pierce top with the tines of a fork.

Bake in a 400° oven for 25 or 30 minutes or until pastry is puffed and top is rich golden brown. To serve, cut into wedges and serve with Salad Cucumber. Serves 6.

Salmon Mushroom Filling (continued)

2 tablespoons butter
1 onion, chopped
4 shallots, minced
1/2 pound mushrooms, thinly sliced
1/2 teaspoon dill weed

1/2 cup dry white wine
1/2 pound salmon, fileted and thinly sliced

2 tablespoons flour

1 cup sour cream
2 tablespoons chopped parsley
   salt to taste
2 tablespoons lemon juice

In a large skillet, saute together first 5 ingredients until onions are tender. Add the white wine and the salmon, cover pan and simmer mixture until salmon flakes easily, about 15 minutes. Remove cover and cook over high heat until liquid is practically evaporated. Stir in the flour and cook for 2 minutes, turning and stirring. Add the remaining ingredients and cook for 2 minutes.

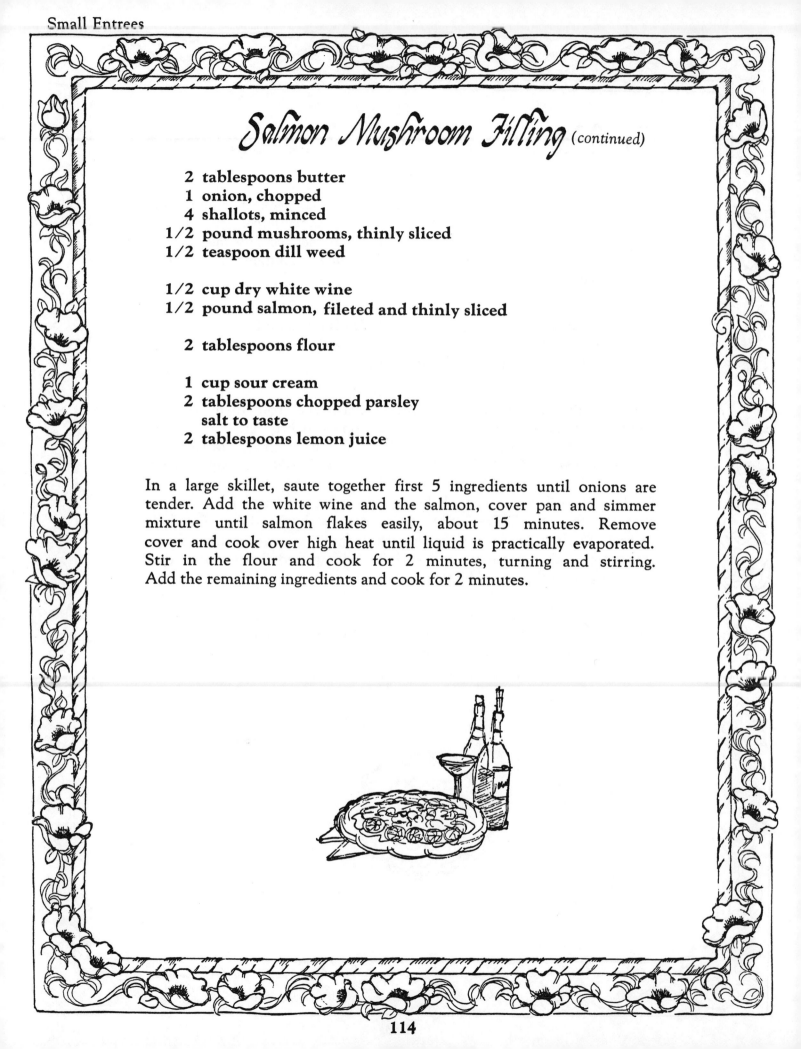

Royal Roulade of Creamed Chicken in Puff Pastry & Hollandaise Sauce

This small entree is as elegant and exciting as you could wish. Using the frozen puff pastry makes it especially easy . . . and foolproof.

- 2 tablespoons butter
- 1 onion
- 3 shallots
- 2 cloves garlic

- 2 tablespoons flour

- 1 cup cream
- 1/2 cup sour cream
- 1 teaspoon Dijon mustard

- 2 cups diced cooked chicken (white meat is better for this dish)
- 1 cup grated Swiss cheese
- 1/2 cup grated Parmesan cheese
- 2 tablespoons chopped parsley
  salt to taste
- 1 sheet frozen puff pastry, about 9x12-inches. Allow to thaw about 20 minutes and then roll out on a floured cloth to measure approximately 10x14-inches.
- 1 egg, beaten and 4 tablespoons grated Parmesan cheese for topping

In a large skillet, saute onion, shallots and garlic in butter until onion is soft. Stir in the flour and cook for 2 minutes, stirring. Add the cream, sour cream and mustard and cook, stirring, until sauce thickens. Allow sauce to cool and stir in chicken, cheeses, parsley and salt.

Roll out the puff pastry and place chicken mixture down the center. Pick up one side to cover and then turn roll over, ending seam side down. Seal the edges with the tines of a fork and then scallop them. The finished roll should measure 4x14-inches. Place in a baking pan and brush top with beaten egg and grated Parmesan cheese. With the tines of a fork, pierce top every 1/2-inch.

Royal Roulade of Creamed Chicken (continued)

Bake in a 350° oven for about 40 minutes or until top is golden brown. Cut into slices to serve. Serve warm, "natural" or with a spoonful of Hollandaise Sauce. Serves 6 as a small entree or 12 as an hors d'oeuvre.

Note: - Roll can be prepared earlier in the day and stored in the refrigerator.
- You can substitute baby shrimp for the chicken.

Sauce Hollandaise

3 egg yolks
1 1/2 tablespoons lemon juice
pinch of salt

3/4 cup butter (1 1/2 sticks)

1 tablespoon chopped chives

Place egg yolks, lemon juice and salt in a blender container and blend for 10 seconds at high speed.

Heat butter until it is sizzling hot and bubbly, but be careful not to brown it. Add the hot, sizzling butter very, very slowly and in a steady stream, while the blender continues running at high speed. When the butter is completely incorporated, stir in chopped chives. Serve at once. Yields about 1 cup sauce.

Royal Roulade Souffle with Pink Caviar & Dill Cream

There are few hors d'oeuvres that one could make that are more elegant, more festive or more exciting than this one. Serve it with chilled champagne as a splendid accompaniment.

Souffle Roll:

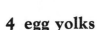

    4 **tablespoons butter**
  1/2 **cup flour**
1 1/2 **cups milk**
  1/2 **cup cream**

    4 **egg yolks**
    4 **egg whites, beaten with 1 teaspoon sugar, until stiff but not dry**
    1 **tablespoon grated Parmesan cheese**

In a saucepan, cook together butter and flour for about 2 minutes, stirring all the while. Add the milk and cream and continue cooking for about 5 minutes, stirring constantly, until sauce is thick. Remove from heat and beat in the egg yolks. Gently fold in the beaten egg whites.

Butter a 10x15-inch jellyroll pan. Line it with wax paper extended 2 inches longer on each end. Butter the wax paper. Spread batter evenly in a prepared pan and bake it in a 350° oven for about 35 to 40 minutes or until top is golden and souffle is set. Sprinkle top of souffle roll with grated cheese.

Invert pan onto overlapping strips of wax paper that are about 18-inches long. Carefully remove the baking paper. Spread top with Royal Caviar Filling, reserving about 1/2 cup. Carefully, roll up the souffle, lifting the wax paper to help you. Place filled souffle on a lovely porcelain server, seam side down, and decorate top with reserved filling. Garnish with green leaves, lemon slices and green onion frills. Slice at the table and serve 12 as an hors d'oeuvre.

Royal Roulade Souffle (continued)

Royal Caviar Filling:

  2 packages (3 ounces, each) cream cheese with chives
3/4 cup sour cream
1/3 cup finely chopped green onions
  3 tablespoons lemon juice
1/2 teaspoon dill weed

  1 jar (4 ounces) pink caviar

Beat together first 5 ingredients until blended. Stir in the caviar.

Soups & Garnitures

Easiest & Best Hungarian Goulash Soup-Stew

This is a very thick soup, almost a stew. It is a lovely main course for dinner and it is a grand choice for a frosty night when the weather is roaring outside. Be sure to serve some crusty bread to dip in the delicious broth.

2 tablespoons brown sugar
2 large onions, chopped
4 cloves garlic, minced
1 red pepper, chopped
2 carrots, peeled and thinly sliced
3 tablespoons butter

1 can (1 pound) stewed tomatoes, chopped
3 cans (10 1/2 ounces, each) chicken broth
1 1/2 pounds lean boneless beef or veal, cut
        into 3/4-inch cubes
2 tablespoons paprika
  salt and pepper to taste

2 potatoes, cut into small dice
1 cup sour cream

In a Dutch oven casserole, saute first 6 ingredients together until onions are transparent. Add the next 5 ingredients and bring mixture to a boil. Cover pan and lower the heat and simmer mixture for about 1 1/2 hours. Cooking time will depend on the choice of meat.

About 30 minutes before meat is tender, add the potatoes and continue cooking. When meat and potatoes are tender, stir in the sour cream. Heat the soup, but do not let it boil. Serve in deep bowls with crusty bread and creamy sweet butter. Serves 6.

Note: - This soup is excellent when made a day earlier and stored in the refrigerator. However, add the sour cream just before serving.

Chestnut & Apple Soup with Honey Sesame Crisps

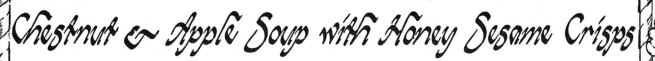

This is an exotic soup, in name only. Actually, it is very simple to prepare and can be assembled in minutes. It is gloriously rich, so keep the portions small. The Honey Sesame Crisps are the perfect accompaniments.

- **2 onions, chopped**
- **3 shallots, minced**
- **2 cloves garlic, minced**
- **4 tablespoons butter**

- **1 can (10 ounces) chestnuts packed in water (not syrup), drained**
- **2 apples, peeled, cored and chopped**
- **2 cans (10 1/2 ounces, each) chicken broth**

- **1/2 cup cream**
- **1/2 cup sour cream**
- **salt to taste**

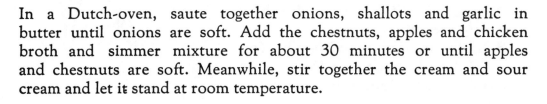

In a Dutch-oven, saute together onions, shallots and garlic in butter until onions are soft. Add the chestnuts, apples and chicken broth and simmer mixture for about 30 minutes or until apples and chestnuts are soft. Meanwhile, stir together the cream and sour cream and let it stand at room temperature.

Puree the soup, in batches, in a blender or food processor, until it is smooth. (Pour the soup in a bowl as you puree it, and then return it to the Dutch-oven pan.) Stir in the cream mixture and salt. Heat the soup through, but do not let it boil. Serve with Honey Sesame Crisps as a delightful accompaniment. Serves 6.

Honey Sesame Crisps

- **3 pita breads, split**
- **6 teaspoons butter**
- **6 teaspoons honey**
- **3 teaspoons sesame seeds**

Spread each half of pita bread with 1 teaspoon of butter, 1 teaspoon honey and sprinkle with 1/2 teaspoon sesame seeds. Place the pita bread under the broiler for a few seconds or until the sesame seeds are lightly browned. Watch carefully so that it does not get too dark. The bread will have become very crisp. Serves 6.

Best Apple, Onion & Carrot Creamed Soup

This fragrant, highly aromatic soup is a grand beginning for a holiday dinner. It is an especially good introduction to either turkey or chicken. Serve it warm, with Spiced Orange Bread, and creamy sweet butter as an excellent accompaniment.

3 **large onions, about 4 cups, chopped**
3 **carrots, peeled and grated**
3 **cloves garlic, minced**
3 **shallots, minced**
1/2 **apple, peeled, cored and grated (large)**
       or 1 medium apple
1/4 **cup chopped celery**
6 **tablespoons butter**

1/4 **teaspoon poultry seasoning**
      salt and pepper to taste

2 **cans (10 1/2 ounces, each) chicken broth**
1 **cup cream**
3 **tablespoons chopped parsley (or**
      1 tablespoon dried)
2 **tablespoons lemon juice**

In a large skillet, saute together first 7 ingredients until vegetables are very soft, but not brown. Do this over very low heat, stirring now and again. Stir in the seasonings.

In a processor or blender, puree the vegetables with a little chicken broth until the mixture is almost smooth. (The faintest amount of texture should remain.)

Place pureed mixture into a sauce pan, add the remaining ingredients and simmer soup for 2 or 3 minutes or until it is piping hot. Adjust seasonings and serve with a dollup of whipped cream or sour cream sprinkled with a few chives on top. Serves 6.

Note: - Soup can be made 1 day earlier and stored in the refrigerator. Warm over low heat, stirring now and again.

Cold Zucchini & Onion Soup with Buttered Crisps

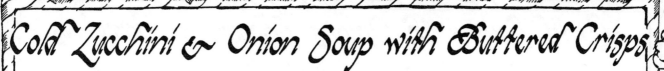

1 1/2 pounds zucchini, peeled and sliced
2 large onions, coarsely chopped
2 cloves garlic, minced
2 shallots, chopped
2 cans (10 1/2 ounces, each) chicken broth

1 cup cream
1 cup sour cream
1 cup buttermilk
1/2 teaspoon dill weed
    salt to taste

In a saucepan, simmer together the first 5 ingredients until the vegetables are very soft. Puree them in a processor or in a blender, in batches, until smooth. Return pureed vegetables to saucepan.

Stir in the remaining ingredients until blended. Simmer the soup for about 2 minutes, allow to cool and refrigerate. Remove from the refrigerator about 10 minutes before serving. Serve cold with Buttered Crisps. Serves 10 to 12.

Note: - Soup can be made 1 day earlier and stored in the refrigerator.

Buttered Crisps with Dill & Cheese

6 slices white bread, crusts removed. Roll flat with
    a rolling pin and cut diagonally into
    2 triangles.
6 tablespoons melted butter
6 tablespoons grated Parmesan cheese
1/2 teaspoon dill weed

Place rolled bread slices on a buttered cookie sheet. Stir together butter, cheese and dill weed until blended. Brush bread slices with this mixture and bake in a 350° oven until crisped. Turn bread and baste other side. Continue baking until toasted crisp.

Note: - Crisps can be made earlier in the day and when cool, stored in an air-tight container.

Lentil Soup with Onions, Bacon & Tomatoes

This soup is thick and sturdy and is just delicious with some good peasant bread served warm with creamy butter.

- 1 pound lentils, rinsed in a strainer and drained
- 3 onions, chopped
- 3 carrots, grated
- 1 can (1 pound) stewed tomatoes, finely chopped
- 2 cloves garlic, cut in half
- 3 cans (10 1/2 ounces, each) chicken broth
  salt and pepper to taste
- 1 tablespoon olive oil
- 3 strips bacon, cooked crisp, drained and crumbled

In a Dutch oven, place the first 8 ingredients and bring soup to a boil, with the cover slightly ajar. Lower heat and simmer soup for about 1 1/2 hours or until lentils are tender, adding a little broth if the soup is too thick. Stir in the crumbled bacon. Remove the garlic (if you can find it) and serve this lovely soup with crusty warm bread. Serves 6.

Creamed Pea Soup with Bacon, Garlic & Cheese

- 2 packages (10 ounces, each) frozen baby peas
- 2 large onions, chopped
- 2 carrots, grated
- 2 shallots, minced
- 3 cloves garlic, minced
- 4 tablespoons butter

- 3 cans (10 1/2 ounces, each) chicken broth
- 3 strips bacon, cooked crisp, drained and crumbled
  salt and pepper to taste
- 1 teaspoon sugar
- 1/4 teaspoon dried dill weed
- 1 cup cream
- 1 cup grated Swiss cheese

In a Dutch oven, place first 6 ingredients and saute mixture until onions are transparent. Add the broth, bacon, salt, pepper, sugar and dill weed and simmer mixture, with cover slightly ajar for 40 minutes to 1 hour or until vegetables are very soft. Just before serving, add the cream and Swiss cheese and heat through, stirring. Serve hot with a dollup of sour cream sprinkled with a bit of dill. Serves 6.

Red Gazpacho, Spanish Soup with Sour Cream

This is a delicious cold soup which very much resembles a salad. It is a grand beginning to paella or chicken with rice. And if you own a food processor, chopping the vegetables is effortless.

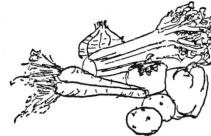

- 1 cucumber, peeled and chopped
- 4 tomatoes, fresh or canned, chopped
- 1 green pepper, seeded and chopped
- 1 stalk celery, chopped
- 1/2 cup chopped green onions
- 1/2 cup chopped onions
- 1 clove garlic, minced
- 2 tablespoons chopped parsley
- 1/2 cup sliced mushrooms

Soup Base :
- 2 cups tomato juice
- 2 cans (10 1/2 ounces, each) beef broth
- 1/4 cup red wine vinegar
- 1/4 cup salad oil
- 3 tablespoons lemon juice
- 2 or 3 tablespoons sugar
- salt and pepper to taste

In a large glass bowl or soup tureen, toss together first 9 ingredients. Combine soup base ingredients and pour over the vegetables. Refrigerate overnight. Serve in soup bowls with a spoonful of sour cream on top. Another nice touch would be to float a cube of frozen tomato juice on the top. Serve with Roulades of Chiles & Cheese for a smashing accompaniment. Serves 6.

Gazpacho Blanco Salad Soup

To the vegetables above, use the following soup base for a very delicious variation.

- 2 cans (10 1/2 ounces, each) chicken broth
- 1 cup cream
- 1 cup sour cream
- 2 tablespoons red wine vinegar
- 2 tablespoons lemon juice or more to taste
- salt and pepper to taste

Stir together all the ingredients until blended. Pour over the chopped vegetables and refrigerate until chilled through, several hours or overnight. Serves 6.

Roulades of Chiles & Cheese

This is a lovely accompaniment to Gazpacho. The cold soup is especially well balanced with these crisp roulades of chiles and melted cheese.

8 **slices white bread, crusts removed. Roll each slice flat with a rolling pin.**
1 **can (4 ounces) diced green chiles**
1/4 **pound Monterey Jack cheese, grated**
1/4 **pound Cheddar cheese, grated**
1/4 **cup finely chopped green onions**

4 **tablespoons melted butter**

Lay bread slices out. Divide the chiles, cheese and green onions evenly over each slice of bread. Roll these up tightly and brush with melted butter on all sides. Place in a baking pan, seam side down and bake at 400° for about 15 minutes or until bread is crisped and cheeses are melted. Serves 8.

Note: - Roulades can be assembled earlier in the day and stored in the refrigerator. Bake just before serving.

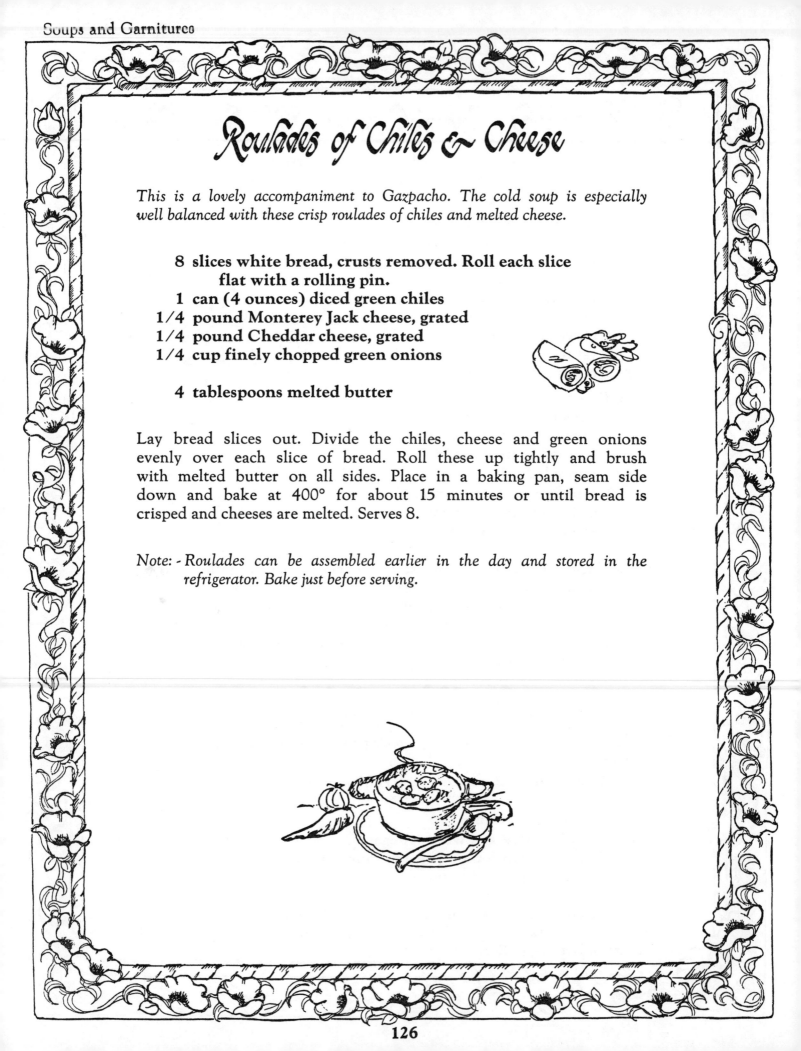

126

Salads
&
Dressings

Fresh Vegetable Salad with Royal Sauce Verte

Arrange a large platter of carrots, celery, cucumbers, radishes, green onions, mushrooms, zucchini, cherry tomatoes, jicama, etc., in any combination. Add excitement by slicing the vegetables straight, on the diagonal, into circles, sticks, curls, etc. Arrange on a bed of lettuce. Dip the ends of the leaves in paprika for an attractive effect. Place Royal Sauce Verte in the center for dipping.

Royal Sauce Verte with Creme Fraiche

1/2   **cup cream**
1/2   **cup sour cream**

1   **cup mayonnaise**
1/3   **cup chopped parsley**
3   **green onions**
2   **tablespoons lemon juice**
1/4   **teaspoon garlic powder**
    salt and pepper to taste

1   **package (10 ounces) frozen chopped spinach, defrosted. Place spinach in a strainer and press out the liquid.**

In a glass jar, stir together cream and sour cream until blended. Allow to stand at room temperature for about 1 hour or until cream has thickened.

In a blender, beat together mayonnaise, parsley, onions, lemon juice and seasonings until mixture is pureed. In a glass bowl, stir together cream mixture, mayonnaise mixture and drained spinach, until blended. Refrigerate until serving time. Yields about 3 cups.

Chinese Chicken Salad with Honey Sesame Crisps

This is such a popular salad lately, that I thought you might enjoy trying it. I start with a very simple salad and then you could choose from the few optionals which add a touch of glamor and interest. The Honey Crisps are outstanding.

1/2 (6 3/4 ounce) package rice sticks (also called
    Maifun), broken into 3-inch pieces

3 cups shredded cooked chicken
1/2 cup chopped green onions
1 large head iceberg lettuce (about 6 cups, chopped)

1/2 cup toasted slivered almonds (optional)
2 tablespoons lightly toasted sesame seeds (optional)
1 package (8 ounces) frozen Chinese pea pods,
    snipped into fourths (optional)
1/2 cup water chestnuts, sliced (optional)

In a French fryer, heat about 3-inches of oil to about 375° to 400°. Divide rice sticks into 4 or 5 batches. Deep fry each batch in the hot oil. (They will puff in a few seconds upon touching the hot oil.) With 2 spoons, turn them over so that the rice sticks on top will puff evenly. As soon as the rice sticks stop puffing, remove them to a paper towel to drain.

In a large salad bowl, combine rice sticks, chicken, onions, lettuce and any combination of the remaining ingredients. (You can use all the "optionals" if you like.) Pour Chinese Honey Dressing over the salad and toss to coat evenly. Serve with Honey Sesame Crisps for an excellent accompaniment. Serves 4.

Chinese Chicken Salad (continued)

Chinese Honey Dressing:
- 1/2 teaspoon dry mustard
- 2 tablespoons honey
- 2 tablespoons sugar
- 1 tablespoon soy sauce
- 2 tablespoons sesame oil
- 1/2 cup salad oil
- 1/2 cup rice vinegar

In a jar with a tight-fitting lid, combine and shake until blended.

Honey Sesame Crisps

Split 4 Pita breads. On each cut side, spread 2 teaspoons butter, 2 teaspoons honey and 1/2 teaspoon sesame seeds. Broil for about 1 minute or until top is beginning to brown. Bread will become very crisp. Serves 4.

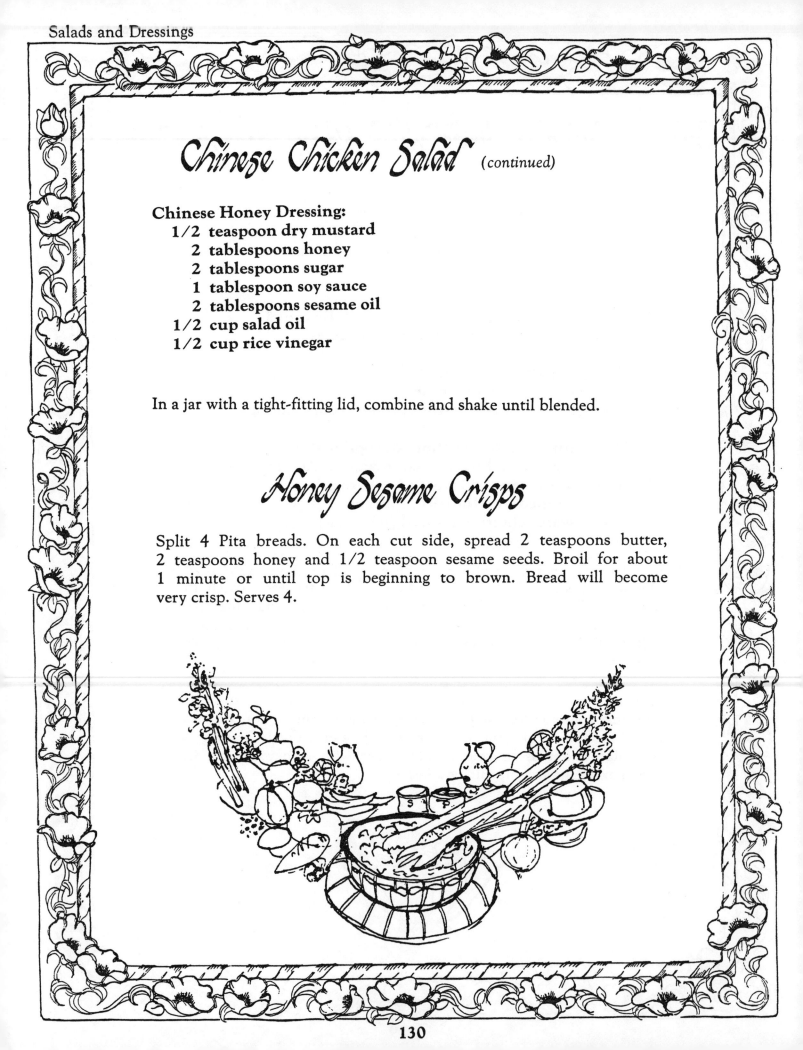

Mexican Fiesta Salad with Mixed Vegetables & Lemon Vinaigrette

4 tomatoes, seeded and chopped
1 cucumber, unpeeled and thinly sliced
1/2 cup chopped green onions
1 onion, chopped
1/2 green pepper, seeded and chopped
1/2 cup sliced mushrooms
1/4 cup chopped parsely
1 clove garlic, minced

1/3 cup oil
1/4 cup wine vinegar
4 tablespoons lemon juice
1 tablespoon sugar
salt and pepper to taste

In a large salad bowl, place all the vegetables and toss to combine. Add the remaining ingredients and mix and toss until the vegetables are nicely coated. Adjust seasonings.

Serve salad with a dollup of sour cream on top. Serves 5 or 6.

Curried Chicken Salad
with Pineapple, Almonds & Bananas

4 cups cooked, diced chicken
1 can (1 pound) crushed pineapple, drained dry,
  Reserve juice for another use.
3/4 cup toasted slivered almonds
1/2 cup yellow raisins, plumped in orange juice
  and drained

1/2 cup mayonnaise
1/2 cup sour cream
2 tablespoons lemon juice
1/2 teaspoon curry powder

2 bananas, thinly sliced and tossed in 2 tablespoons
  lemon juice

salt to taste

In a large bowl place first 4 ingredients. Stir together mayonnaise, sour cream, lemon juice and curry powder until blended. Pour dressing over chicken mixture and toss until blended. Refrigerate until serving time. Just before serving, toss in bananas and seasonings. Serve on a bed of lettuce or melon halves. Serves 5 or 6.

Lomi Lomi Salad
with Salmon, Tomatoes & Green Onions

1/2 pound smoked salmon, finely chopped
6 green onions, finely chopped
4 tomatoes, peeled, seeded and finely chopped
2 tablespoons salad oil
2 tablespoons cider vinegar
salt and pepper to taste

In a glass bowl, combine all the ingredients and toss until everything is nicely mixed. Refrigerate for several hours. Serve with thin slices of rye or black bread.

3~Bean Salad with Lemon Vinaigrette Dressing

- 1 can (1 pound) kidney beans, rinsed and drained
- 1 can (1 pound) garbanzo beans, drained
- 1 can (1 pound) cut green beans, drained
- 1/2 cup chopped green onions

- 1/2 cup oil
- 3 tablespoons lemon juice
- 2 tablespoons red wine vinegar
- 1 clove garlic, minced
- 1 teaspoon Dijon mustard
  salt and pepper to taste

In a bowl, place the 3 beans and green onions. In a glass jar, with a tight-fitting lid, place the remaining ingredients and shake to blend. Pour dressing to taste, over the beans. (Unused dressing can be stored in the refrigerator and used over salad greens.) Toss, so that the beans are nicely coated with dressing.

Cover bowl and refrigerate for several hours or overnight. Serves 8.

Cauliflower & Broccoli with Lemon Dill Dressing

- 1 package (10 ounces) frozen cauliflower, cooked
    until firm tender
- 1 package (10 ounces) broccoli spears, cooked until
    firm tender and cut into 1-inch pieces
- 1/2 cup chopped green onion
- 1 jar (2 ounces) pimento strips, drained

- 1/2 cup mayonnaise
- 1/2 cup sour cream
- 1 tablespoon lemon juice
- 1 green onion
- 2 stalks parsley
- 1/4 teaspoon dill weed
  salt and pepper to taste

In a bowl, toss together first 4 ingredients. Place remaining ingredients in a blender or processor and blend until mixture is smooth. Pour dressing to taste over the vegetables. (Unused dressing can be stored in the refrigerator and used over tomato slices.) Serves 6 to 8.

Salad of Celery Root in Creamed Mustard Mayonnaise

If you are looking for something a little different to serve as a salad, this is an excellent first course to a "substantial" dinner. I also enjoy serving it for lunch, to accompany a quiche or an omelette.

Creamed Mustard Mayonnaise:
4 tablespoons mayonnaise ¼C
4 tablespoons sour cream ¼C
1 tablespoon Dijon-style mustard
1 tablespoon lemon juice
1 tablespoon chopped chives
salt and white pepper to taste

Combine all the ingredients in a glass bowl and stir until they are thoroughly combined. Refrigerate.

1 celery root, about 3-inches in diameter and
weighing about 3/4 to 1 pound
2 tablespoons lemon juice

Peel the celery root and please use a very sharp knife. Place it in a saucepan with the lemon juice. Add boiling water to cover. Blanche it for about 7 to 8 minutes.

If your mixer has a grating attachment, use it on the julienne blade. Or use a food processor or Mouli grater. This is one of the times it is not satisfactory to grate by hand.

Immediately upon grating, place celery root in a bowl and pour in the reserved dressing. Toss it until it is nicely combined and store it in the refrigerator overnight. Serve on a bed of lettuce or as a cold vegetable. Serves 4 to 6.

Note: - Salad can be prepared 2 days earlier and stored in the refrigerator.

Cold Rice Salad with Mushrooms & Green Onions & Red Wine Vinaigrette

    1 cup long grain rice
    2 cups chicken broth (totally void of fat),
         homemade or canned

1/2 cup chopped green onions
    1 cup thinly sliced mushrooms
    1 tomato, peeled and finely chopped
    4 tablespoons chopped parsley
1/4 cup salad oil
    2 tablespoons red wine vinegar (or to taste)
    2 tablespoons lemon juice
1/2 teaspoon sugar
       salt and pepper to taste

In a saucepan, simmer rice in broth, covered over low heat until rice is tender and liquid is aborsbed. Place rice in a large bowl and toss to separate grains. To the bowl, add the onions, mushrooms, tomato and parsley.

In a glass jar with a tight-fitting lid, shake together the salad oil, vinegar, lemon juice, sugar and seasonings. Pour dressing over the salad and toss until everything is nicely mixed.

Cover and refrigerate for several hours, stirring now and again. Serves 5 or 6.

Buckwheat Salad with Green Onions & Tomatoes

This is a very interesting and unusual salad. Buckwheat, also called Bulgur or Kasha is a form of cracked wheat. Keep some on hand for nibbling.

    1 cup buckwheat, medium grain
    2 cups boiling water

    1/2 cup vinegar
    1/2 cup oil
    1/4 cup lemon juice
    1/4 cup chopped parsley
    4 green onions
    2 tomatoes, chopped
    salt and pepper to taste

Combine buckwheat and boiling water, stir and allow to stand for about 1 hour or until liquid is absorbed. (If any water is not absorbed, discard it.)

Combine buckwheat with the remaining ingredients and stir until well mixed. Refrigerate until serving time. Serves 8 as a side dish.

Note: - If you like, you can add any number of vegetables to the salad. Grated cooked carrots, sliced steamed zucchini, cooked green beans, cooked peas, etc. are especially good.

Warm Cauliflower Salad with Herbed Vinaigrette

Very often when we were children, Mom served delicious warm salads. I was never quite certain if it was planned this way or if there simply wasn't enough time to chill the vegetables. But it really was quite good and I serve warm salads often. They are very good as an accompaniment to lunch.

2 packages (10 ounces, each) frozen cauliflower. Separate each flower into smaller florets. Cook them according to the directions on the package until they are firm tender. Drain and place in a bowl. Pour Herbed Vinaigrette over the warm vegetables, toss and turn them until they are evenly coated and serve them warm. Serves 6 to 8.

Herbed Vinaigrette Dressing

1/3 cup oil (can use part olive oil)
2 tablespoons red wine vinegar
2 tablespoons lemon juice
1 green onion (use the whole onion)
1 clove garlic
4 tablespoons chopped parsley
salt and pepper to taste

1 teaspoon Dijon mustard
2 tablespoons finely chopped pimento

In a blender or food processor, place first 7 ingredients and blend until the onion is very finely chopped. Stir in the mustard and pimento. Pour dressing over warm vegetables. Yields about 1/2 cup dressing.

Fresh Vegetable Salad with Creamy Blue Cheese Dressing

1 pound broccoli, steamed until tender and cut
    into 1-inch pieces
1 pound cauliflower (about) steamed until tender
    and separated into florets
3 tomatoes, peeled and sliced
1 onion, sliced thinly. Cut each slice in half
    and separate rings.

1 cup sour cream
4 tablespoons lemon juice
1/8 teaspoon garlic powder
1 teaspoon finely grated lemon peel
    salt and pepper to taste
1/4 pound blue cheese, mashed or crumbled
2 tablespoons chopped chives

Place vegetables in a large bowl. In a glass jar, stir together the remaining ingredients until blended. Pour dressing over the vegetables and toss to combine. Refrigerate for several hours or overnight. Serves 8.

Note: - Dressing can be prepared several days earlier and stored in the refrigerator.

Tomato, Mushroom & Onion Salad with Lemon & Mustard Dressing

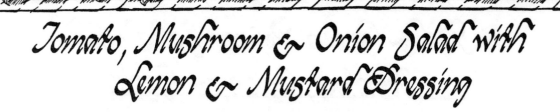

    4 tomatoes, peeled and coarsley chopped
    1 pound mushrooms, thinly sliced
    1 onion, thinly sliced. Cut each slice in half
        and separate rings.

    1 egg, beaten
    1 teaspoon Dijon mustard
    4 tablespoons lemon juice
    1 clove garlic, minced
  1/2 cup oil (use part olive oil)
        salt and pepper to taste
    2 tablespoons grated Parmesan cheese

Place tomatoes, mushrooms and onions in a large bowl and toss to combine. Place the remaining ingredients in a glass jar, with a tight-fitting lid and shake until thoroughly blended. Pour dressing over the salad and toss to blend. Refrigerate for at least 4 hours, tossing and turning once or twice during that time. Serves 8.

Red & Green Pepper Salad with Tomatoes, Onion & Garlic

2 green peppers, cut into 1/2-inch thick slices
2 red peppers, cut into 1/2-inch thick slices
1 onion, cut into 1/4-inch thick slices and separated
    into rings
4 tomatoes, peeled, seeded and chopped. Discard
    the juice.
3 cloves garlic, minced
4 tablespoons oil (use part olive oil)

2 tablespoons red wine vinegar *balsamic*
2 tablespoons chopped parsley
  salt and pepper to taste
1 teaspoon crushed basil

In a large skillet, saute peppers, onion, tomatoes and garlic in oil until vegetables are tender. Place vegetables in a bowl and toss with vinegar, parsley and seasonings. Refrigerate overnight. Serve as an accompaniment to chicken or veal, roasted with garlic and herbs.

Salad Cucumber with Sour Cream & Dill

    1/3 cup chopped green onion
      1 pint sour cream
      4 tablespoons lemon juice
      1 teaspoon sugar
    1/2 teaspoon dill weed

      3 cucumbers, peeled, seeded and grated

In a bowl, stir together first 5 ingredients. Drain cucumbers and stir into sour cream mixture. Store in the refrigerator until serving time. Serves 6.

Note: - Dressing can be made earlier in the day and stored in the refrigerator. Cucumbers can be grated earlier in the day and stored in the refrigerator. An hour before serving, drain cucumbers and combine with the dressing.

Green Pea, Onion & Tomato Salad

      2 packages (10 ounces, each) baby green peas,
            defrosted and cooked in 4 tablespoons water
            until firm tender. Drain.

    1/3 cup chopped green onions
      2 medium tomatoes, chopped
      1 tablespoon chopped parsley

    1/2 cup salad oil
    1/4 cup red wine vinegar
    1/4 teaspoon coarsely ground garlic powder
      4 tablespoons grated Parmesan cheese
            salt and pepper to taste

In a large bowl, combine peas, green onions, tomatoes and parsley. In a jar with a tight-fitting lid, place oil, vinegar, garlic, cheese and seasonings and shake until blended. Pour dressing to taste over the vegetables and toss until they are nicely coated. Refrigerate for several hours or overnight to allow flavors to blend. Unused dressing can be stored in the refrigerator and used over salad greens.

Serve as a salad or a cold vegetable side dish. Serves 8.

Salad Cucumber with Green Onion, & Yogurt Dressing

1 cup plain yogurt
1 clove garlic, put through a press
2 green onions, finely chopped. Use the
    whole onion.
1 tablespoon chopped parsley
2 tablespoons lemon juice
1/4 teaspoon dried dill weed

2 cucumbers, peeled and thinly sliced
  salt to taste

Combine first 6 ingredients and mix until blended. Toss cucumbers with yogurt dressing just before serving. Serves 4.

Tomato Zucchini Salad with Garlic & Lemon Dressing

6 zucchini, unpeeled. Cut into thin slices.
3 tomatoes, peeled, seeded and coarsely chopped
1/2 cup green onions, finely chopped
1/4 cup parsley, finely chopped
6 slices bacon, cooked crisp, drained and crumbled
   (optional)

1/3 cup salad oil
1/3 cup lemon juice
1 clove garlic, minced
  salt and pepper to taste

Combine all the ingredients in a large bowl and toss until vegetables are nicely coated. Serve in lettuce-lined bowls. Serves 5 to 6.

Spinach Salad with Mushrooms, Bacon & Tomatoes & Special Dressing

1 pound fresh spinach, wash thoroughly to remove
every trace of sand. Snip off the stems and tear
into bite-size pieces.
1/4 pound mushrooms, thinly sliced
1/2 cup chopped green onions
2 tomatoes, peeled and chopped
8 strips bacon, cooked crisp, drained and crumbled

1 cup mayonnaise
1/4 cup cream
2 green onions
2 sprigs of parsley, stems removed
2 tablespoons lemon juice
1/8 teaspoon garlic powder
salt and pepper to taste

In a large bowl, toss together first 5 ingredients. In a blender or processor place the remaining ingredients and blend until smooth. Pour dressing to taste over the salad and store unused dressing in the refrigerator. Garnish salad with sieved egg yolks.   Serves 4.

Carrot, Broccoli & Cauliflower Salad Vinaigrette

1 package (10 ounces) frozen baby carrots, defrosted
1 package (10 ounces) frozen broccoli spears, cut
    into 1-inch lengths
1 package (10 ounces) frozen cauliflower, separated
    into small florets
  salt to taste

1/2 cup oil
1/4 cup red wine vinegar
2 tablespoons water
1 teaspoon sugar
1/4 cup finely chopped chives
1/4 teaspoon dill weed
1/8 teaspoon garlic powder
  salt and pepper to taste

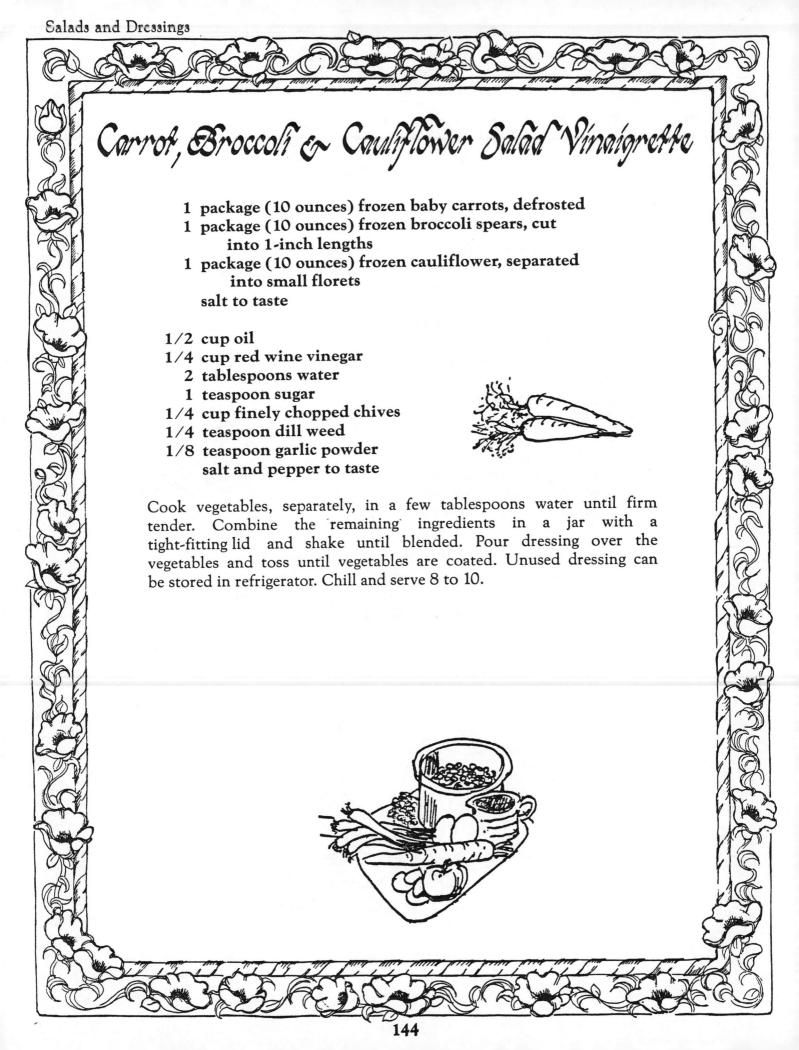

Cook vegetables, separately, in a few tablespoons water until firm tender. Combine the remaining ingredients in a jar with a tight-fitting lid and shake until blended. Pour dressing over the vegetables and toss until vegetables are coated. Unused dressing can be stored in refrigerator. Chill and serve 8 to 10.

Poached Celery & Tomatoes in Lemon Herbed Vinaigrette

1 bunch celery, peeled with a vegetable peeler to remove threads. Cut into 1-inch pieces. Poach in 1-inch boiling water for about 7 minutes or until celery is firm tender.
3 medium tomatoes, peeled and chopped
1/2 cup finely chopped green onions
1 clove garlic, minced
1/4 cup oil
4 tablespoons lemon juice
2 tablespoons vinegar
1/2 teaspoon oregano
1/4 teaspoon thyme
1/2 bay leaf

In a large bowl, combine all the ingredients and toss until blended. Refrigerate salad for at least 6 hours to allow flavors to blend. Serves 6.

Greek Salad with Lemon Dill Dressing

2 cups cut lettuce leaves (about 1/2 head)
4 medium tomatoes, chopped
1 large cucumber, cut into thin slices
1/4 cup pitted olive slices
4 ounces feta cheese, crumbled
3 green onions, finely chopped
    (use the whole onion)
2 tablespoons chopped parsley
salt and freshly ground pepper to taste
2 mashed anchovies, (optional)

Combine all the ingredients in a large salad bowl and toss to mix. Pour Lemon Dill Dressing over salad and toss to coat evenly. Serves 6.

Lemon Dill Dressing:
4 tablespoons lemon juice
1 tablespoon water
2 teaspoons wine vinegar
5 ounces oil
1/2 teaspoon dried dill weed
1/4 teaspoon garlic powder
2 tablespoons grated Parmesan cheese
salt and pepper to taste

Combine all the ingredients in a glass jar with a tight lid and shake thoroughly. Refrigerate until ready to use. Makes about 1 cup dressing.

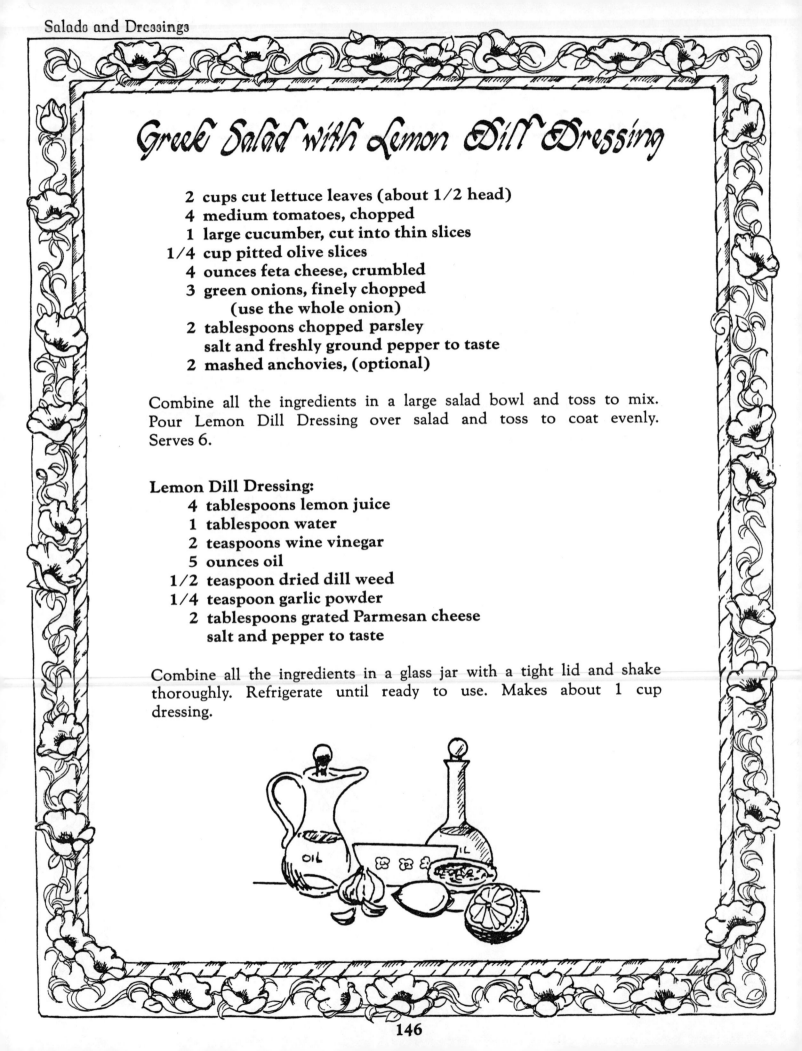

Desserts

Fresh Apple Pecan Torte with Lemon Orange Glaze

This is a particularly moist and fruity torte. There are few cakes you can make that are more delicious than this one. It is a lovely dessert, and not very sweet or cloying.

        6 eggs
        1 cup sugar

  1 1/2 cups finely grated pecans
        1 cup vanilla wafer crumbs
        1 teaspoon baking powder

        1 large apple, peeled, cored and grated
      1/2 medium orange, grated (about 4 tablespoons peel,
              fruit and juice)
      1/4 lemon grated (about 1 tablespoon peel,
              fruit and juice)

In the large bowl of an electric mixer, beat eggs with sugar for 5 minutes or until eggs are very light and creamy.

Toss pecans, crumbs and baking powder until blended and fold into egg mixture. (You can do this in your mixer, but you must do this on very low speed, and just until blended, so as not to deflate the eggs.) By hand, fold in the remaining ingredients, just until blended.

Pour batter into a buttered 10-inch springform pan and spread to even. Bake in a 350° oven for 45 minutes or until a cake tester, inserted in center, comes out clean. Allow cake to cool and then drizzle with Lemon Orange Glaze. Serves 8.

Lemon Orange Glaze

        1 cup sifted powdered sugar
        1 tablespoon orange juice
        2 teaspoons lemon juice
        1 tablespoon grated orange peel
        2 tablespoons chopped pecans

Stir together all the ingredients until blended. Add a little orange juice or sugar to make a glaze a drizzling consistency.

The World's Best Velvet Chocolate Brownies

I must admit that this is the best chocolate fantasy and it elevates a simple brownie to gastronomical heights. The Chocolate Rum Buttercream is an especially good accompaniment and the little chocolate shavings on top add a touch of glamor.

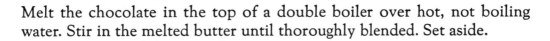

- 2/3 cup semi-sweet chocolate chips
- 1/3 cup melted butter

- 4 eggs
- 1 cup sugar

- 3/4 cup finely ground walnuts
- 1/3 cup flour
- 2 tablespoons rum
- 1 teaspoon vanilla

Melt the chocolate in the top of a double boiler over hot, not boiling water. Stir in the melted butter until thoroughly blended. Set aside.

In the large bowl of an electric mixer, beat the eggs with the sugar until mixture is light and fluffy, about 10 minutes. Fold in the walnuts, flour, rum and vanilla until blended. Do not overmix. (This can be done on the lowest speed setting.) Fold in the chocolate mixture.

Pour batter into a 10-inch buttered springform pan and bake in a 350° oven for about 25 minutes or until a cake tester, inserted in center, comes out clean. Allow cake to cool in pan.

Remove metal ring and frost cake with Chocolate Rum Buttercream. Swirl it around in a decorative fashion and sprinkle top with shaved chocolate and a bit of powdered sugar. Serves 10.

Chocolate Rum Buttercream

- 1/2 cup butter
- 1/2 cup melted semi-sweet chocolate chips, cooled
- 1 tablespoon rum
- 1/2 teaspoon vanilla

Beat butter until light and creamy. Beat in the chocolate until blended. Beat in the rum and vanilla. Will frost 1 layer.

Royal Chocolate Gateau with Mocha Mousse Frosting

If you are looking for a chocolate cake that is sheer ecstacy and one that will delight the most ardent chocolate lover, then this heavenly creation is a good choice. It is not a high cake but low and dense.

> 1/2 **cup butter (1 stick)**
> 1 **cup sugar**
>
> 6 **eggs**
>
> 1 **cup semi-sweet chocolate chips, melted and cooled**
>
> 1 3/4 **cups finely grated walnuts**
> 1/2 **cup vanilla wafer crumbs**
> 1/2 **teaspoon baking powder**
>
> 1 **teaspoon vanilla**

Cream butter with sugar until mixture is light and fluffy, about 3 or 4 minutes. Add eggs, one at a time, beating well after each addition. Beat in the melted chocolate.

Toss together walnuts, crumbs and baking powder until blended, and beat this into the egg mixture. Beat in vanilla.

Pour batter into a buttered 10-inch springform pan and bake at 350° for about 45 minutes or until a cake tester, inserted in center, comes out clean. Allow cake to cool in pan.

Remove the metal ring and pour Mocha Mousse Frosting over the cake, and spread it on the sides, carefully. Refrigerate until firm. Remove from the refrigerator about 10 minutes before serving. Serves 10.

Mocha Mousse Frosting

> 1 **cup semi-sweet chocolate chips**
> 1/2 **cup cream**
> 1 **teaspoon instant coffee**
> 1 **tablespoon Kahlua liqueur**

Place chocolate in blender container. Heat cream with instant coffee and bring it to boiling point. Pour into blender container and beat for 1 minute or until chocolate is melted. Blend in liqueur. Allow to cool for a few minutes and pour over the cake.

Buttery Coffee Cake with Chocolate Chips, Pecans & Raisins

This delicious coffee cake is filled with pecans and raisins and chocolate chips. The dough is buttery and the Sour Cream Glaze is the perfect accompaniment. It is a little more work, but worth every bit the effort.

> 1 package dry yeast
> 1/4 cup warm water (105° to 110°)
> 1 teaspoon sugar
>
> 2 egg yolks
> 1/4 cup milk
>
> 1 3/4 cups flour (may need 1/4 cup more)
> 3 tablespoons sugar
> 1/2 teaspoon salt
> 1/2 cup butter
>
> 1 egg white
> 1 cup chopped pecans
> 1 cup chocolate chips
> 1 cup raisins
> 1/2 cup cinnamon sugar

In a glass measuring cup, stir together yeast, water and sugar and allow to stand until yeast is bubbly. (This is called "proofing" the yeast and if yeast does not foam, it is inactive, and should be discarded.) Stir in the yolks and milk until blended.

In the large bowl of an electric mixer, beat together flour, sugar, salt and butter until mixture resembles coarse meal. Beat in the yeast mixture and continue beating for 3 minutes. (If dough is very soft, beat in a little more flour.) Scrape the dough together in a ball and drizzle a few drops of oil on the top. Cover the bowl with plastic wrap and refrigerate it overnight.

Buttery Coffee Cake (continued)

On a floured pastry cloth, roll the dough out to measure a 15x10-inch rectangle. Beat egg white until soft peaks form. Stir in pecans, chocolate chips and cinnamon sugar until blended. Spread this filling over the dough. Roll the dough up, jelly roll fashion and place it in a 9-inch, greased tube pan, seam side down. Overlap the ends a bit and pinch them together. Allow to stand 1 hour.

Bake in a 350° oven for about 55 to 65 minutes or until top is golden brown. Allow to cool in pan. When cool, remove pan and drizzle top with Sour Cream Glaze. Serves 8 to 10.

Sour Cream Glaze: Stir together 1 tablespoon sour cream, 1/2 teaspoon vanilla and 1 cup sifted powdered sugar until blended.

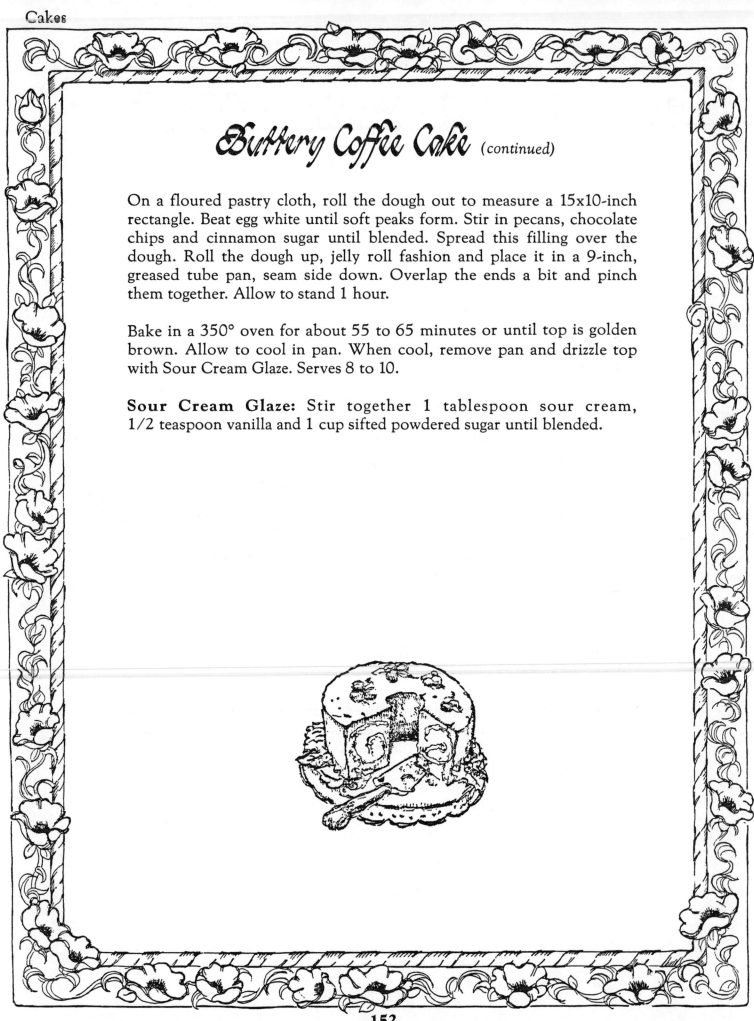

Imperial Chocolate Torte with Raspberries & Chocolate Chip Whipped Cream

      6 egg whites, at room temperature
1/2 cup sugar

      6 egg yolks, at room temperature
1/2 cup sugar

1 1/2 cups finely grated walnuts
    2 tablespoons cocoa
    1 teaspoon baking powder
    1 teaspoon vanilla

Preheat oven to 350°. Butter a 10x15-inch jelly roll pan. Line it with waxed paper extending 4-inches beyond the ends of the pan. Butter the waxed paper. Set aside. Wet a towel and squeeze it until it is damp-dry.

Beat whites until foamy. Gradually add 1/2 cup sugar and continue beating until whites are stiff and glossy. Beat yolks with 1/2 cup sugar until mixture is very thick. Beat in nuts, cocoa, baking powder and vanilla. Fold in beaten egg whites. Pour batter into prepared pan and bake at 350° for about 25 minutes or until top is golden and a cake tester, inserted in center, comes out clean. Immediately cover cake with damp towel. Allow cake to cool and then refrigerate. Leave towel on cake. This can be done 2 days ahead.

The day before serving, turn cake out on 2 overlapping strips of waxed paper that have been sprinkled with sifted powdered sugar. Remove baking paper and trim edges of cake. Cut cake into thirds, yielding 3 strips measuring 14x3-inches. Fill and frost with Chocolate Chip Whipped Cream and Raspberries. Sprinkle extra chocolate bits over the top and decorate with whole raspberries. Refrigerate overnight. Serves 12 very special friends.

Chocolate Chip Whipped Cream & Raspberries

(continued)

1 pint whipping cream
2 tablespoons sugar
2 tablespoons Grand Marnier Liqueur
1 cup semi-sweet chocolate chips, coarsely chopped
    in blender or processor
1 package (10 ounces) frozen raspberries, drained.
    Reserve juice for another use

Beat cream with sugar and liqueur until stiff. Beat in chopped chocolate bits. Stir in drained raspberries. Will fill and frost above cake.

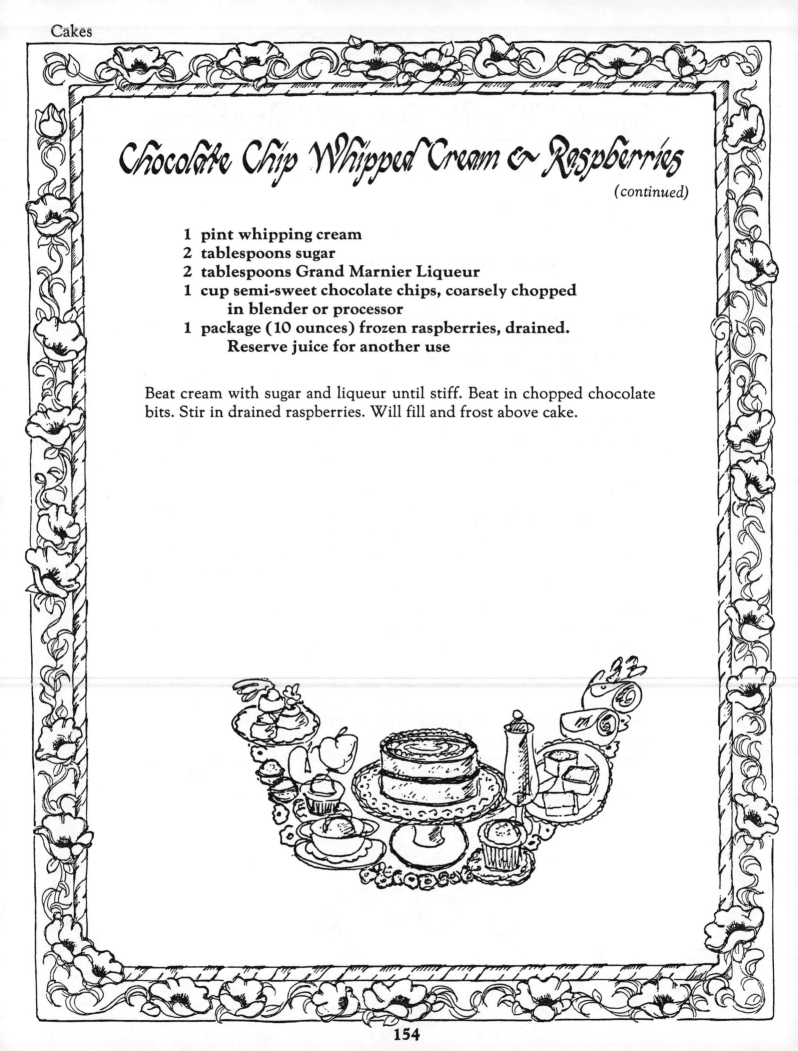

The Everything Carrot Cake with Pineapple, Coconut & Walnuts

Some carrot cakes have pineapple or coconut or walnuts for additional fillups. This carrot cake has all of these and it is very good. Frosted with Butter Cream Cheese Frosting makes it a perfect combination.

      2 cups flour
      2 teaspoons baking powder
      1 teaspoon baking soda
  1/2 teaspoon salt
2 1/2 teaspoons cinnamon

      4 eggs
1 1/4 cups oil
      2 cups sugar
      2 teaspoons vanilla

2 1/2 cups grated carrots
      1 can (8 ounces) crushed pineapple, drained
  1/2 cup coconut flakes
      1 cup chopped walnuts

In a bowl, combine flour, baking powder, baking soda, salt and cinnamon.

Beat together eggs, oil, sugar and vanilla. Beat in flour mixture until blended. Do not overbeat. Stir in carrots, pineapple, coconut and walnuts. Pour batter into 2 greased 9-inch tube pans. Bake in a 350° oven for about 40 minutes or until a cake tester inserted in center comes out clean. Frost with Butter Cream Cheese Frosting when cool. (This will produce 2 cakes. Use one and freeze the other.) Each cake will serve 8 to 10.

Butter Cream Cheese Frosting

  1/2 cup butter, at room temperature
      1 package (8 ounces) cream cheese, at room
            temperature
      1 teaspoon vanilla
      3 cups sifted powdered sugar

Beat together all the ingredients until blended.

Cinnamon Carrot Cake with Oranges & Walnuts

The addition of the orange gives this carrot cake a totally different character. And the frosting is simply delicious with a touch of orange and walnuts.

1/2 cup butter (1 stick)
  2 cups sugar
  3 eggs

  2 cups flour
1/2 teaspoon salt
  2 teaspoons baking powder
  2 teaspoons baking soda
  2 teaspoons cinnamon

  1 medium orange, grated
  1 cup chopped walnuts
  2 cups grated carrots
  1 teaspoon vanilla

Beat together butter and sugar until mixture is light and fluffy. Beat in eggs, one at a time, beating well after each addition.

Beat in flour, baking powder, soda and cinnamon until blended. Do not overbeat. Beat in the remaining ingredients until blended.

Pour batter into 2 10-inch greased cake pans with removable bottoms and bake at 350° for about 45 minutes or until a cake tester, inserted in center, comes out clean. Allow to cool in pan.

When cool, fill and frost with Orange Cream Cheese Frosting. Will serve 10.

Orange Cream Cheese Frosting

  1 package (8 ounces) cream cheese
1/2 cup butter (1 stick)
  3 tablespoons grated orange peel
1/2 cup chopped walnuts
  2 cups sifted powdered sugar

Beat cream cheese and butter until blended. Beat in the remaining ingredients until blended.

Sour Cream Chocolate Chip Chocolate Cake with Chocolate Mousse Frosting

There are few chocolate cakes that you can make that are easier or better than this one. It is super moist, fudgy and beautiful to behold.

1/2	cup butter (1 stick) at room temperature
1 1/2	cups sugar
3	eggs
2	teaspoons vanilla
2	cups flour
6	tablespoons cocoa
3	teaspoons baking powder
1/2	teaspoon baking soda
1/2	teaspoon salt
1 1/2	cups sour cream
3/4	cup chocolate chips, coarsely crushed. (This can be done by placing the chocolate chips in a plastic bag and rolling them with a rolling pin.)

In the large bowl of an electric mixer, place all the ingredients and beat them together for about 5 minutes. Divide the batter between two 10-inch springform pans that have been lightly buttered. Bake the layers in a 350° oven for about 35 to 40 minutes or until a cake tester, inserted in center comes out clean. Do not overbake or cake will not be moist. (The two layers can be baked together.)

Allow layers to cool. Spread Chocolate Mousse Frosting between the layers and on the top and sides.

This can be prepared earlier in the day or 1 day earlier and stored in the refrigerator, but bring to room temperature before serving as the Chocoalte Mousse Frosting will firm up. Serves 10.

Chocolate Mousse Frosting (continued)

1 1/3 cups semi-sweet chocolate chips (8 ounces)
   1 cup whipping cream
 1/4 cup butter (1/2 stick), at room temperature
   3 egg yolks
 1/2 teaspoon vanilla (or 1 tablespoon rum if you want
          to sparkle it a bit)

Place chocolate chips in a blender container. Heat cream to boiling point and pour into the blender. Blend for about 1 minute. Beat in butter for another 30 seconds. Beat in yolks and vanilla for another 30 seconds. Will fill and frost one 10-inch layer cake.

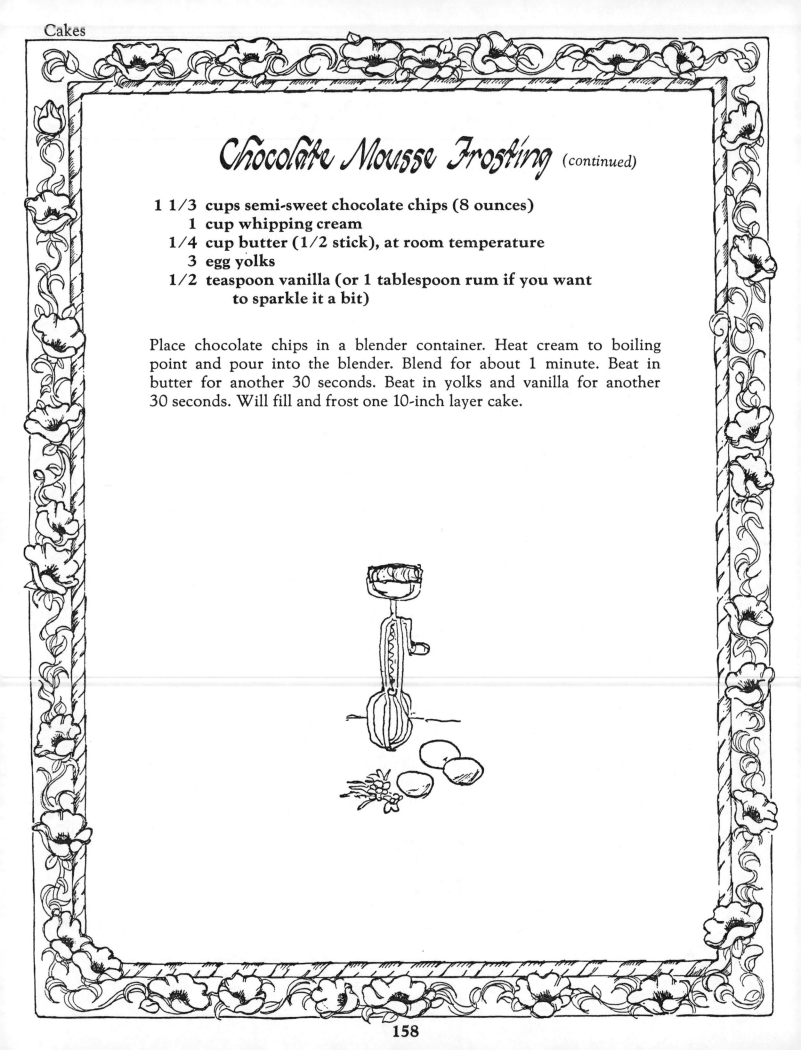

Fresh Apple Butter Cake with Raisins, Walnuts & Buttermilk Glaze

1 1/3 cups sugar
   2 cups flour
   2 teaspoons cinnamon
   1 teaspoon baking powder
      pinch salt
 2/3 cup melted butter
   3 eggs
 1/2 cup sour cream

   3 apples, peeled, cored and then thinly sliced.
   2 cups chopped walnuts
 3/4 cup yellow raisins

Combine first 8 ingredients in a large mixer bowl and beat for 3 minutes. Stir in the fruit and walnuts. Pour batter into a greased 9-inch tube pan and bake at 350° for 50 minutes to 1 hour. Allow to cool in pan. When cool, drizzle top decoratively with Buttermilk Glaze. Serves 10.

Buttermilk Glaze:
   1 cup sifted powdered sugar
   1 tablespoon buttermilk
   1 teaspoon lemon juice
 1/2 cup chopped yellow raisins

Stir together all the ingredients, adding a little more sugar or buttermilk, until glaze is a drizzling consistency.

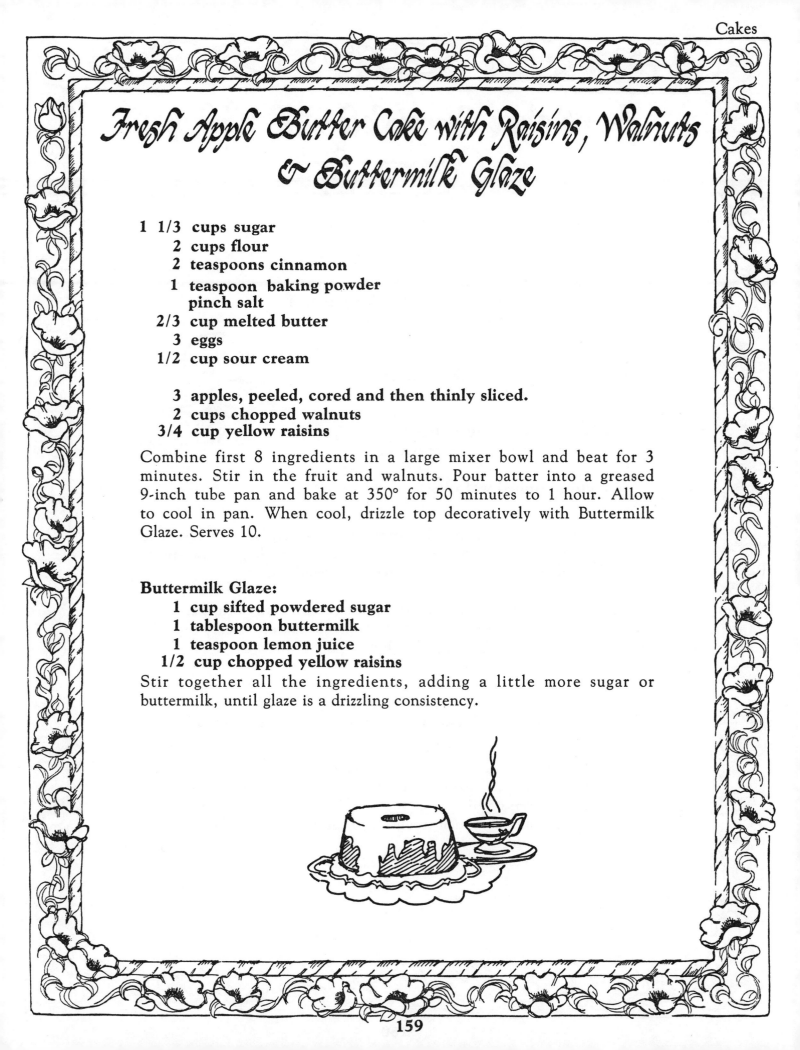

French Apple Orange Cake with Walnuts & Cinnamon Sugar

3 eggs
3/4 cup sugar

1 cup flour
1/2 orange, grated. Remove any large pieces
    of membrane
1 teaspoon vanilla

1/2 cup butter (1 stick), melted
    pinch of salt

2 apples, very thinly sliced
3 tablespoons cinnamon sugar

1 cup chopped walnuts

Beat eggs and sugar for about 5 minutes or until they are very light and tripled in volume. Beat in the flour, orange and vanilla, at low speed, until blended. Slowly beat in the melted butter and salt.

Butter a 10-inch springform pan and pour batter evenly into pan. Toss together apples and cinnamon sugar and spread mixture evenly over the batter. Sprinkle top with chopped walnuts.

Bake in a 350° oven for 40 minutes or until a cake tester, inserted in center, comes out clean. Sprinkle top lightly with sifted powdered sugar when cool. Serve with a dollup of sour cream, if desired. Serves 10.

Note: - This recipe produces a very low cake (about 1-inch in height) so don't feel that anything went wrong. It very much resembles a fruit tart with a cake crust.
* - An excellent substitution would be to use frozen pitted bing cherries instead of apples.*
* - Cake can be prepared one day earlier.*

Spiced Apple Cake with Raisins, & Walnuts

This cake is especially good for those who love a moist, spicy, fruity cake. With a cup of coffee or a glass of hot cider, it is sublime. The mayonnaisse is the secret ingredient, but it is masked with the cinnamon, apples and oranges.

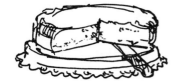

     2 cups flour
1 1/2 cups sugar
    2/3 cup mayonnaise
    1/4 cup sour cream
     2 eggs
     1 teaspoon baking soda
1 1/2 teaspoons cinnamon

     2 apples, peeled, cored and grated
    1/2 orange, grated. Remove any large pieces
         of membrane.
    1/2 cup yellow raisins
     1 cup chopped walnuts

In the large bowl of an electric mixer, combine first 7 ingredients and beat until blended, about 1 to 2 minutes. Stir in the remaining ingredients until blended.

Pour batter into a 10-inch springform pan, that has been lightly greased. Bake in a 350° over for about 50 minutes, or until a cake tester, inserted in center, comes out clean. Allow to cool in pan.

Frost with Orange Cream Cheese Frosting. Serves 10.

Orange Cream Cheese Frosting

1/4 cup (1/2 stick) butter
1/4 pound (4 ounces) cream cheese
  1 teaspoon vanilla
  2 cups sifted powdered sugar
  2 tablespoons grated orange peel

Beat butter and cream cheese until blended. Beat in the remaining ingredients until mixture is smooth. Will frost 1 10-inch cake.

Date Nut Cracker Pie with Lemon Creme Fraiche

3 eggs
3/4 cup sugar

2 cups vanilla wafer crumbs
1/4 cup sugar
1 teaspoon baking powder
1 teaspoon vanilla

1 cup chopped dates
1 cup chopped walnuts
2 tablespoons grated orange peel

Beat eggs with 3/4 cup sugar for about 5 minutes or until very light and fluffy. Stir in the remaining ingredients until blended.

Pour mixture into a buttered 9-inch pie plate and bake at 350° for 30 minutes or until a cake tester inserted in center comes out clean. Frost with Lemon Creme Fraiche and refrigerate overnight. Serves 8.

Lemon Creme Fraiche

1/2 cup sour cream
1/2 cup cream
2 tablespoons lemon juice
2 tablespoons sugar

Stir together all the ingredients and allow to stand at room temperature for about 30 minutes. Mixture will have thickened.

Note: - This pie can be frozen, unfrosted. Wrap in double thicknesses of plastic wrap and foil. Remove wrappers while thawing. Frost and refrigerate for several hours before serving.

Spiced Pumpkin Gateau with Praline Whipped Cream

6 egg yolks
1/2 cup sugar

2/3 cup canned pumpkin puree
1/3 cup vanilla wafer crumbs
2 teaspoons pumpkin pie spice
2 tablespoons grated orange peel
1 teaspoon vanilla
1 tablespoon Cognac
1 1/2 cups finely grated walnuts
1 teaspoon baking powder

6 egg whites, at room temperature
1/2 cup sugar

3/4 cup apricot jam, heated and pureed

Preheat oven to 350°. Heavily grease a 10x15-inch jelly roll pan. Line it with waxed paper extending 4-inches beyond the ends of the pan. Grease the waxed paper and set it aside. Wet a dish towel and squeeze it until it is damp dry.

In a large mixing bowl, beat yolks with 1/2 cup sugar until the mixture is very thick. Beat in the next group of 8 ingredients until blended. In another bowl, with clean beaters, beat the egg whites with 1/2 cup sugar until whites are stiff and glossy. Fold whites gently into yolk mixture.

Pour batter into prepared pan and spread evenly. Bake at 350° for about 25 minutes or until top is golden and a cake tester, inserted in center, comes out clean. Immediately, cover cake with the slightly dampened towel. Allow cake to cool, remove towel and cut cake, on the 15-inch side, into 3 even parts. You will have 3 layers, 5x10-inches, each.

Place first layer on serving dish and brush with apricot jam. Spread with Praline Whipped Cream. Repeat for the next 2 layers and frost the sides with the whipped cream. Decorate top with rosettes of whipped cream and a drizzle of apricot jam. Serves 10 to 12.

Praline Whipped Cream: Beat together 2 cups cream with 1/2 cup brown sugar and 2 tablespoons Cognac until cream is stiff. Beat in 1/2 cup finely chopped walnuts.

Fudge Almond Cake with Chocolate Mousse Frosting

This is a deliciously simple cake to prepare and the results will truly amaze you. The Chocolate Mousse Frosting is the essence of simplicity and this grand cake will brighten up a casual meal to stellar heights.

- 4 eggs
- 1 cup sugar
- 1 teaspoon vanilla

- 1/3 cup sifted cocoa
- 1/3 cup flour
- 3/4 cup almond meal (can be purchased at health food stores or finely grind in a food processor)
- 4 tablespoons melted butter

Beat together eggs, sugar and vanilla, until mixture is very light and fluffy, about 10 minutes. Combine cocoa, flour and ground almonds and mix until blended. Gently fold this into the beaten eggs. Fold in the melted butter.

Pour batter into a 10-inch springform pan that has been buttered and lightly floured. Bake in 350° oven for 30 to 35 minutes or until a cake tester, inserted in center, comes out clean. Do not overbake. Allow cake to cool in pan, remove metal ring and pour Chocolate Mousse Frosting over the top. Allow some of the frosting to flow down the sides. Refrigerate. (Cake will settle a bit in the center so don't think anything went wrong. The frosting will cover this fact nicely.)

As if all this were not enough, you could gild the lily by decorating the top with shaved chocolate. Serves 12.

Chocolate Mousse Frosting

- 1 cup semi-sweet chocolate chips
- 3/4 cup cream
- 2 egg yolks
- 1 teaspoon vanilla or 1 tablespoon Grand Marnier Liqueur

In a blender container, place chocolate chips. Heat cream to boiling point and pour into blender. Blend for about 1 minute or until chocolate is melted and smooth. Beat in yolks and vanilla and continue beating for about 2 minutes. Pour frosting over cooled cake.

Bittersweet Chocolate Spongecake with Sour Cream Chocolate Topping

This is not a sweet cake. It has a bittersweet taste, and a longlasting delicious after taste. The texture is light as air and could be, literally, cut with a feather.

   4 eggs
3/4 cup sugar

1/2 cup flour
   3 tablespoons cornstarch
   4 tablespoons cocoa
   2 tablespoons melted butter
   1 teaspoon vanilla

In the large bowl of an electric mixer, beat together the eggs and sugar for about 10 minutes or until mixture is very thick and creamy.
Fold in the cornstarch, flour and cocoa until blended. Fold in the melted butter and vanilla. (This can be done carefully with the mixer running at the lowest speed. Don't run it quickly or the batter will deflate. If your machine does not have a very slow setting, then you must fold by hand.)

Place batter into a buttered 10-inch springform pan and bake in a 350° oven for about 20 to 25 minutes or until a cake tester inserted in center comes out clean. Allow cake to cool. Spread Sour Cream Chocolate Topping on cake and swirl it in a decorative fashion.

To serve, cut into wedges and have some cold milk close by. Serves 8 to 10.

Sour Cream Chocolate Topping

1/2 cup semi-sweet chocolate chips
1/2 cup sour cream

Melt chocolate in the top of a double boiler over hot, not boiling water. Stir in the sour cream, 1 tablespoon at a time, until mixture is blended. This is a delicious frosting that stays creamy even after being refrigerated.

Butter Cake with Chocolate Chips & Walnuts

This is a very old-fashioned recipe. It is a very simple cake, much like a pound cake and the children will love it with milk.

1/2	cup butter (1 stick)
3/4	cup sugar
2	eggs
1 1/2	cups self-rising flour
1/4	cup milk
1	cup chocolate chips (semi-sweet)
1	cup chopped walnuts

In the large bowl of an electric mixer, cream butter and sugar until it is light and fluffy. Add eggs, one at a time, beating well after each addition. Beat in the flour, milk, chocolate chips and walnuts. (Batter will be stiff.)

Spoon batter into a 9-inch tube pan that has been lightly greased and spread it evenly into the pan. Bake in a 350° oven for 30 minutes or until a cake tester, inserted in center comes out clean. Allow to cool in pan.

Remove cooled cake from pan and drizzle Vanilla Cream Glaze decoratively over top. Serves 8.

Vanilla Cream Glaze

1 cup sifted powdered sugar
2 tablespoons cream
1 teaspoon vanilla

Stir together all the ingredients until blended. Add only enough cream to make it of drizzling consistency.

Chocolate Fudge Cake with Chocolate Whipped Cream

What a wonderful way to greet the children when they trudge home after a weary day at school. But this cake is so light and moist that it will serve beautifully for a special dinner party.

3/4 cup cocoa
1/2 cup boiling water

3/4 cup butter
1 3/4 cups sugar
1 teaspoon vanilla

3 eggs

2/3 cup sour cream

2 cups flour
1 teaspoon baking soda
1/2 teaspoon salt

Place cocoa in a bowl and stir in the boiling water. Set bowl aside.

In the large bowl of an electric mixer, cream butter and sugar until butter is light and fluffy. Beat in vanilla. Add eggs, 1 at a time, beating well after each addition. Beat in the sour cream, cocoa mixture, flour, baking soda and salt and beat for an additional 2 minutes. Batter will be very light and creamy.

Divide the batter between 2 greased 10-inch springform pans and bake in a 350° oven for about 30 minutes or until a cake tester inserted in center comes out clean. Do not overbake. Allow cakes to cool in pan and remove layers. Fill and frost with Chocolate Whipped Cream. Decorate with shaved chocolate or drizzle top with chocolate syrup. Serves 10.

Chocolate Whipped Cream

2 cups cream
1 cup sifted powdered sugar
1 teaspoon vanilla
4 tablespoons sifted cocoa

Beat all the ingredients together until cream is stiff.

Dark Fudge Chocolate Cake with Chocolate Mousse Buttercream Frosting

If you are looking for a rich, dark, moist chocolate cake, please consider this one. It is the essence of simplicity to prepare and a bit unusual with the use of mayonnaise.

- 2 cups flour
- 1 egg
- 1/3 cup oil
- 1 cup sugar
- 1/3 cup cocoa
- 1 teaspoon baking soda
- 1/8 teaspoon salt
- 1 cup water
- 2 teaspoons vanilla
- 1/2 cup mayonnaise

Combine all the ingredients in the large bowl of an electric mixer and beat until mixture is thoroughly blended, about 1 minute. Pour batter into 2 greased 10-inch layer pans with removable bottoms. Bake at 350° for about 35 minutes or until a cake tester, inserted in center, comes out clean. Cool layers in pan, but do place them on a rack.

Remove layers from pan, using a sharp knife. Place bottom layer onto a lovely footed platter and fill with Chocolate Mousse Frosting. Place second layer on top and frost with remaining frosting. Decorate top with a little grated chocolate and serve with pride. Serves 10.

Chocolate Mousse Buttercream Frosting

- 1 1/2 cups semi-sweet chocolate chips
- 1 1/4 cups cream
- 6 tablespoons butter, at room temperature
- 1 teaspoon vanilla (or 1 tablespoon rum)

Place chocolate in blender container. Heat cream to the boiling point and pour it into the blender. Blend for 1 minute or until chocolate is melted. Blend in butter and vanilla. Allow to cool a little and when it firms up enough to spread, fill and frost the layers. Will fill and frost 1 10-inch layer cake.

Hungarian Walnut Torte with Apricot & Chocolate Buttercream Glaze

This lovely torte is a delicate blend of apricot and chocolate butter cream on a moist, delectable nut torte. It is an elegant choice for a dinner party, and easy enough to make at any time.

- **4 egg whites**
- **1/3 cup sugar**

- **4 egg yolks**
- **1/3 cup sugar**
- **2 cups very finely grated walnuts (Use a nut grater for best results.)**
- **4 tablespoons fresh bread crumbs**
- **1/2 teaspoon baking powder**
- **1 teaspoon vanilla**

- **3/4 cup apricot jam, heated**
  Chocolate Buttercream Glaze

Beat egg whites with sugar until whites are stiff and glossy. Continue beating and add the yolks, one at a time, beating well after each addition. (Yes, this is correct, albeit unconventional.) Beat in the additional 1/3 cup sugar.

Toss together the walnuts, crumbs and baking powder until blended. Beat this into the egg mixture. Beat the vanilla. Pour batter into a buttered 10-inch springform pan and bake in a 350° oven for about 30 to 35 minutes or until a cake tester, inserted in center, comes out clean. Allow cake to cool.

Remove metal sides and spread cake with a coating of apricot jam. (Warming the jam makes it easier to spread.) With a spoon, swirl top with warm Chocolate Buttercream Glaze, allowing some of the apricot to show. Cut into wedges to serve. Serves 8.

Chocolate Buttercream Glaze: Melt 4 ounces semi-sweet chocolate over hot, not boiling water. Stir in 1/4 cup (1/2 stick) butter, 1 tablespoon at a time, until blended. Stir in 1/2 teaspoon vanilla or 1 teaspoon Grand Marnier Liqueur. Swirl on cake while glaze is still warm or it will firm up.

Chocolate Chip Pecan Pie with Creme de Chocolate

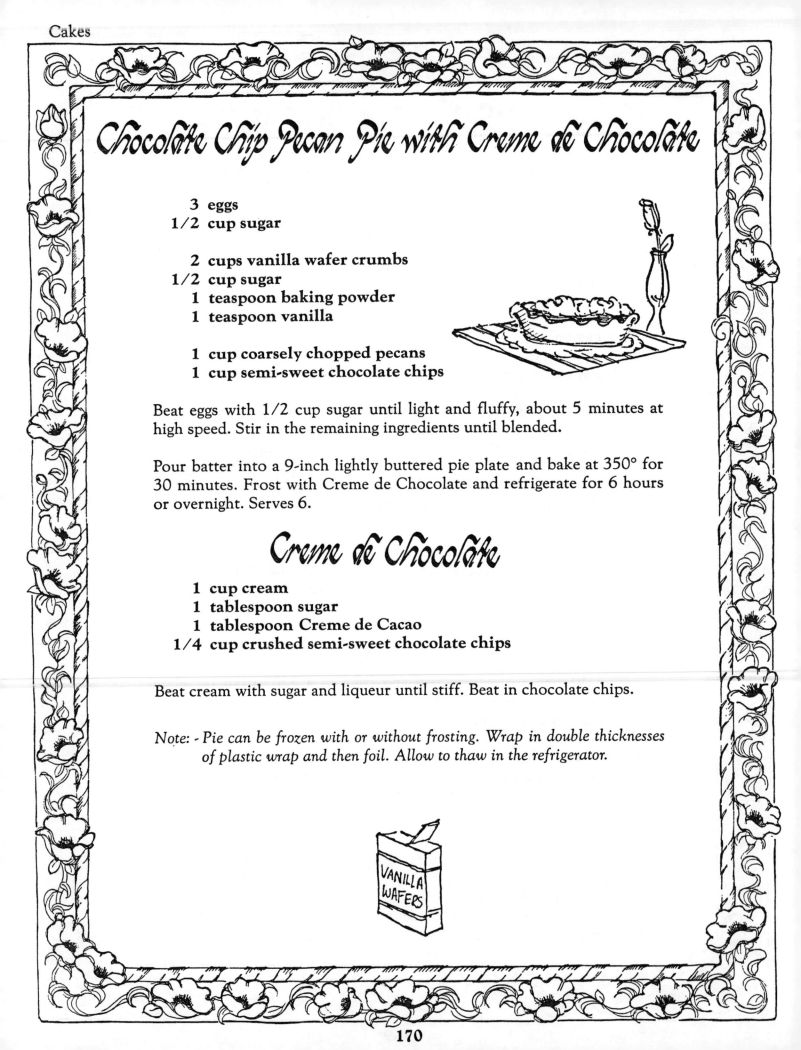

    3 eggs
1/2 cup sugar

    2 cups vanilla wafer crumbs
1/2 cup sugar
    1 teaspoon baking powder
    1 teaspoon vanilla

    1 cup coarsely chopped pecans
    1 cup semi-sweet chocolate chips

Beat eggs with 1/2 cup sugar until light and fluffy, about 5 minutes at high speed. Stir in the remaining ingredients until blended.

Pour batter into a 9-inch lightly buttered pie plate and bake at 350° for 30 minutes. Frost with Creme de Chocolate and refrigerate for 6 hours or overnight. Serves 6.

Creme de Chocolate

    1 cup cream
    1 tablespoon sugar
    1 tablespoon Creme de Cacao
1/4 cup crushed semi-sweet chocolate chips

Beat cream with sugar and liqueur until stiff. Beat in chocolate chips.

Note: - Pie can be frozen with or without frosting. Wrap in double thicknesses of plastic wrap and then foil. Allow to thaw in the refrigerator.

Velvet Chocolate Chip Cake with Chocolate Cream

    1 cup butter (2 sticks)
    2 cups sugar

    5 eggs
    2 teaspoons vanilla
    1 cup sour cream

    10 tablespoons cocoa
1 1/4 cups flour
    1 teaspoon baking powder
    1 teaspoon baking soda
 1/4 teaspoon salt

1 1/2 cups grated walnuts
    1 cup semi-sweet chocolate chips

Cream butter with sugar until mixture is light and fluffy. Beat in eggs, one at a time, beating well after each addition. Beat in the sour cream until blended.

In a bowl, sift together cocoa, flour, baking powder, baking soda and salt. Add these dry ingredients to the egg mixture and beat until blended. Beat in the nuts and chocolate.

Divide the batter between 2 buttered 10-inch springform pans and spread it evenly. Bake in a 325° oven for about 45 minutes or until a cake tester, inserted in center comes out clean. Allow to cool in pan. Remove layers and fill and frost with Chocolate Cream. Sprinkle top with shaved chocolate. Serves 10 to 12.

Chocolate Cream

    1 cup butter, slightly softened
 3/4 cup sifted powdered sugar
    3 tablespoons sifted cocoa
    1 teaspoon vanilla

Beat butter until light and creamy. Beat in the remaining ingredients until thoroughly blended. Will fill and frost a 10-inch layer cake.

These are 2 variations of oldies, but goodies. The Fudge whips up in minutes and the Bourbon Balls are sparkled with raisins and pecans.

Fantasy Fudge with Raisins & Walnuts

- 4 cups miniature marshmallows
- 2/3 cup evaporated milk
- 1/2 cup butter (1 stick)
- 1 1/2 cups sugar
- 1/4 teaspoon salt

- 1 package (12 ounces) semi-sweet chocolate chips
- 1 cup chopped walnuts
- 1/2 cup chopped raisins
- 1 teaspoon vanilla

Combine first 5 ingredients in a saucepan and bring mixture to a boil. Boil mixture for 5 minutes, stirring constantly. Stir in chocolate chips, remove from heat, and continue stirring until chocolate is melted. Stir in the walnuts, raisins and vanilla until blended.

Pour mixture evenly into a greased 9x9-inch pan and refrigerate until firm. Cut into small squares and place in bon bon paper liners. Yields about 2 pounds fudge.

Bourbon Balls with Pecans & Raisins

- 1 package (1 pound) vanilla wafer crumbs
- 1 cup raisins
- 2 cups pecans
- 2 cups sifted powdered sugar
- 2 heaping tablespoons cocoa
- 3/4 cup Bourbon
- 1/3 cup light corn syrup

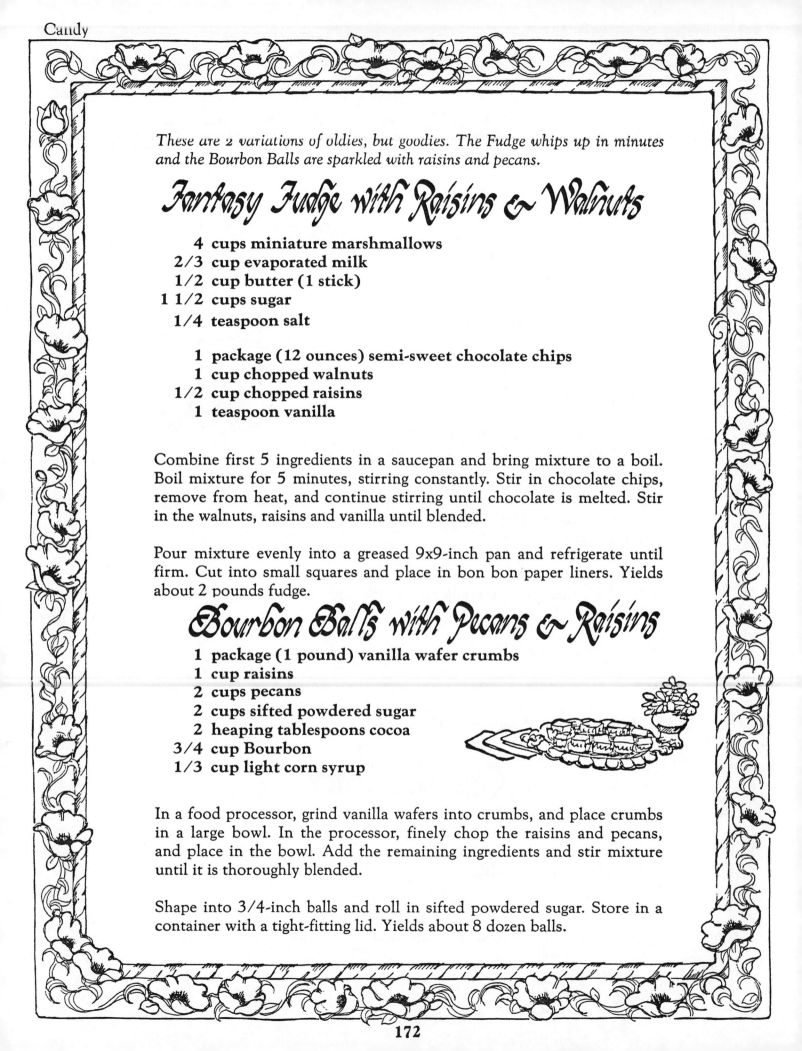

In a food processor, grind vanilla wafers into crumbs, and place crumbs in a large bowl. In the processor, finely chop the raisins and pecans, and place in the bowl. Add the remaining ingredients and stir mixture until it is thoroughly blended.

Shape into 3/4-inch balls and roll in sifted powdered sugar. Store in a container with a tight-fitting lid. Yields about 8 dozen balls.

Pecans with Pralines & Cream

3/4 **cup brown sugar**
3/4 **cup sugar**
1/2 **cup sour cream**

2 **teaspoons vanilla**
2 **cups pecan halves**

In a saucepan, over medium heat, stir together sugars and sour cream until sugar is dissolved. Continue cooking, without stirring, until temperature reaches 238° on a candy thermometer (soft ball stage.)

Stir in the vanilla and pecans and stir to coat evenly. Pour mixture onto waxed paper and with a tooth pick, separate the nuts. Allow to dry. Store in a tin or a jar with a tight-fitting lid. Do not refrigerate, Yields about 1 1/4 pounds.

Caramel Glazed Walnuts

1/2 **cup brown sugar**
1/2 **cup sugar**
1/2 **cup light corn syrup**
1/2 **cup cream**
2 **tablespoons butter**

1 **teaspoon vanilla**
2 **cups walnut halves**

In a saucepan, over medium heat, stir together first 5 ingredients until sugar is dissolved. Continue cooking until temperature reaches 245° on a candy thermometer (firm ball stage.)

Stir in the vanilla and pecans and stir to coat evenly. Pour mixture onto waxed paper and separate nuts with a tooth pick. Allow to dry. Store in a tin or a jar with a tight-fitting lid. Do not refrigerate. Yields about 1 pound.

Velvet Creamy Chocolate Fudge

1/2 cup cream
3 cups miniature marshmallows
1/2 cup sugar
1/4 cup butter
6 ounces milk chocolate (use a good quality chocolate)
1 teaspoon vanilla

1/4 cup chopped walnuts

In a saucepan, combine cream, marshmallows, sugar and butter and bring mixture to boil. Lower heat a little and continue cooking (mixture should be bubbling), stirring for 5 minutes. Add the chocolate and stir until it is melted. Stir in the vanilla and chopped walnuts.

Place fudge in a foil lined 6x9-inch pan and spread to even. Refrigerate until firm. Cut into small squares and place in bon bon paper liners. Yields about 3/4 pound fudge.

Note: - Recipe can be doubled.
 - You can substitute semi-sweet chocolate for the milk chocolate. Or you can use half milk and half semi-sweet.
 - To facilitate lining the pan with foil, turn the pan upside down and shape the foil against the bottom of the pan. (This makes for neater corners.) Then all you need do is set the foil into the pan.

Milk Chocolate Bar with Raisins & Almonds

1 package (12 ounces) milk chocolate chips

1 cup sweetened condensed milk
1 cup soft raisins
1 cup toasted slivered almonds
1 teaspoon vanilla

In the top of a double boiler, over hot, not boiling water, melt the chocolate. Stir in the condensed milk until blended. Stir in the raisins, nuts and vanilla.

Pour chocolate mixture on a foil-lined cookie sheet and spread, irregularly to 1/4-inch thickness. Refrigerate and when firm, cut into chunks. Yields about 1 pound candy.

Easiest Chocolate Fudge

        1 can (14 ounces) condensed milk
    1/2 cup butter (1 stick), salted

        1 pound semi-sweet chocolate chips
    1 1/2 cups chopped toasted walnuts
        2 teaspoons vanilla

Heat together milk and butter and bring mixture to a boil. Add chocolate chips and stir until chocolate is melted. Stir in walnuts and vanilla. Pour into a wax-paper lined 8x8-inch pan and spread to even. Refrigerate until firm. Remove from pan, peel off paper and cut into 1-inch squares. Place in paper bon bon liners. Can be stored in the freezer for several months. Yields 64 squares.

Rocky Road Rum Candy

        8 ounces semi-sweet chocolate chips

        2 eggs, beaten
        1 teaspoon vanilla
        1 tablespoon rum

    1 1/2 cups chopped toasted walnuts or almonds
        2 cups miniature marshmallows

    1 1/2 cups vanilla wafer crumbs

In top of double boiler, melt chocolate. Beat in eggs, vanilla and rum. Stir in nuts and marshmallows.

On a large piece of wax paper, sprinkle 1/4 cup crumbs along one side. Spoon 1/3 of the candy mixture over the crumbs, shaping a log about 10-inches long. Sprinkle 1/4 cup crumbs over the top of the roll. With the help of the wax paper, roll up the candy logs, making certain that the chocolate is well covered with crumbs. Place wax paper rolled logs in refrigerator until chocolate is firm. Repeat procedure for remaining 2 logs.

When ready to use, cut with a serrated knife into 1/2-inch slices. Serve in paper bon bon liners. Can be stored in the refrigerator for 1 week or in the freezer for several months. Yields 60 slices.

Dreamy, Creamy California Cheesecake

I call this a California cheesecake only because of the wonderful hint of orange and lemon in the filling. It is very delicious and the texture is creamy (and dreamy.) As it does not have a crust, it is exceedingly light, and a good choice for dessert after a hardy meal.

- 3 packages (8 ounces, each) cream cheese, at room temperature
- 2 cups sour cream
- 1 cup sugar
- 2 tablespoons flour
- 5 eggs
- 1 teaspoon vanilla
- 3 tablespoons lemon juice
- 1 tablespoon grated orange peel
- 2 teaspoons grated lemon peel

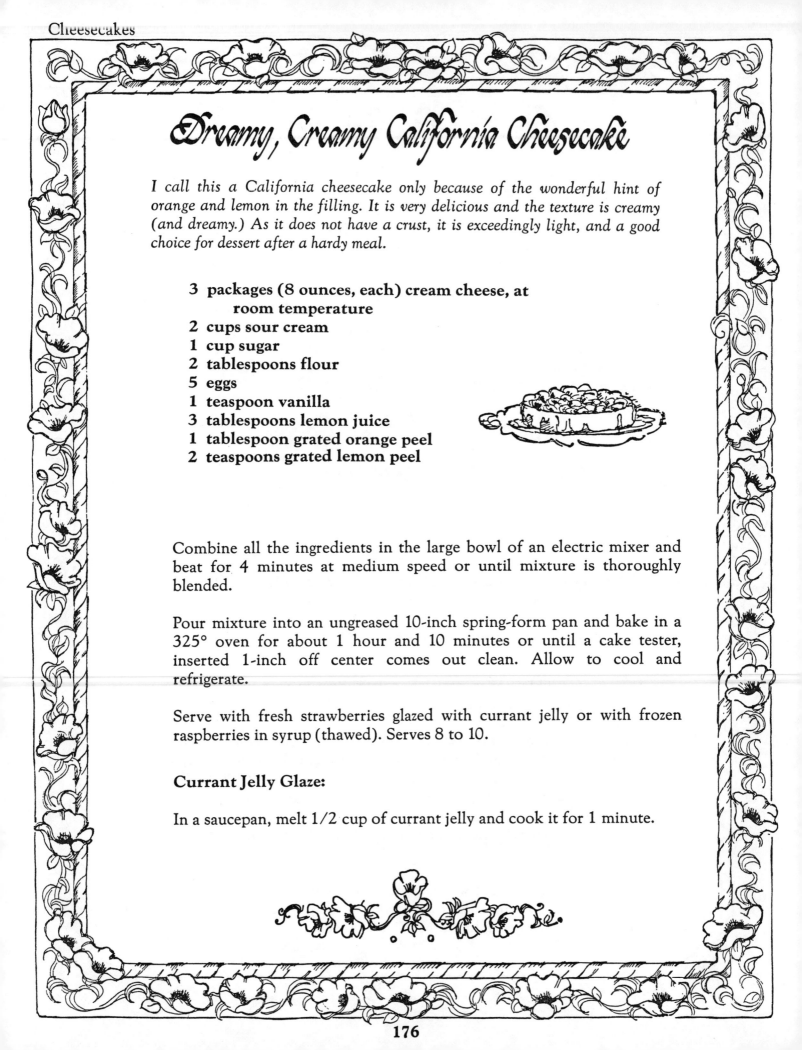

Combine all the ingredients in the large bowl of an electric mixer and beat for 4 minutes at medium speed or until mixture is thoroughly blended.

Pour mixture into an ungreased 10-inch spring-form pan and bake in a 325° oven for about 1 hour and 10 minutes or until a cake tester, inserted 1-inch off center comes out clean. Allow to cool and refrigerate.

Serve with fresh strawberries glazed with currant jelly or with frozen raspberries in syrup (thawed). Serves 8 to 10.

Currant Jelly Glaze:

In a saucepan, melt 1/2 cup of currant jelly and cook it for 1 minute.

Chocolate Cappuccino Cheesecake with Kahlua & Brandy

3 packages (8 ounces, each) cream cheese, at
    room temperature
1 cup sugar
2 cups sour cream
3 eggs

1 cup semi-sweet chocolate chips (6 ounces) melted
2 teaspoons instant espresso or regular instant
    coffee, dissolved in 1/2 cup boiling water
1 teaspoon vanilla
1 tablespoon brandy
1 tablespoon Kahlua liqueur

1 10-inch Chocolate Cinnamon Crust

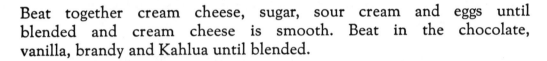

Beat together cream cheese, sugar, sour cream and eggs until blended and cream cheese is smooth. Beat in the chocolate, vanilla, brandy and Kahlua until blended.

Pour mixture into prepared crust and bake in a 350° oven for about 50 minutes or until a cake tester, inserted in center comes out clean, no longer. Do not overbake. Cheesecake will firm up when it chills. Cool in pan and refrigerate for at least 6 hours. Overnight is good too. Decorate top with chocolate leaves and little rosettes of whipped cream flavored with chocolate and brandy. Serves 10.

Chocolate Cinnamon Crust

1 1/2 cups chocolate cookie crumbs
6 tablespoons (3/4 stick) butter, melted
1/4 teaspoon cinnamon
1/3 cup grated chocolate

Combine all the ingredients and pat mixture firmly on the bottom and 1-inch up the sides of a 10-inch springform pan. Bake in a 350° oven for 8 minutes.

Chocolate Brandy Whipped Cream: Beat together 1/2 cup cream, 6 tablespoons chocolate syrup and 2 teaspoons brandy until cream is stiff.

Chocolate Cheese Cake Darling

When you are looking for a dessert to please the most discriminating chocolate lover you know, I recommend you try this magnificent chocolate cheesecake. It is a variation of my favorite chocolate cheesecake pie.

12 ounces semi-sweet chocolate chips
1 cup cream

2 packages cream cheese (8 counces, each), softened
4 eggs, at room temperature
1/2 cup sugar
2 teaspoons vanilla

Chocolate Cookie Crust

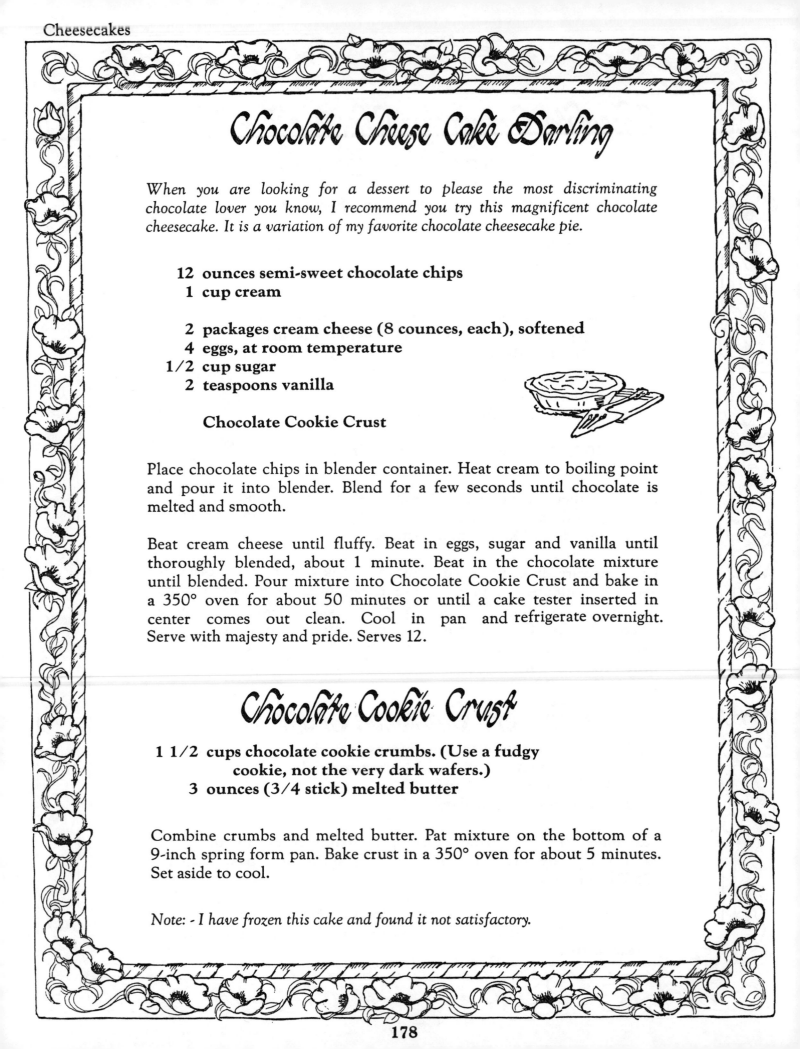

Place chocolate chips in blender container. Heat cream to boiling point and pour it into blender. Blend for a few seconds until chocolate is melted and smooth.

Beat cream cheese until fluffy. Beat in eggs, sugar and vanilla until thoroughly blended, about 1 minute. Beat in the chocolate mixture until blended. Pour mixture into Chocolate Cookie Crust and bake in a 350° oven for about 50 minutes or until a cake tester inserted in center comes out clean. Cool in pan and refrigerate overnight. Serve with majesty and pride. Serves 12.

Chocolate Cookie Crust

1 1/2 cups chocolate cookie crumbs. (Use a fudgy
cookie, not the very dark wafers.)
3 ounces (3/4 stick) melted butter

Combine crumbs and melted butter. Pat mixture on the bottom of a 9-inch spring form pan. Bake crust in a 350° oven for about 5 minutes. Set aside to cool.

Note: - I have frozen this cake and found it not satisfactory.

Cheesecake Gateau with Glazed Brandied Apricots

If you are looking for a dessert that is light, refreshing and incredibly delicious, I hope you will try this one. The combination of an ethereal cloud-like cheesecake with the glazed apricots sparkled with brandy is simply marvelous.

2 tablespoons butter
1 cup vanilla wafer crumbs

2 tablespoons gelatin
1/2 cup milk

2 packages (8 ounces, each) cream cheese, at room temperature
2 cups sour cream
1 cup sugar
3 tablespoons lemon juice
1 tablespoon grated lemon peel
1 teaspoon vanilla

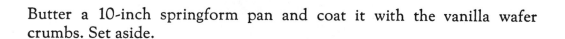

1 cup cream, whipped

Butter a 10-inch springform pan and coat it with the vanilla wafer crumbs. Set aside.

Soften gelatin in milk and place over hot water until gelatin is liquefied. A metal measuring cup makes this easy.

Beat together the next 6 ingredients until mixture is light, about 3 or 4 minutes. Beat in the whipped cream. Beat in the liquefied gelatin until blended.

Pour mixture into prepared pan and refrigerate until firm. At serving time, run a knife along the edge and remove metal ring. Coat top with Brandied Apricots. Cut into wedges and serve with pride. Serves 10.

Glazed Brandied Apricots

1 package (6 ounces) dried apricots, chopped
1 cup apricot nectar or orange juice
1/3 cup sugar

2 tablespoons apricot brandy

In a saucepan, cook together apricots, juice and sugar for about 20 minutes or until apricots are very tender and liquid is syrupy. Apricots should look pureed. Stir in the apricot brandy. Spread apricot mixture over cooled cheesecake and spread to even.

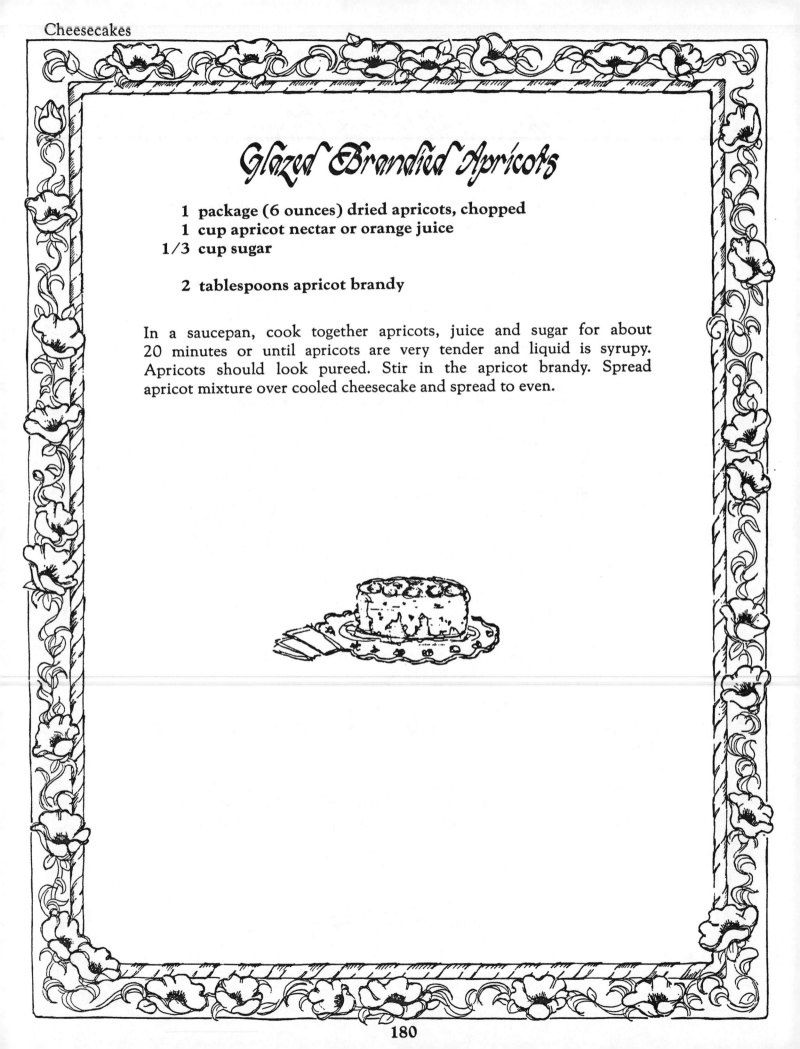

Creamy, Dreamy Chocolate Chip Chocolate Cheesecake

As you probably have guessed, I love chocolate and cheesecakes. I'm forever experimenting to find "the ultimate" chocolate cheesecake. This is a current favorite. It is light, it is delicate, it is creamy and chocolaty. You will enjoy the fact that it doesn't have to be baked and it whips up very easily.

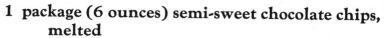

2 eggs
1/2 cup sugar

1 package (8 ounces) cream cheese
3/4 cup sour cream
1/4 cup sugar

1 package (6 ounces) semi-sweet chocolate chips, melted
1/3 cup semi-sweet chocolate chips, crushed

Beat together eggs and 1/2 cup sugar for at least 10 minutes until mixture is very light and frothy. Set aside. Do not underbeat.

In another bowl (you can use the same beaters), beat together the cream cheese, sour cream and 1/4 cup sugar until mixture is very light and creamy, about 5 minutes. Beat in the semi-sweet melted chocolate until blended. Slowly beat in the egg mixture until blended. Stir in the crushed chocolate chips.

Pour mixture into prepared Chocolate Chip Crust and spread to even. Refrigerate until firm. Decorate with additional crushed chocolate chips or a few sprinklings of shaved chocolate. Heavenly! Serves 8 to 10.

Chocolate Chip Crust

1 1/4 cups chocolate chip cookie crumbs
1/3 cup melted butter

Combine crumbs and butter until blended. Press mixture evenly on the bottom of a 9-inch springform pan. Bake in a 350° oven for 8 minutes or until lightly browned. Allow to cool before filling.

Note: - Cookie crumbs can be made in your processor, in batches, in a blender or a grater. In absence of these, place cookies in a plastic bag and crush with a rolling pin. Enjoy!

Orange Date Nut Cookies with Raisins

3 eggs
3/4 cup sugar
1 teaspoon vanilla

3/4 cup flour
3/4 teaspoon baking powder
1/4 teaspoon salt

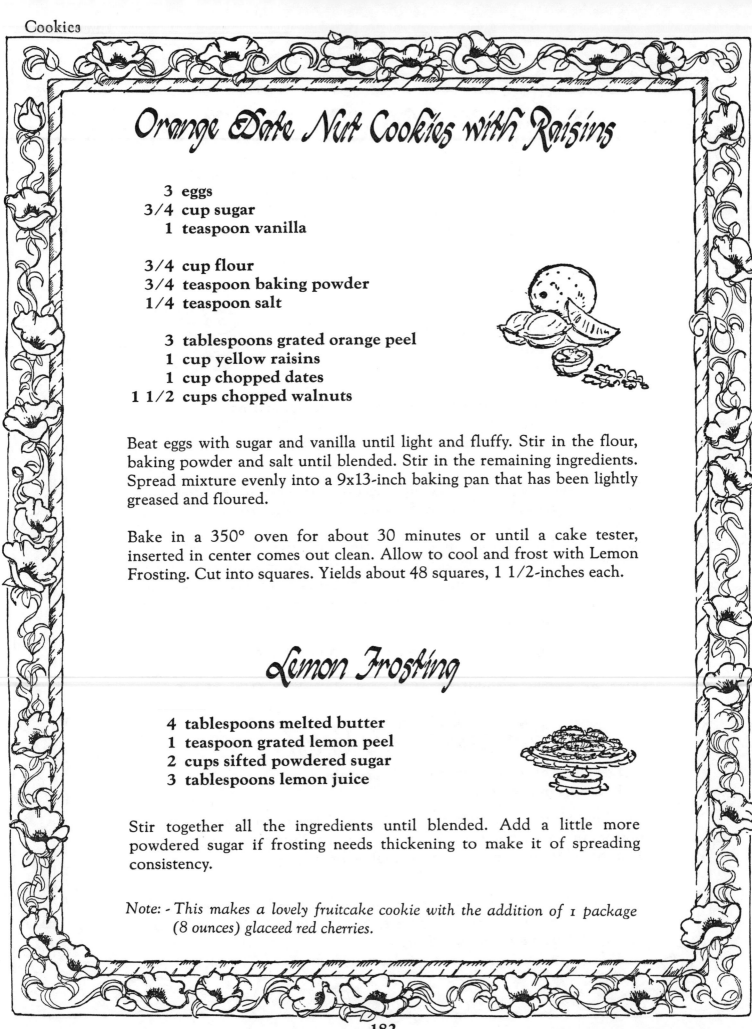

3 tablespoons grated orange peel
1 cup yellow raisins
1 cup chopped dates
1 1/2 cups chopped walnuts

Beat eggs with sugar and vanilla until light and fluffy. Stir in the flour, baking powder and salt until blended. Stir in the remaining ingredients. Spread mixture evenly into a 9x13-inch baking pan that has been lightly greased and floured.

Bake in a 350° oven for about 30 minutes or until a cake tester, inserted in center comes out clean. Allow to cool and frost with Lemon Frosting. Cut into squares. Yields about 48 squares, 1 1/2-inches each.

Lemon Frosting

4 tablespoons melted butter
1 teaspoon grated lemon peel
2 cups sifted powdered sugar
3 tablespoons lemon juice

Stir together all the ingredients until blended. Add a little more powdered sugar if frosting needs thickening to make it of spreading consistency.

Note: - This makes a lovely fruitcake cookie with the addition of 1 package (8 ounces) glaceed red cherries.

The World's Best Chocolate Chunk Nut Cookies

These are the best chocolate chunky cookies. Serve them warm with milk or coffee for a never-to-be-forgotten treat. Baking them in a jelly-roll pan makes them exceedingly simple to prepare . . . although they can be prepared as individual cookies, as well.

2 1/4 **cups flour**
1 **teaspoon baking soda**
1 **teaspoon baking powder**
1/2 **teaspoon salt**

1 **cup butter, at room temperature**
1 **cup sugar**
1 **cup brown sugar**
1 **teaspoon vanilla**

2 **eggs**
3 **bars (5 ounces, each) Cadbury's milk chocolate,**
or other good quality milk or semi-sweet
chocolate, coarsely chopped with a knife
1 1/2 **cups chopped walnuts**

Combine flour, soda, baking powder and salt in a bowl and stir to mix.

In the large bowl of an electric mixer, cream together butter, sugars and vanilla until mixture is creamy. Beat in eggs, one at a time, beating well after each addition. Beat in flour mixture until well combined. Stir in nuts and chocolate.

Spread batter (it will be thick) in a 10x15-inch jelly-roll pan and bake in a 375° oven for about 20 to 25 minutes or until top is lightly browned. Cool in pan and cut into 1 1/2-inch squares. Yields about 60 cookies.

Note: - The best way to chop the chocolate is to have it come to room temperature and then coarsely chop it with a knife. You cannot use the processor for this recipe.
- If you choose to make individual cookies, then drop the batter by the teaspoonful on a buttered cookie sheet. Bake for about 8 or 10 minutes or until very lightly browned.

Old Fashioned Raisin Nut Cookies with Orange Glaze

2 eggs
2 cups brown sugar
2 tablespoons grated orange peel
2 teaspoons vanilla

1 cup flour
1/2 teaspoon baking soda
1/4 teaspoon salt
1/4 teaspoon cinnamon

1 cup chopped walnuts
1 cup yellow raisins

Beat together first 4 ingredients until blended. Combine flour, baking soda, salt and cinnamon and add all at once to egg mixture. Stir until blended. Stir in walnuts and raisins. Pour batter and spread it evenly, in a greased 9x13-inch baking pan and bake in a 350° oven for about 20 minutes or until cookies are set. You might have to probe it a little with a cake tester, as the top will appear dry before cookies are set.

Allow cookies to cool in pan. When cool, drizzle top with Orange Glaze. Cut into squares to serve. Yields about 4 dozen cookies.

Orange Glaze: Stir together 1 tablespoon orange juice with about 1 cup sifted powdered sugar, until glaze is a drizzling consistency. Add 1 teaspoon grated orange peel and stir until blended. Drizzle glaze on cooled cookies and allow to dry, about 30 minutes, before cutting cookies.

Note: - Cookies freeze beautifully. If you are planning to freeze them, I would prefer you not to glaze these until after they have defrosted.

Swiss Butter Cookies with Chocolate Chips & Chocolate Dip

What a treat for dunking in milk after school... These delicate cookies are an excellent accompaniment to ice cream. If you are looking to add a bit of glamor for a dinner party, then dip half the cookie in melted chocolate and serve with pride.

- **1 cup butter (2 sticks)**
- **1 cup sifted powdered sugar**
- **1 teaspoon vanilla**
  pinch of salt

- **2 cups flour**
- **1 package (6 ounces) semi-sweet chocolate**
- **1/2 cup finely chopped walnuts**

Beat butter and sugar together until light. Beat in vanilla and salt. Add flour and beat until mixture is blended. Stir in chocolate chips and nuts.

Shape dough into 3/4-inch balls and flatten slightly with the palms of your hand or with the bottom of a glass. Place cookies on a lightly greased cookie sheet and bake in a 350° oven for about 15 minutes or until the edges are just beginning to turn a light brown. (Cookies should be pale.)

Remove cookies to a brown paper bag to cool. Yields about 3 dozen cookies. When cool, sprinkle lightly with sifted powdered sugar.

Chocolate Dip

- **3/4 cup semi-sweet chocolate chips**
- **4 tablespoons butter**
- **1 1/2 tablespoons cream**
  pinch of salt

Place all the ingredients in top of double boiler. Over hot, not boiling water, stir until chocolate is melted. Use to dip cookies or chilled fruit. Dip cookies half-way into chocolate, place on waxed paper and refrigerate until firm. Chocolate Dip can also be used to drizzle over cookies to decorate.

Note: - If you are planning to dip the cookies in melted chocolate, do not sprinkle with powdered sugar until after dipping... and then only the very faintest sprinkle.

Apricot, Pecan & Cinnamon Chewies

1 package (6 ounces) dried apricots, chopped
1 cup orange juice
1/4 cup sugar

2 1/2 cups yellow cake mix (use the regular cake mix
not the pudding mix)
1/2 cup butter (1 stick)
1 cup chopped pecans
4 tablespoons cinnamon sugar

1 can (14 ounces) sweetened condensed milk

In a saucepan, cook together apricots, orange juice and sugar until apricots are soft. Drain apricots.

In a 9x13-inch pan, melt the butter and spread it evenly. Sprinkle the cake mix evenly over the butter and pat it down with a fork. Sprinkle apricots, pecans and cinnamon sugar evenly over the cake mix. Drizzle the condensed milk evenly over all.

Bake in a 350° oven for about 30 minutes or until top is nicely browned. Allow to cool, and then cut into squares. Sprinkle top with a faint dusting of sifted powdered sugar. Yields 48 cookies.

Note: - Cookies freeze beautifully. Wrap in double thicknesses of plastic wrap and then, foil. Remove wrappers to defrost.

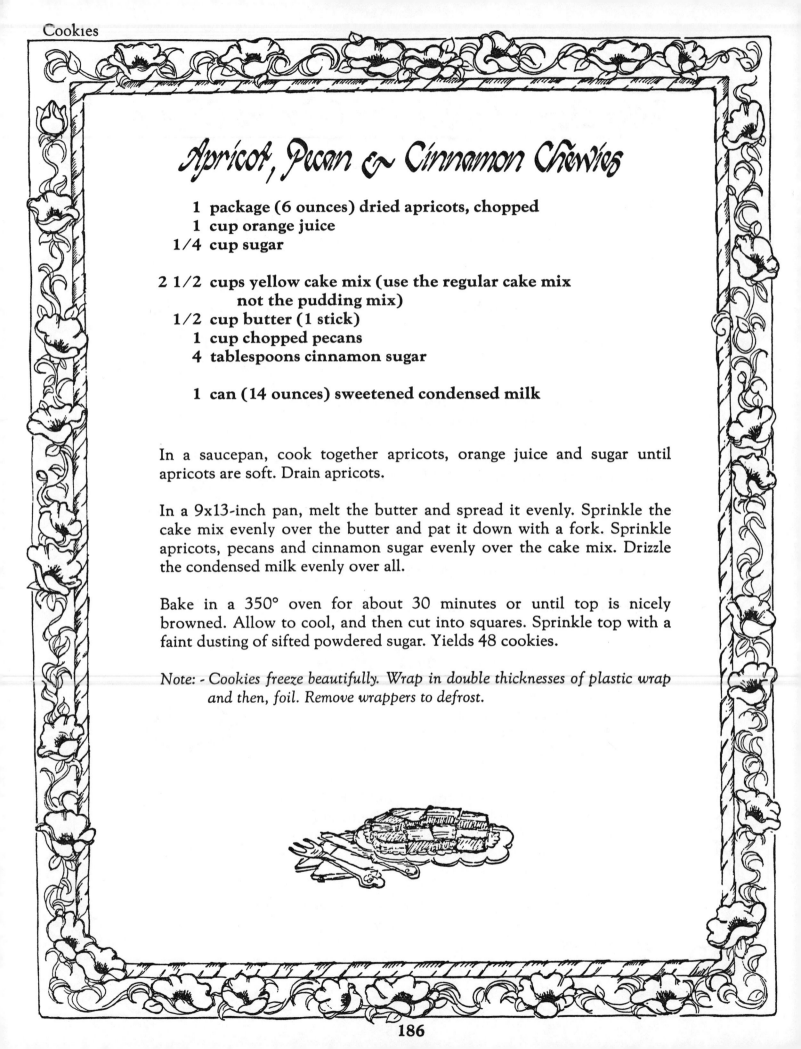

Chewy Chocolate Chip Macaroons

This is an incredibly easy and very delicious cookie that is chewy AND crunchy. It assembles in seconds and bakes in minutes.

- 3 **cups coconut meal (from the health food stores)**
- 1 **teaspoon vanilla**
- 1 **can (14 ounces) sweetened condensed milk**
- 1 **package (6 ounces) semi-sweet chocolate chips**

Combine all the ingredients and stir until they are blended. Drop batter by the teaspoonful on a generously greased cookie sheet. Bake for 12 minutes at 350° or until lightly browned. Remove from cookie pan immediately and place cookies on a brown paper bag to cool. Yields about 48 cookies.

Almond Raisin Macaroons

A variation of the above, but very different in taste and texture.

- 3 **cups almond meal (from the health food stores)**
- 1 **teaspoon vanilla**
- 1/2 **teaspoon almond extract**
- 1 **can (14 ounces) sweentened condensed milk**
- 1/2 **cup raisins**

Combine all the ingredients and stir until they are blended. Drop batter by the teaspoonful on a generously greased cookie sheet. Bake for 12 minutes at 350° or until lightly browned. Remove from cookie pan immediately and place cookies on a brown paper bag to cool. Yields about 48 cookies.

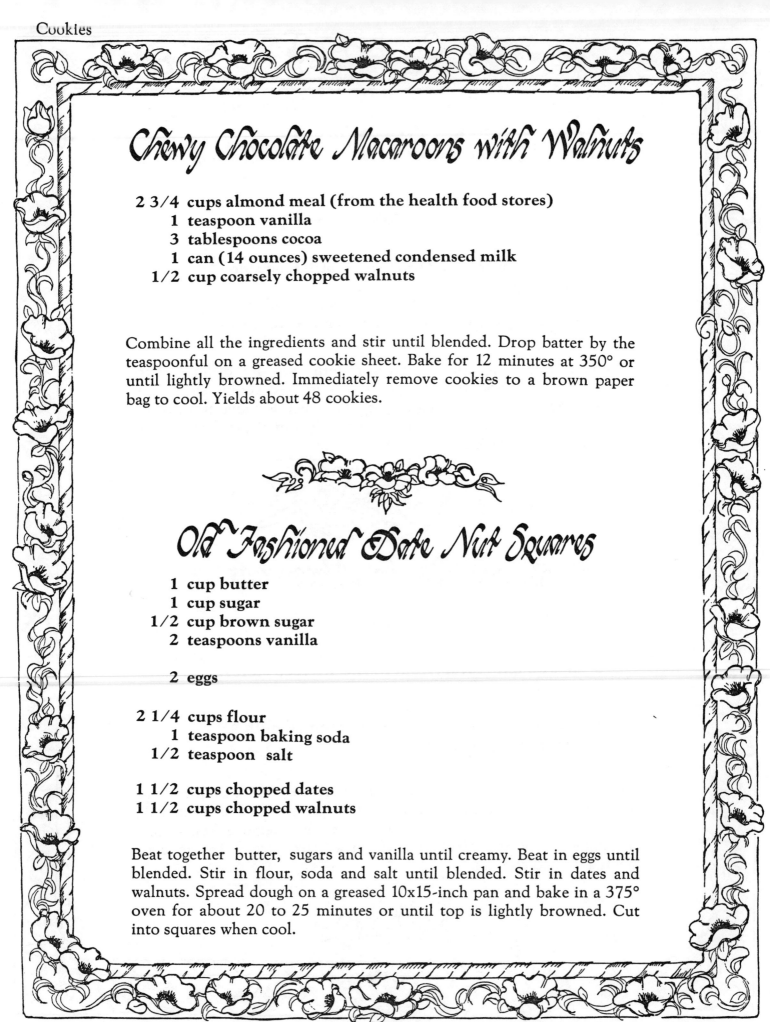

Chewy Chocolate Macaroons with Walnuts

2 3/4 cups almond meal (from the health food stores)
   1 teaspoon vanilla
   3 tablespoons cocoa
   1 can (14 ounces) sweetened condensed milk
 1/2 cup coarsely chopped walnuts

Combine all the ingredients and stir until blended. Drop batter by the teaspoonful on a greased cookie sheet. Bake for 12 minutes at 350° or until lightly browned. Immediately remove cookies to a brown paper bag to cool. Yields about 48 cookies.

Old Fashioned Date Nut Squares

   1 cup butter
   1 cup sugar
 1/2 cup brown sugar
   2 teaspoons vanilla

   2 eggs

2 1/4 cups flour
   1 teaspoon baking soda
 1/2 teaspoon salt

1 1/2 cups chopped dates
1 1/2 cups chopped walnuts

Beat together butter, sugars and vanilla until creamy. Beat in eggs until blended. Stir in flour, soda and salt until blended. Stir in dates and walnuts. Spread dough on a greased 10x15-inch pan and bake in a 375° oven for about 20 to 25 minutes or until top is lightly browned. Cut into squares when cool.

German Chocolate Chip Walnut Cookies

A wonderfully crisp cookie layer topped with a crunchy nut and chocolate topping is delightful with milk or coffee.

1/2 cup butter
2/3 cup sugar
   1 cup flour
   2 tablespoons cocoa, sifted

   1 cup sugar <
   1 teaspoon vanilla
1/4 cup flour
   2 eggs, beaten
   1 cup chopped walnuts or pecans
3/4 cup flaked coconut
   1 cup milk chocolate chips

Beat together butter and sugar until creamy. Stir in flour and cocoa until blended. Pat dough on the bottom of a greased 9x13-inch pan. Bake at 350° for 15 minutes.

Meanwhile, beat together sugar, vanilla, flour and eggs until blended. Stir in walnuts, coconut and chocolate chips. Spread mixture evenly over baked crust. Return to oven and continue baking for 25 minutes or until topping is set. Cut into squares when cool. Yields 4 dozen squares.

Easiest & Best Blender Brownie Bars

These delicious fudge bars whip up in seconds in your blender and are so good as an after school snack with a glass of cold milk.

2 cups semi-sweet chocolate chips

3/4 cup butter
1 1/2 cups sugar
1/4 cup water

4 eggs
2 teaspoons vanilla
1 1/2 cups flour
1/2 teaspoon baking soda
1/4 teaspoon salt

1 1/2 cups chopped walnuts

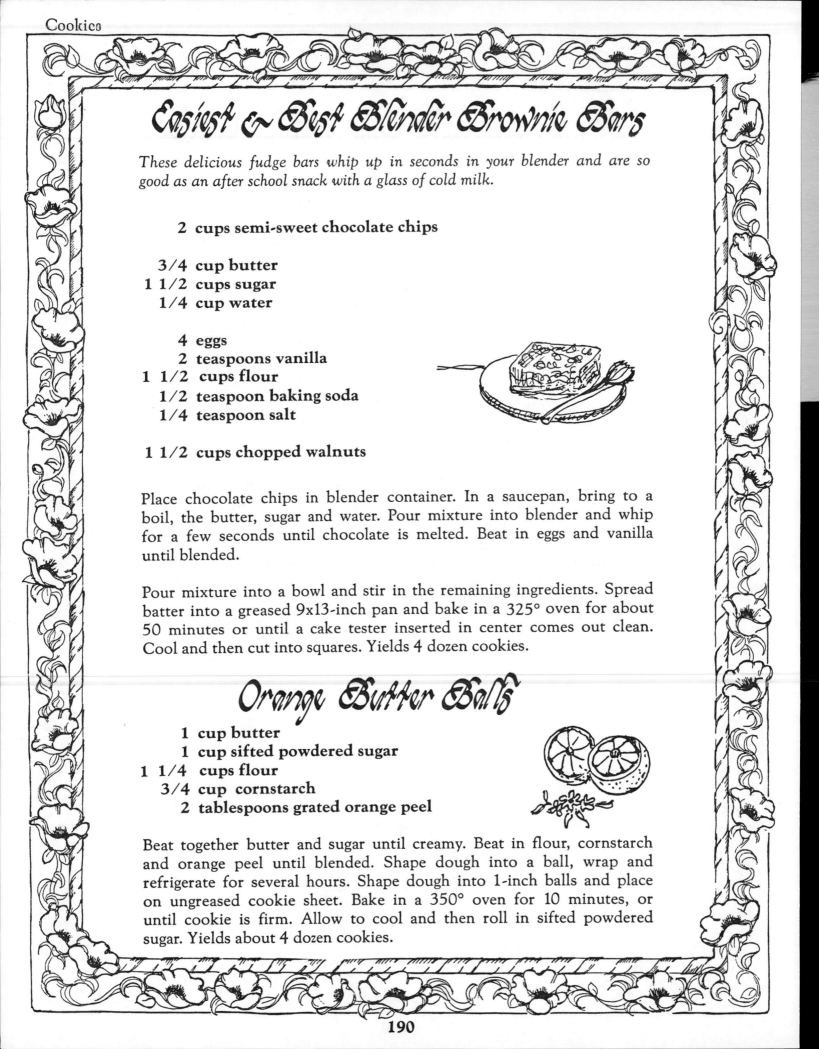

Place chocolate chips in blender container. In a saucepan, bring to a boil, the butter, sugar and water. Pour mixture into blender and whip for a few seconds until chocolate is melted. Beat in eggs and vanilla until blended.

Pour mixture into a bowl and stir in the remaining ingredients. Spread batter into a greased 9x13-inch pan and bake in a 325° oven for about 50 minutes or until a cake tester inserted in center comes out clean. Cool and then cut into squares. Yields 4 dozen cookies.

Orange Butter Balls

1 cup butter
1 cup sifted powdered sugar
1 1/4 cups flour
3/4 cup cornstarch
2 tablespoons grated orange peel

Beat together butter and sugar until creamy. Beat in flour, cornstarch and orange peel until blended. Shape dough into a ball, wrap and refrigerate for several hours. Shape dough into 1-inch balls and place on ungreased cookie sheet. Bake in a 350° oven for 10 minutes, or until cookie is firm. Allow to cool and then roll in sifted powdered sugar. Yields about 4 dozen cookies.

German Chocolate Bars with Pecans & Coconut Topping

What a delicious cookie to greet friends coming over for coffee, or to surprise the children trudging home from school. The crust is a delicate cookie, topped with coconuts and pecans and a drizzle of milk chocolate.

1/2	cup butter (1 stick)
1/4	cup sugar
1	egg
1 1/3	cups flour
	pinch of salt
1/2	teaspoon vanilla

Beat together butter and sugar until nicely blended. Beat in egg. Beat in flour, salt and vanilla. Pat the mixture on the bottom of a greased 8x12-inch pan and bake in a 350° oven for 15 minutes. Pour Coconut Pecan Topping on the baked crust and continue baking for 25 minutes. Allow to cool slightly and drizzle melted chocolate over the top in a decorative fashion. Cut into squares and sprinkle with a little powdered sugar. Yields about 24 cookies.

Coconut Pecan Topping:

2	eggs
1	cup sugar
2	tablespoons flour
1/2	teaspoon baking powder
1 1/2	cups chopped pecans
1/2	cup sweetened flaked coconut

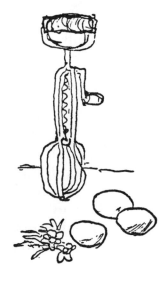

Beat all the ingredients together until blended.

Frosting:
   1/2 cup milk chocolate chips, melted

Note: - Cookies can be frozen.

Orange Spice Cookies with Walnuts & Lemon Orange Glaze

There is no cookie that you can make that is easier or more delicious than this spicy, fruity, nutty bar. It is exceedingly easy to prepare, starting, as it does, with a prepared cake mix.

    1 package (18 1/2 ounces) spice cake mix (not
          the pudding variety, but the regular cake mix)
    2 teaspoons pumpkin pie spice
  1/4 cup butter, melted
    2 eggs
  1/3 cup sour cream
  1/4 cup sugar
  1/2 orange, grated (use the fruit, peel and juice)
    1 cup chopped walnuts

Combine all the ingredients in the large bowl of an electric mixer and beat until mixture is blended, about 1 1/2 minutes. Spread mixture evenly into a greased 10x15x1-inch jelly roll pan and bake in a 350° oven for 25 minutes or until a cake tester, inserted in center, comes out clean. Remove from oven and allow to cool in pan.

When cool, spread Lemon Orange Glaze over the top and allow it to set for about 30 minutes. Cut into squares or bars and serve with a tall glass of milk. Yields 48 cookies.

Lemon Orange Glaze

    2 tablespoons lemon juice
    2 tablespoons orange juice
    2 tablespoons grated orange peel
  1/2 cup finely chopped walnuts
    1 tablespoon sour cream
    2 cups sifted powdered sugar (about)

Combine all the ingredients and stir until blended. Glaze should be quite thick. Add a little extra sifted powdered sugar if necessary.

Viennese Linzer Cookies with Raspberries & Almonds

When I was growing up, these classic cookies were one of my very favorites. How I loved the crisp cookie, filled with raspberry jam and the flavor of butter that was sheer ecstacy. These are heightened with the addition of lemon and almonds and I hope you enjoy them as much as I do.

        1 3/4 **cups flour**
           3/4 **cup sugar**
           3/4 **cup almond meal (ground almonds purchased at a
                    health food store)**
           1/2 **cup butter (1 stick)**

             1 **egg, beaten**
           1/2 **lemon, grated. Use peel, juice and fruit.
                    Remove any large pieces of membrane.**

             1 **cup red raspberry jam**

In the large bowl of an electric mixer, beat together flour, sugar, almond meal and butter until the mixture resembles coarse meal. Combine the egg and lemon and beat this into the flour mixture until just blended.

Remove about 3/4 cup of dough and set aside. With floured hands, pat the remaining dough into a lightly buttered 9x9-inch pan. Spread raspberry jam evenly over the dough.

Divide the reserved dough into 8 balls and with floured hands roll and pat these out to 9-inch strips. Dough is very soft, so you will need to flour your hands often. Lay the strips over the jam, lattice-fashioned. Bake in a 350° oven for about 30 to 35 minutes or until top is golden brown. Allow to cool and cut into squares or bars. Sprinkle lightly with sifted powdered sugar. Yields about 16 cookies.

Note: - There is nothing tricky about this dough except that it is soft. However, if you flour your hands when you pat it, you should have no trouble at all.

Chocolate Fudge Chewies with Nuts & Chocolate

This little confection is a cross between a cookie and a candy. It is fudgy and chewy and fun to eat. Milk is a definite accompaniment.

3 egg whites
  pinch of salt
  pinch of cream of tartar
1 1/2 cups sugar
  2 teaspoons vanilla

1 cup flour
1/2 cup sifted cocoa

1/2 cup (1 stick) butter, melted

2 cups chopped walnuts
1 cup semi-sweet chocolate chips

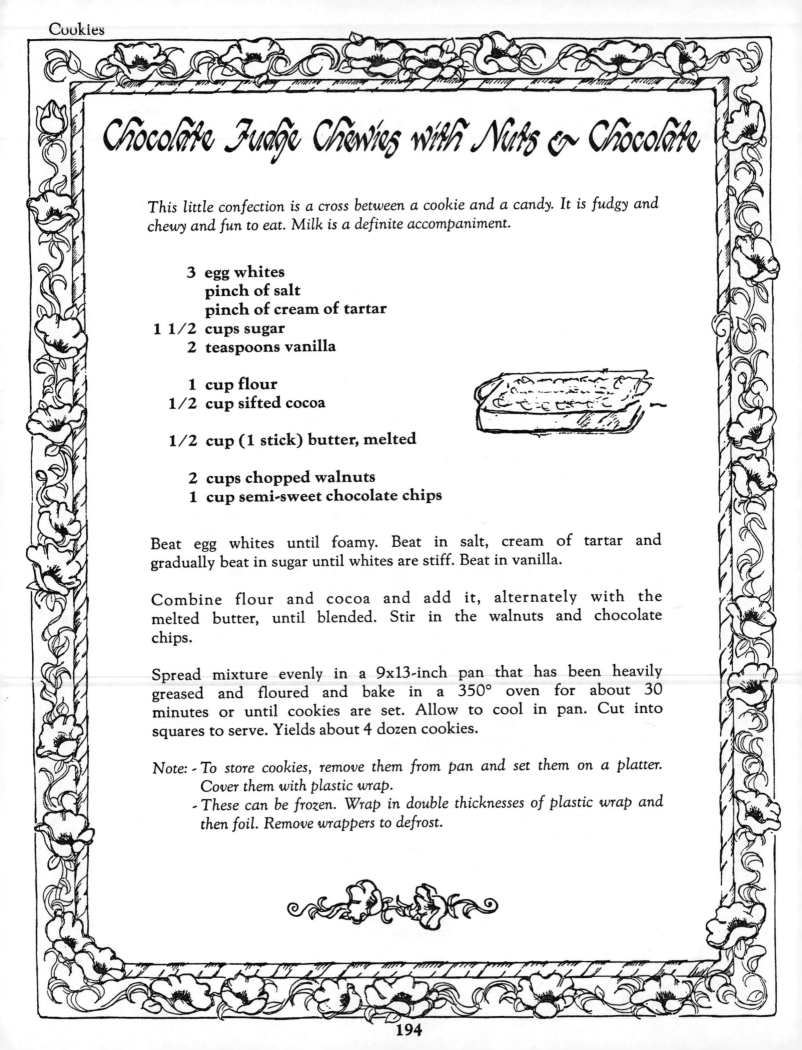

Beat egg whites until foamy. Beat in salt, cream of tartar and gradually beat in sugar until whites are stiff. Beat in vanilla.

Combine flour and cocoa and add it, alternately with the melted butter, until blended. Stir in the walnuts and chocolate chips.

Spread mixture evenly in a 9x13-inch pan that has been heavily greased and floured and bake in a 350° oven for about 30 minutes or until cookies are set. Allow to cool in pan. Cut into squares to serve. Yields about 4 dozen cookies.

Note: - To store cookies, remove them from pan and set them on a platter. Cover them with plastic wrap.
- These can be frozen. Wrap in double thicknesses of plastic wrap and then foil. Remove wrappers to defrost.

Raspberry & Coconut Meringue Cookies

    3/4 cup butter
1 1/2 cups flour
  1/2 cup sifted powdered sugar
    2 egg yolks
    1 tablespoon grated lemon peel

1 1/4 cups raspberry jam
    1 cup chopped walnuts

    2 egg whites
  1/2 cup sugar
  1/2 cup coconut flakes

In the large bowl of an electric mixer, beat together butter, flour, sugar, yolks and lemon peel until mixture is blended. Pat mixture into a buttered 9x13-inch pan. Bake in a 350° oven for 15 minutes. Spread raspberry jam over warm crust and sprinkle with chopped walnuts.

Beat whites with sugar until stiff. Beat in coconut flakes. Spread mixture evenly over jam and nuts. Return to oven and continue baking for about 20 minutes or until meringue is golden brown. Cool and cut into bars. Yields about 48 cookies.

Note: - These cookies are equally delicious made with apricot jam. Use a nice fruity jam and sieve it.

Pecan Butter Balls

    1 cup butter (2 sticks)
  3/4 cup sifted powdered sugar
    1 teaspoon vanilla
1 1/4 cups finely chopped walnuts
    2 cups flour

Cream together butter and sugar. Beat in the remaining ingredients until blended. Shape dough into 3/4-inch balls and place on a lightly buttered cookie sheet. Bake at 350° for about 15 to 20 minutes or until cookies are set, but not browned. Roll in powdered sugar while hot and again when cool. Yields about 60 cookies.

Old-Fashioned Chocolate Chip Walnut Squares

Cookie Crust:
2 1/4 cups flour
1 cup sugar
1 1/4 cups butter (2 1/2 sticks)
1 egg
1/4 cup sour cream
1/2 teaspoon vanilla

Chocolate Chip Walnut Filling:
1 package (12 ounces) semi-sweet chocolate chips
1 1/2 cups chopped walnuts
2 eggs, beaten
3/4 cup sugar
1 teaspoon vanilla

Place flour, sugar and butter in large bowl of mixer and beat until mixture resembles coarse meal. Beat egg with sour cream and vanilla and add to flour mixture. Beat until blended, about 30 seconds. Do not overbeat. With a spatula, spread dough, (it will be soft) on the bottom and 1-inch up the sides of a greased 9x13-inch pan. Bake in a 350° oven for 30 minutes.

Meanwhile, combine chocolate chips, walnuts, beaten eggs, sugar and vanilla until blended. Pour egg mixture over cooked crust and return to oven for an additional 30 minutes or until top is a nice golden brown. Cool in pan and then cut into squares. Sprinkle with a little sifted powdered sugar. Yields 48, 1 1/2-inch squares.

Date Nut Squares

Prepare cookie crust as above, and bake for 30 minutes. Cover cooked crust with Date Nut Filling and bake for an additional 35 minutes or until top is golden and crusty.

Date Nut Filling:
2 cups chopped dates
2 cups chopped walnuts
2 eggs, beaten
1 cup sugar

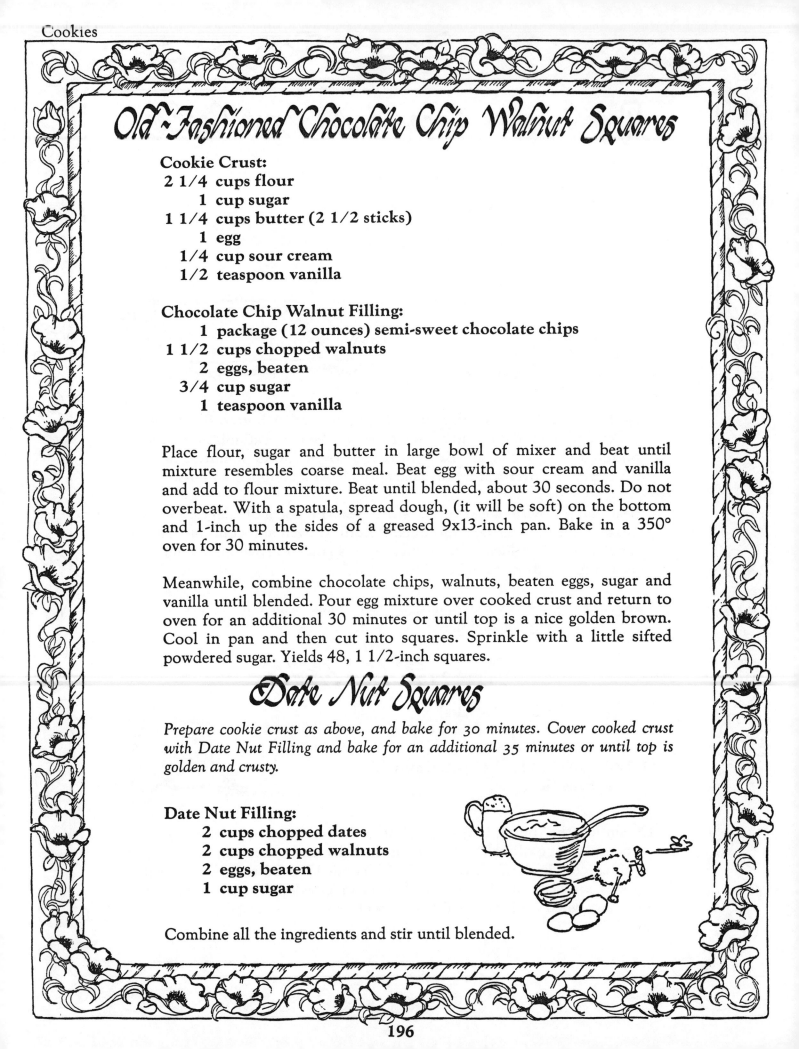

Combine all the ingredients and stir until blended.

Bourbon Fruitcake Cookies with Bourbon Vanilla Icing

    1 1/8 cups flour
    1 1/2 cups sugar
        1 teaspoon baking powder

        3 eggs
      1/2 cup oil
      1/4 cup Bourbon
      1/2 orange, grated (remove any large pieces
             of membrane)
        1 teaspoon vanilla

        1 cup yellow raisins
        1 cup chopped dates
        1 cup chopped glaceed candied mixed fruits
    1 1/2 cups chopped walnuts

In the large bowl of an electric mixer, place flour, sugar and baking powder. Add eggs, oil, Bourbon, orange and vanilla and beat until mixture is blended. Stir in the remaining fruits and nuts.

Spread batter evenly into a greased and floured 9x13-inch pan and bake in a 350° oven for about 30 minutes or until a cake tester, inserted in center, comes out clean.

Allow cookies to cool and spread with Bourbon Vanilla Icing. Cut into squares and serve with milk or cider. Yields 4 dozen 1 1/2-inch squares.

Bourbon Vanilla Icing

        4 tablespoons butter, softened
    2 1/2 cups sifted powdered sugar
        1 tablespoon Bourbon
        1 tablespoon cream
        1 teaspoon vanilla

Beat together all the ingredients until mixture is thoroughly blended. Add a little cream or additional sugar so that the icing is of spreading consistency.

Chocolate Chip Chocolate Walnut Chewies

Chocolate cookies topped with chocolate chips and walnuts and covered with a chewy caramel topping is a heavenly combination.

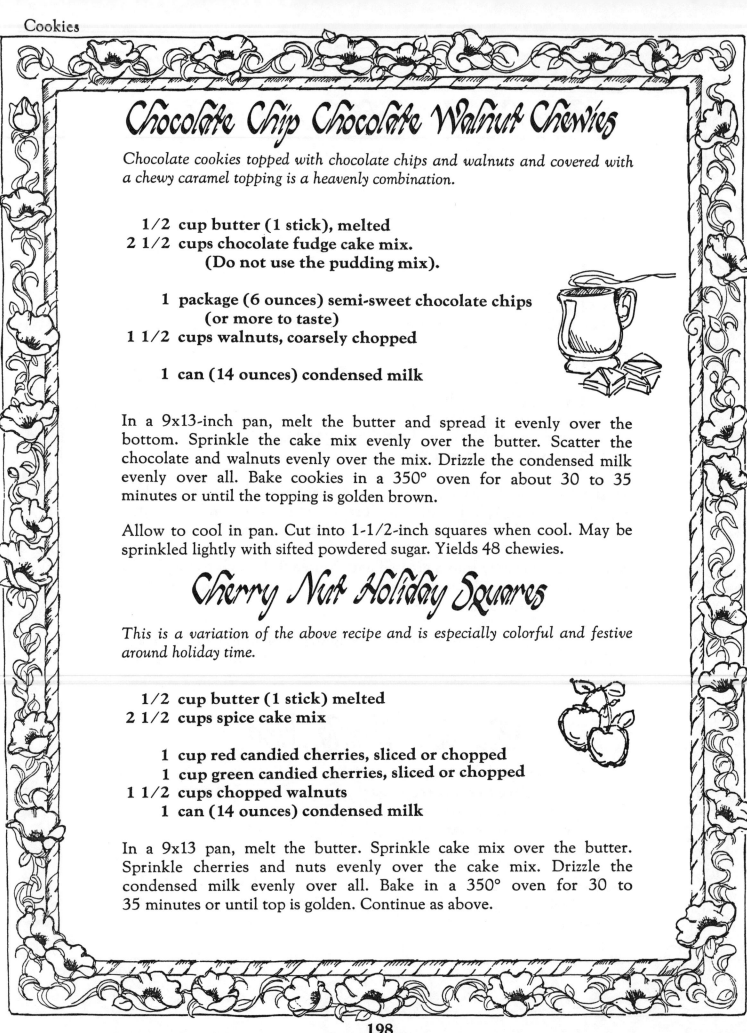

  1/2 **cup butter (1 stick), melted**
2 1/2 **cups chocolate fudge cake mix.**
       (Do not use the pudding mix).

  1 **package (6 ounces) semi-sweet chocolate chips**
     (or more to taste)
1 1/2 **cups walnuts, coarsely chopped**

  1 **can (14 ounces) condensed milk**

In a 9x13-inch pan, melt the butter and spread it evenly over the bottom. Sprinkle the cake mix evenly over the butter. Scatter the chocolate and walnuts evenly over the mix. Drizzle the condensed milk evenly over all. Bake cookies in a 350° oven for about 30 to 35 minutes or until the topping is golden brown.

Allow to cool in pan. Cut into 1-1/2-inch squares when cool. May be sprinkled lightly with sifted powdered sugar. Yields 48 chewies.

Cherry Nut Holiday Squares

This is a variation of the above recipe and is especially colorful and festive around holiday time.

  1/2 **cup butter (1 stick) melted**
2 1/2 **cups spice cake mix**

  1 **cup red candied cherries, sliced or chopped**
  1 **cup green candied cherries, sliced or chopped**
1 1/2 **cups chopped walnuts**
  1 **can (14 ounces) condensed milk**

In a 9x13 pan, melt the butter. Sprinkle cake mix over the butter. Sprinkle cherries and nuts evenly over the cake mix. Drizzle the condensed milk evenly over all. Bake in a 350° oven for 30 to 35 minutes or until top is golden. Continue as above.

Old~Fashioned Date Nut Chewies

This delicious cookie is old-fashioned in taste, but very modern in technique. It assembles in seconds and makes a good, solid after school snack. Of course, they are delicious enough to serve as dessert with some fresh fruit.

    1/2 cup (1 stick) butter
2 1/2 cups yellow cake mix
    2 cups chopped dates
    4 tablespoons cinnamon sugar
    1 cup chopped walnuts

    1 can (14 ounces) condensed milk

In a 9x13-inch pan, melt the butter and spread it evenly over the bottom. Now, layer and sprinkle evenly over the butter, the cake mix, dates, cinnamon sugar and walnuts. Drizzle the condensed milk evenly over all.

Bake in a 350° oven for about 30 to 35 minutes or until the top is a golden brown. Allow to cool in pan. Cut into 1 1/2-inch squares and serve with a faint sprinkling of sifted powdered sugar. Yields 48 delectable chewies.

Note: - Cookies freeze beautifully. Freeze in double plastic bags. Remove wraps while defrosting.

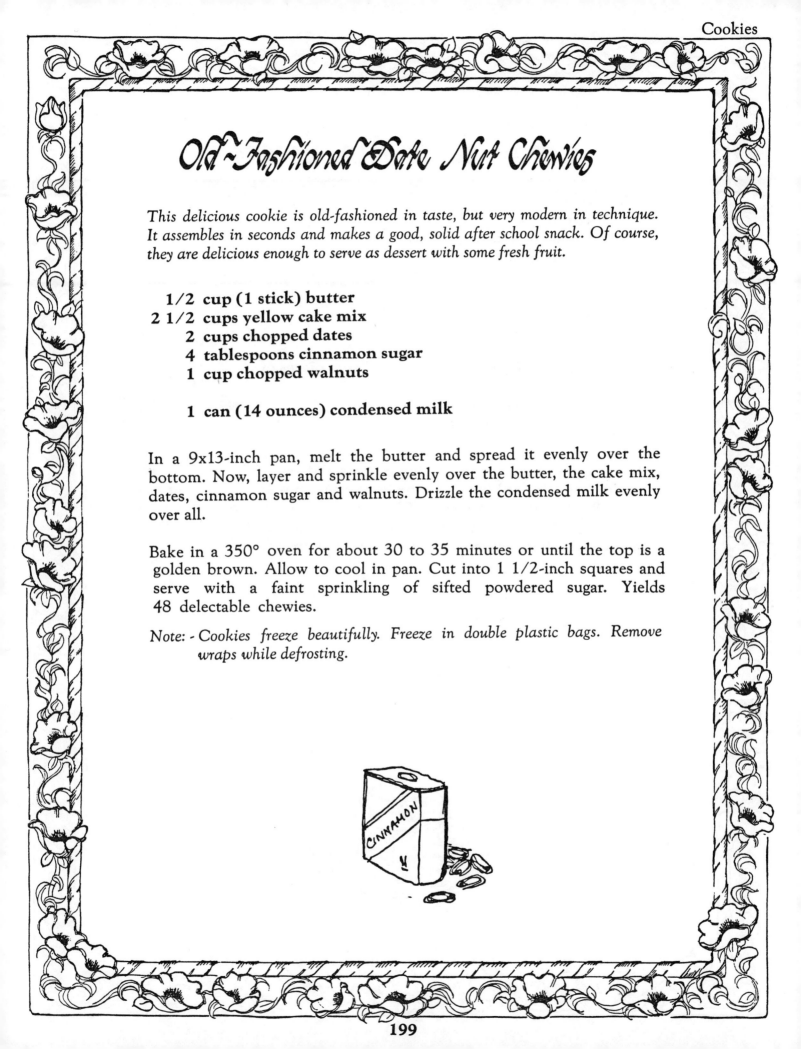

Orange Date Nut Cookies

3/4 cup flour
  1 cup sugar
1/2 teaspoon baking powder
     pinch of salt

  2 eggs, beaten
1/2 cup oil
  1 teaspoon vanilla

1/2 orange, grated. (Remove any large pieces of
       membranes.)
  1 cup chopped dates
  1 cup chopped walnuts

Mix together flour, sugar, baking powder and salt. Add eggs, oil and vanilla and stir until blended. Stir in orange, dates and nuts. Pour into an 8x8-inch pan and bake at 350° for 30 minutes or until a cake tester inserted in center comes out clean. Cut in 1-inch squares and sprinkle lightly with sifted powdered sugar. Makes about 64 cookies.

Mother's Apricot Cloud Cookies

  3/4 cup butter
1 1/2 cups flour
  3/8 cup sifted powdered sugar
    1 tablespoon grated lemon peel

    1 cup dried apricots, boiled in water for 10 minutes.
         Drain and chop.
    3 eggs
1 1/2 cups sugar
    4 tablespoons flour
  3/4 teaspoon baking powder
    1 teaspoon vanilla
  3/4 cup chopped walnuts

Beat butter, flour, sugar and lemon peel together until blended. Pat mixture into a lightly buttered 9x13-inch pan. Bake crust in a 350° oven for about 20 or 25 minutes or until lightly browned.

Meanwhile, beat together the remaining ingredients until blended. Pour egg mixture on baked crust. Continue baking an additional 30 minutes or until topping is set. Cool in pan and cut into squares. Sprinkle generously with sifted powdered sugar. Yields 4 dozen cookies.

Date & Raisins Walnut Chewies with Cinnamon

3 eggs
2/3 cup oil
1 teaspoon vanilla

1 cup flour
1 cup sugar
1 teaspoon baking powder
  pinch salt

1 cup chopped dates
1 cup yellow raisins
1 cup chopped walnuts

2 tablespoons cinnamon sugar

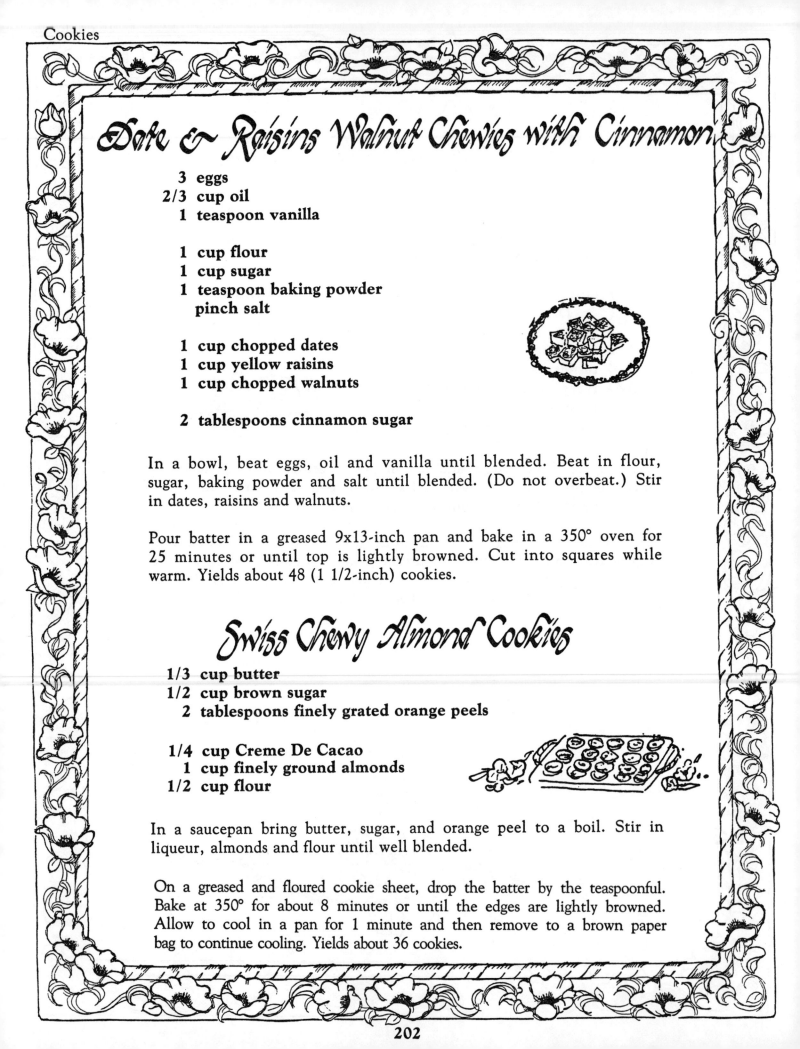

In a bowl, beat eggs, oil and vanilla until blended. Beat in flour, sugar, baking powder and salt until blended. (Do not overbeat.) Stir in dates, raisins and walnuts.

Pour batter in a greased 9x13-inch pan and bake in a 350° oven for 25 minutes or until top is lightly browned. Cut into squares while warm. Yields about 48 (1 1/2-inch) cookies.

Swiss Chewy Almond Cookies

1/3 cup butter
1/2 cup brown sugar
2 tablespoons finely grated orange peels

1/4 cup Creme De Cacao
1 cup finely ground almonds
1/2 cup flour

In a saucepan bring butter, sugar, and orange peel to a boil. Stir in liqueur, almonds and flour until well blended.

On a greased and floured cookie sheet, drop the batter by the teaspoonful. Bake at 350° for about 8 minutes or until the edges are lightly browned. Allow to cool in a pan for 1 minute and then remove to a brown paper bag to continue cooling. Yields about 36 cookies.

Cinnamon Apples with Macaroons & Pecans & Cognac Honey Whipped Cream

What a homey way to serve baked apples with a cookie meringue topping flavored with cinnamon and crunchy with pecans.

- 3 large sweet apples, cut in half lengthwise and cored. Do not peel.
- 1/2 cup cinnamon sugar
- 4 tablespoons melted butter
- 1/2 cup orange juice

- 1/2 pound soft macaroons
- 1/2 cup pecans

- 1 egg white
- 3 tablespoons cinnamon sugar
- 1 teaspoon vanilla

In an 8x3-inch round baking pan, place the apples in one layer, cut side up. Combine the sugar, butter and orange juice and pour this mixture over the apples. Bake apples in a 350° oven for about 20 minutes or until almost tender.

In a blender or food processor, blend together the remaining ingredients until the macaroons and pecans are coarsely ground. Spoon crumb mixture over the apples and pat them down gently with spoon.

Continue baking apples for about 20 minutes or until tops are nicely browned. (If the syrup is getting too brown, add a little orange juice.)

Serve in a bowl with a spoonful of syrup and dollup of Cognac Honey Whipped Cream. Serves 6.

Cognac Honey Whipped Cream:
- 1/2 cup cream
- 2 teaspoons honey
- 2 teaspoons Cognac

Beat together all the ingredients until cream is stiff.

Apples Baked in Grand Marnier with Cinnamon

In the world of simple desserts, there is perhaps none more satisfying than a baked apple...serve warm with a dollup of whipped cream. Well, here is that simple baked apple, elevated to celestial heights with the addition of Grand Marnier, raisins, almonds, butter and wine. The grated orange peel is the perfect balance.

6 medium-sized apples. Core, but leave about 1/4-inch on the bottom. Take off about 1-inch peel from the top.

1/4 cup cinnamon sugar
1/2 cup chopped almonds
1/2 cup chopped raisins
1 tablespoon Grand Marnier liqueur
2 tablespoons cream

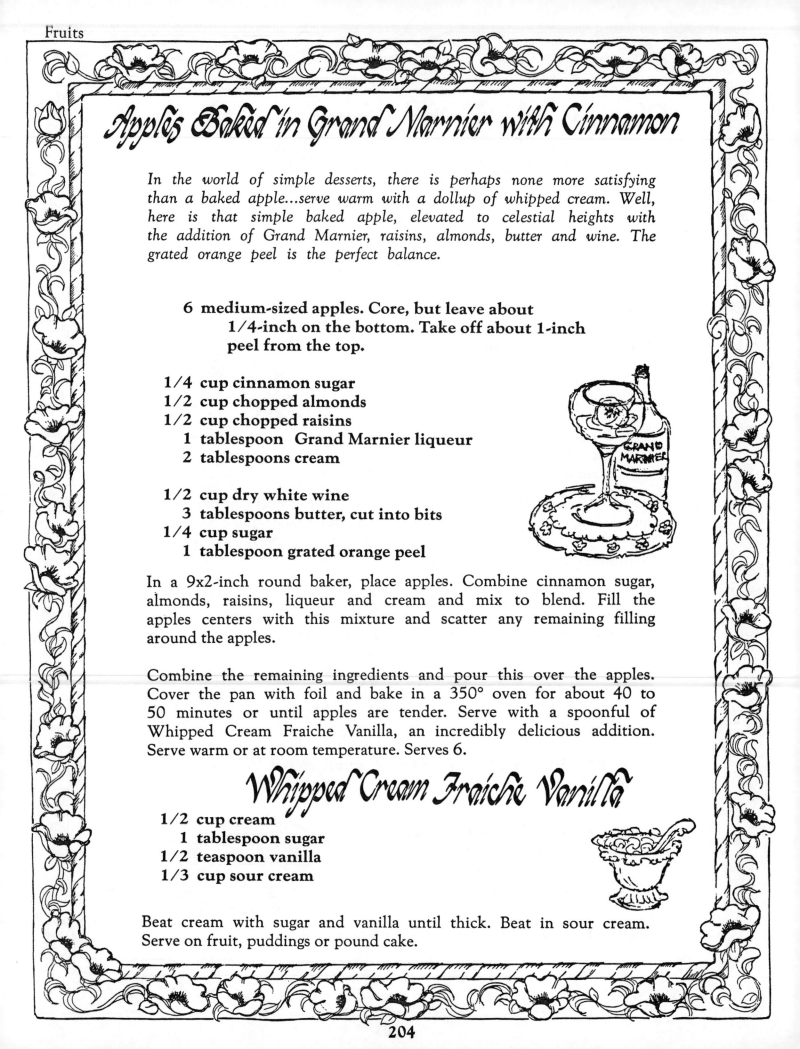

1/2 cup dry white wine
3 tablespoons butter, cut into bits
1/4 cup sugar
1 tablespoon grated orange peel

In a 9x2-inch round baker, place apples. Combine cinnamon sugar, almonds, raisins, liqueur and cream and mix to blend. Fill the apples centers with this mixture and scatter any remaining filling around the apples.

Combine the remaining ingredients and pour this over the apples. Cover the pan with foil and bake in a 350° oven for about 40 to 50 minutes or until apples are tender. Serve with a spoonful of Whipped Cream Fraiche Vanilla, an incredibly delicious addition. Serve warm or at room temperature. Serves 6.

Whipped Cream Fraiche Vanilla

1/2 cup cream
1 tablespoon sugar
1/2 teaspoon vanilla
1/3 cup sour cream

Beat cream with sugar and vanilla until thick. Beat in sour cream. Serve on fruit, puddings or pound cake.

Iced Pecan Praline & Cream Cheese Pie with Kahlua

1 package cream cheese (8 ounces) at
   room temperature
1/4 cup cream
3 tablespoons brown sugar
2 tablespoons Kahlua liqueur

1 quart Pecan, Praline & Cream Ice Cream, slightly
   softened
1 9-inch Graham Cracker Pie Crust

In the large bowl of an electric mixer, beat together cream cheese, cream, sugar and liqueur until blended. Beat in the softened ice cream. Pour mixture into prepared pie crust and freeze until firm. Remove from the refrigerator about 10 minutes before serving.

Cut into wedges and serve with a spoonful of Kahlua liqueur. Serves 8.

Graham Cracker Pie Crust

1/3 cup butter, melted
1 1/4 cups graham cracker crumbs
1/2 cup coarsely chopped pecans
3 tablespoons brown sugar

In a 9-inch pie pan, combine all the ingredients and mix to thoroughly combine. Press crumbs evenly along the bottom and the sides of the pie pan. Bake in a 350° oven for about 8 minutes. Cool before filling.

Note: - Pie can be prepared and frozen up to 1 week before serving. To store, wrap frozen pie in double thicknesses of plastic wrap and then foil. Remove from the freezer about 10 minutes before serving.

Gateau of Fresh Peach Iced Cream

This is an exciting dessert and serves with glamour and style. Use any fresh fruit that is in season. Peaches, apricots or strawberries are especially good. Mangoes are just lovely if you are planning a luau.

4 peaches, peeled, stoned and chopped
1/2 cup sugar
2 tablespoons lemon juice

6 egg whites, at room temperature
1/2 cup sugar

2 cups cream
4 tablespoons sugar
1 teaspoon vanilla
2 tablespoons orange liqueur

In a saucepan, cook together peaches, sugar and lemon juice for about 5 minutes or until sugar is completely dissolved. Puree mixture in a processor or in a blender in batches. Beat egg whites with 1/2 cup sugar until a stiff meringue. Beat cream with sugar, vanilla and liqueur until stiff.

In a large bowl, fold together pureed fruit, beaten egg whites and whipped cream until blended. Pour mixture into Vanilla Crumb Crust and place in freezer until firm. Cover and store with double thicknesses of plastic wrap and foil.

To serve, remove from the freezer about 15 minutes before serving. Cut into wedges and serve with a spoonful of whipped cream on top. Serves 8 to 10.

Vanilla Crumb Crust: Spread 2 tablespoons butter onto the bottom and sides of a 10-inch springform pan. Sprinkle with 3 tablespoons vanilla wafer crumbs and tilt pan to coat it evenly with crumbs.

Note: - A lovely accompaniment, instead of the whipped cream, would be to spoon Peach Syrup on iced cream, at time of serving. To make Peach Syrup, cook together 4 peaches, peeled, stoned and chopped; 1/2 cup sugar; 1/2 cup orange juice and 2 tablespoons lemon juice, until liquid is syrupy.

Mousse au Kahlua with Brandied Creme de Cafe

    4 eggs
3/4 cup sifted powdered sugar

    1 tablespoon gelatin
1/4 cup Kahlua liqueur

1/3 cup hot milk
    1 heaping teaspoon powdered instant coffee

    1 cup cream, beaten until stiff

In the large bowl of an electric mixer, beat eggs with sugar until eggs are thick and lemon colored, about 5 minutes at high speed.

Meanwhile, in a metal measuring cup, soften gelatin in liqueur and place over hot water, until gelatin is liquefied. Stir together the hot milk and instant coffee until coffee is dissolved. Stir together coffee and gelatin mixtures.

At low speed, beat the gelatin mixture and whipped cream into the egg mixture. Spoon mousse into lovely glass bowl and refrigerate until firm. Decorate with rosettes of Brandied Creme de Cafe and the faintest sprinkling of powdered instant coffee. Serves 6.

Brandied Creme de Cafe

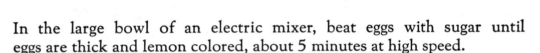

1 cup cream
1 teaspoon powdered instant coffee
2 tablespoons sifted powdered sugar
1 tablespoon Kahlua liqueur
1 teaspoon brandy

Beat cream, with the remaining ingredients, until stiff. Place whipped cream in a pastry bag and decorate top of mousse with large rosettes.

Note: - You may divide the mousse into 6 individual lovely stemmed glasses and refrigerate these until firm. Decorate as above.

Raspberry Mousse with Grand Marnier & Chocolate

There are few desserts you can make that are more exciting than this raspberry cloud sparkled with Grand Marnier. The vanilla crust has a layer of pure chocolate making it totally irresistable.

2 packages (10 ounces, each) frozen raspberries
   in syrup.

2 envelopes (2 tablespoons) unflavored gelatin
1/3 cup Grand Marnier liqueur

6 eggs, at room temperature
3/4 cup sugar

2 cups cream, beaten until stiff

1 cup grated chocolate (about 4 ounces)

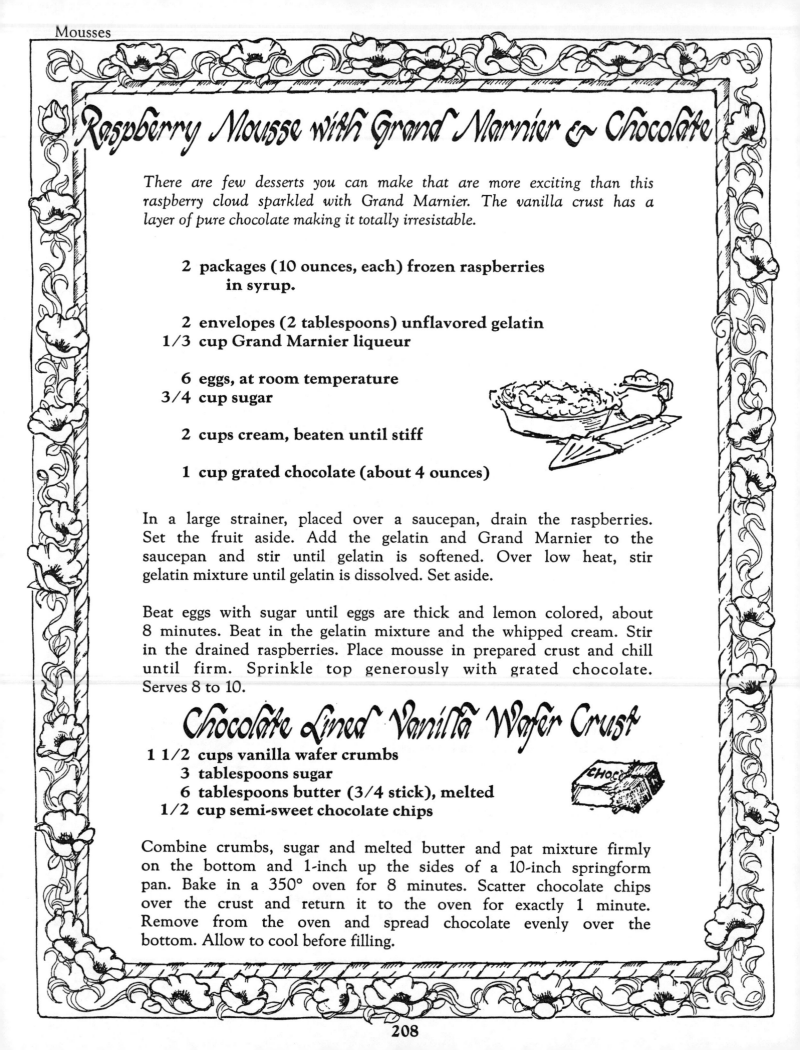

In a large strainer, placed over a saucepan, drain the raspberries. Set the fruit aside. Add the gelatin and Grand Marnier to the saucepan and stir until gelatin is softened. Over low heat, stir gelatin mixture until gelatin is dissolved. Set aside.

Beat eggs with sugar until eggs are thick and lemon colored, about 8 minutes. Beat in the gelatin mixture and the whipped cream. Stir in the drained raspberries. Place mousse in prepared crust and chill until firm. Sprinkle top generously with grated chocolate. Serves 8 to 10.

Chocolate Lined Vanilla Wafer Crust

1 1/2 cups vanilla wafer crumbs
   3 tablespoons sugar
   6 tablespoons butter (3/4 stick), melted
1/2 cup semi-sweet chocolate chips

Combine crumbs, sugar and melted butter and pat mixture firmly on the bottom and 1-inch up the sides of a 10-inch springform pan. Bake in a 350° oven for 8 minutes. Scatter chocolate chips over the crust and return it to the oven for exactly 1 minute. Remove from the oven and spread chocolate evenly over the bottom. Allow to cool before filling.

Chocolate Chestnut Mousse with Macaroons & Chestnut Rum Whipped Cream

If you are looking for glamor, excitement and a standing ovation, this is a wonderful choice for a holiday dinner. The combination of chocolate and chestnuts and rum is incredibly good (and quite different) and the macaroon crust is the perfect accompaniment. I would prefer you to make the macaroons for this one . . . but if you prefer to buy them, purchase a good quality, soft macaroon.

2 **tablespoons butter**
1 1/2 to 2 **cups macaroon cookie crumbs (use soft macaroons)**

1/4 **cup rum**
1 **package (1 tablespoon) unflavored gelatin**

4 **eggs, at room temperature**
1/2 **cup sugar**

3/4 **cup canned sweetened chestnuts puree**
1 **cup semi-sweet chocolate chips, melted**
1 **cup cream, beaten until stiff**

Butter a 10-inch spring form pan and spread the cookie crumbs evenly in pan. Pat the crumbs down to form a crust.

In a metal measuring cup, soften the gelatin in the rum. Place the cup in a pan with 1-inch of simmering water, and stir until the gelatin is dissolved.

Meanwhile beat the eggs with the sugar until they are light and fluffy, about 10 minutes. Beat in the chestnut puree, melted chocolate and whipped cream, blending well after each addition. Beat in the gelatin mixture until thoroughly blended and pour mousse into the prepared pan.

Refrigerate mousse until firm. Spread a thin layer of Chestnut Rum Whipped Cream over the mousse and decorate the top by piping large rosettes of the remaining cream. Sprinkle the top with grated chocolate and if you have the time, make some chocolate leaves. It is lovely on this dessert. Cut into wedges when serving. Serves 10 to 12.

Chestnut Rum Whipped Cream

1 cup cream
2 tablespoons brown sugar
2 tablespoons chestnut puree
1 tablespoon rum

Beat cream with sugar until it is stiff. Beat in the chestnut and the rum until blended.

These are the macaroons I made for the crust. They are very easy and very good. Blend or process about 16 of the cookies and use the rest for munching.

Chewy, Soft Macaroons

**3 cups macaroon coconut meal (from the health
    food stores) or finely shredded coconut**
1 teaspoon vanilla
1 can (14 ounces) sweetened condensed milk

Combine all the ingredients in a bowl and stir until they are blended. Drop batter by the spoonful on a generously greased cookie sheet. (Parchment paper-lined pan is very good for this.) Bake for 15 minutes in a 350° oven or until tops are golden brown. Remove from pan immediately and place cookies on a brown paper bag to cool. Yields about 24 large cookies.

Chocolate Leaves

**6 camellia leaves (or other non-toxic leaves), rubbed,
    tubbed and scrubbed clean. Dry with paper
    towelling.**
1/4 cup semi-sweet chocolate chips (Nestle's), melted

With the back of a spoon or with a small spatula, spread chocolate on the *back* of the leaves. Place chocolate-side up on waxed paper and place in the refrigerator to firm up. When chocolate is firm, peel off the leaf and Voila! You have the prettiest chocolate leaves.

They must be kept in the refrigerator until ready to use, and they can be prepared a week in advance. Store them in a plastic container, with wax paper to cover and then the lid.

*Note: - Entire dessert should be prepared 1 day earlier and stored in the
    refrigerator until serving time.*
*- Try and find the 8-ounce can of chestnut puree (sweetened) for this
    recipe. It will eliminate the problem of leftover puree.*

Imperial Mousse au Chocolate with Cognac & Creme de Cacao

This dessert is devilishly delicious and totally spectacular. It is a fine choice for an elegant dinner. Serving these in tall stemmed glasses adds a sweet touch of glamor. Keep the cookies on the bottom as a surprise.

- 3 egg yolks, at room temperature
- 2 tablespoons sugar
- 1 teaspoon vanilla
- 1 tablespoon Cognac

- 1 package (6 ounces) semi-sweet chocolate chips
- 1/4 cup butter (1/2 stick) at room temperature

- 3 egg whites, at room temperature
- 2 tablespoons sugar

- 1 cup cream

- 6 macaroons, crumbled
- 6 teaspoons Creme de Cacao

Beat yolks with sugar until they are very thick, about 5 to 6 minutes. Beat in vanilla and Cognac.

Melt the chocolate in the top of a double boiler, over hot, not boiling, water. Stir in the butter, 1 bit at a time, until blended. Beat chocolate into the yolk mixture until blended.

Beat egg whites with 2 tablespoons sugar until stiff. Fold egg whites into chocolate mixture. Beat cream until stiff and fold it into the chocolate mixture.

In each of 6 lovely stemmed glasses (can stretch this to 8), crumble 1 macaroon. Sprinkle it with 1 teaspoon liqueur. Top this with chocolate mousse. Refrigerate until firm. Garnish with a cherry or a raspberry. Serves 6 to 8.

Note: - If you prepare this 1 day earlier, then cover each glass with plastic wrap.

Rum & Chocolate Cheesecake Mousse with Chocolate Almond Crust

1 package (8 ounces) cream cheese, at room temperature
1 1/2 cups sour cream
6 tablespoons sugar
1 teaspoon vanilla

1/4 cup rum
1 package (1 tablespoon) unflavored gelatin

8 ounces semi-sweet chocolate, melted

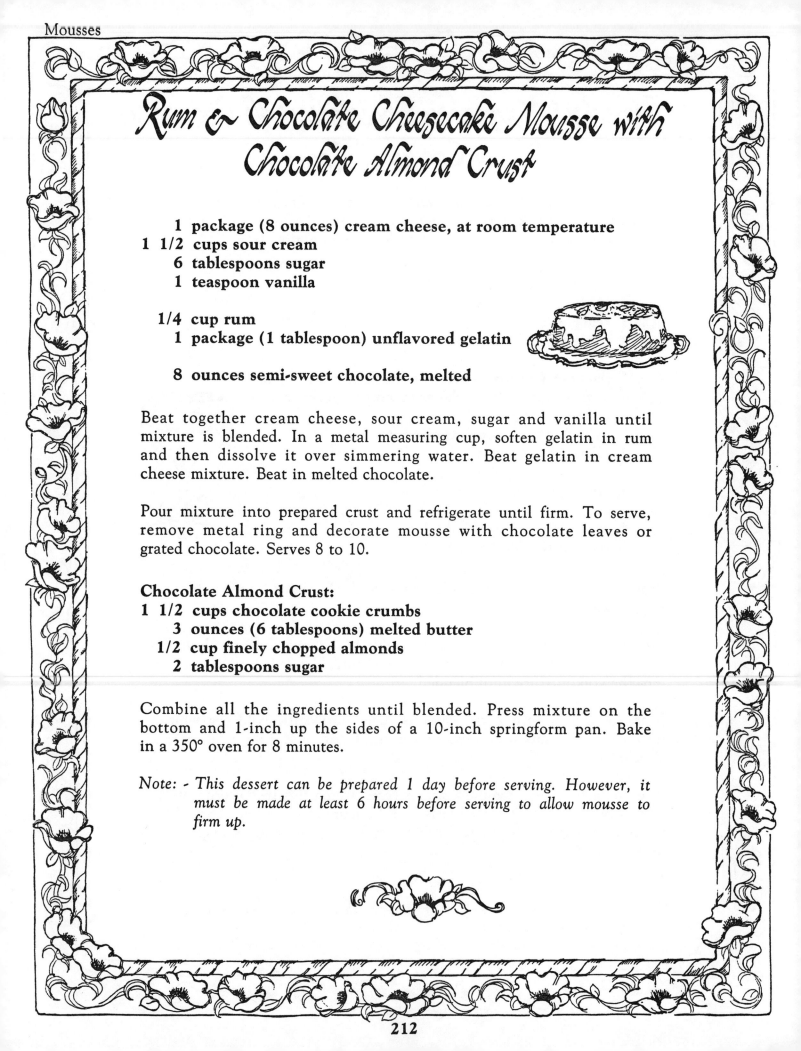

Beat together cream cheese, sour cream, sugar and vanilla until mixture is blended. In a metal measuring cup, soften gelatin in rum and then dissolve it over simmering water. Beat gelatin in cream cheese mixture. Beat in melted chocolate.

Pour mixture into prepared crust and refrigerate until firm. To serve, remove metal ring and decorate mousse with chocolate leaves or grated chocolate. Serves 8 to 10.

Chocolate Almond Crust:
1 1/2 cups chocolate cookie crumbs
3 ounces (6 tablespoons) melted butter
1/2 cup finely chopped almonds
2 tablespoons sugar

Combine all the ingredients until blended. Press mixture on the bottom and 1-inch up the sides of a 10-inch springform pan. Bake in a 350° oven for 8 minutes.

Note: - This dessert can be prepared 1 day before serving. However, it must be made at least 6 hours before serving to allow mousse to firm up.

Mousse au Chocolate with Macaroons & Raspberries & Cognac Cream

This creation is simple, but by no means plain. It is a grand dessert and serves with extraordinary style. The white chocolate leaves and grated chocolate is the perfect accompaniment.

3 1/2 cups miniature marshmallows
1 cup milk

1 1/2 cups semi-sweet chocolate chips

2 cups cream
2 tablespoons Cognac
2 tablespoons sugar

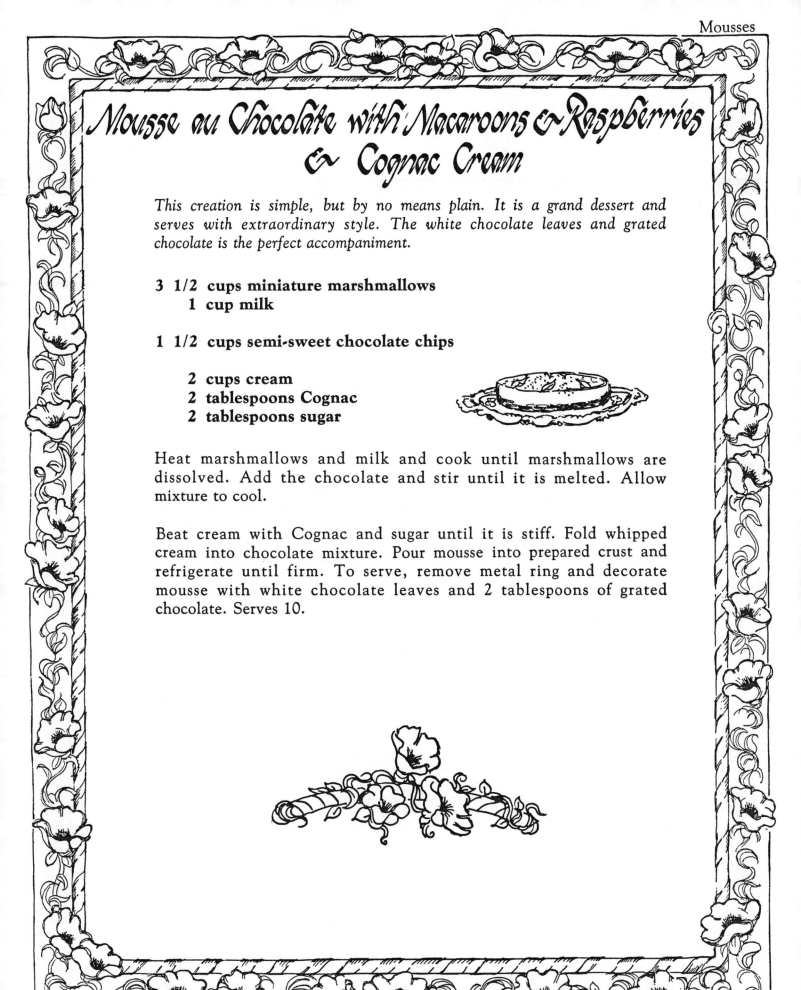

Heat marshmallows and milk and cook until marshmallows are dissolved. Add the chocolate and stir until it is melted. Allow mixture to cool.

Beat cream with Cognac and sugar until it is stiff. Fold whipped cream into chocolate mixture. Pour mousse into prepared crust and refrigerate until firm. To serve, remove metal ring and decorate mousse with white chocolate leaves and 2 tablespoons of grated chocolate. Serves 10.

Mousse au Chocolate (continued)

Macaroon Crust:
1 1/2 cups macaroon cookie crumbs
3 ounces (6 tablespoons) melted butter
3/4 cup chopped walnuts
2 tablespoons sugar

2/3 cup red raspberry jam, sieved

Combine crumbs, butter, walnuts and sugar until blended. Press mixture on the bottom and 1-inch up the sides of a 10-inch springform pan. Bake in a 350° oven for 8 minutes.

Spread raspberry jam on top while crust is still warm. Allow to cool.

White Chocolate Leaves: In the top of a double boiler, over hot not boiling water, melt 1/4 cup white chocolate. With the back of a spoon, spread 1 teaspoon chocolate on the back of washed and thoroughly dried Camellia leaves. Place on waxed paper and refrigerate until firm. When ready to use, peel off the leaf and Voila! beautiful white chocolate leaves. Leaves can be made several days earlier and stored in the refrigerator.

Royal Chocolate Cheesecake Mousse

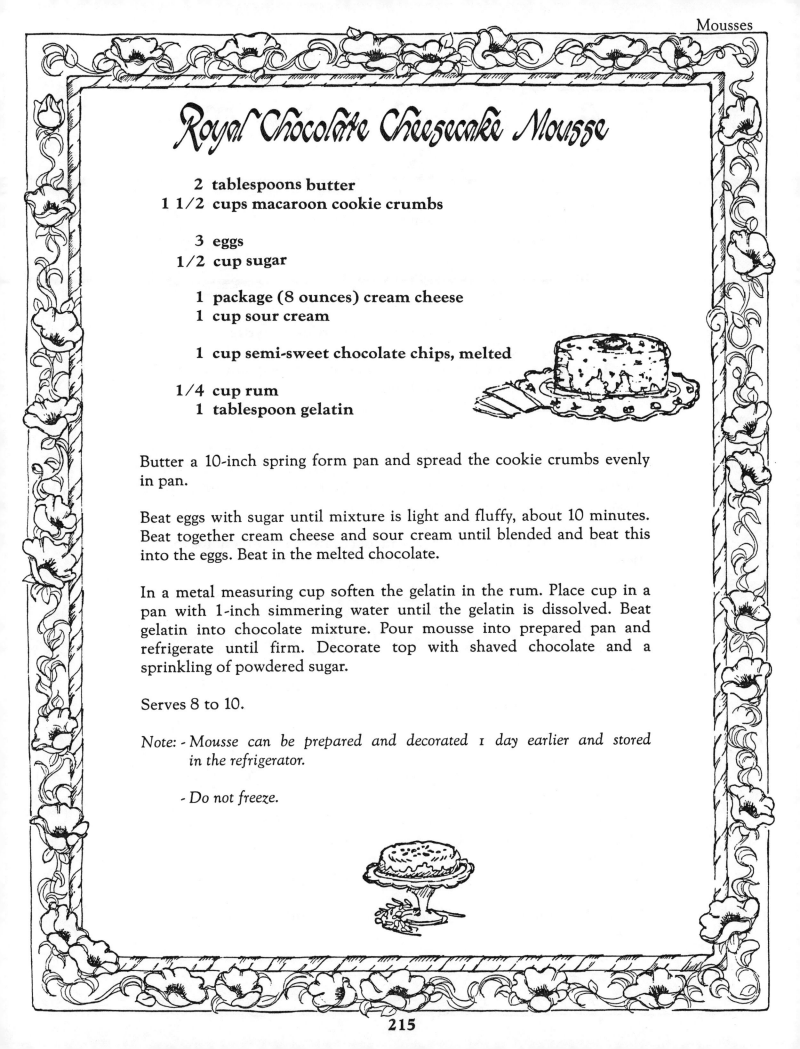

2 tablespoons butter
1 1/2 cups macaroon cookie crumbs

3 eggs
1/2 cup sugar

1 package (8 ounces) cream cheese
1 cup sour cream

1 cup semi-sweet chocolate chips, melted

1/4 cup rum
1 tablespoon gelatin

Butter a 10-inch spring form pan and spread the cookie crumbs evenly in pan.

Beat eggs with sugar until mixture is light and fluffy, about 10 minutes. Beat together cream cheese and sour cream until blended and beat this into the eggs. Beat in the melted chocolate.

In a metal measuring cup soften the gelatin in the rum. Place cup in a pan with 1-inch simmering water until the gelatin is dissolved. Beat gelatin into chocolate mixture. Pour mousse into prepared pan and refrigerate until firm. Decorate top with shaved chocolate and a sprinkling of powdered sugar.

Serves 8 to 10.

Note: - Mousse can be prepared and decorated 1 day earlier and stored in the refrigerator.

- Do not freeze.

Raspberry Mold with Sour Cream, Bananas & Coconut

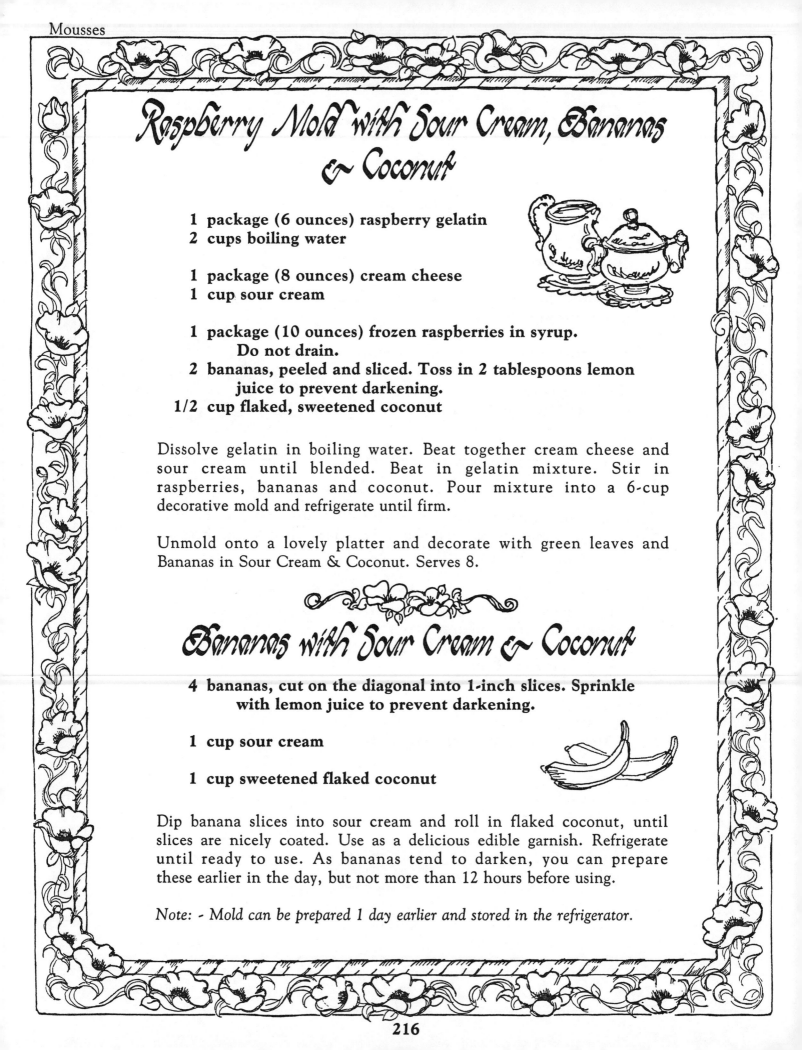

1 package (6 ounces) raspberry gelatin
2 cups boiling water

1 package (8 ounces) cream cheese
1 cup sour cream

1 package (10 ounces) frozen raspberries in syrup.
    Do not drain.
2 bananas, peeled and sliced. Toss in 2 tablespoons lemon
    juice to prevent darkening.
1/2 cup flaked, sweetened coconut

Dissolve gelatin in boiling water. Beat together cream cheese and sour cream until blended. Beat in gelatin mixture. Stir in raspberries, bananas and coconut. Pour mixture into a 6-cup decorative mold and refrigerate until firm.

Unmold onto a lovely platter and decorate with green leaves and Bananas in Sour Cream & Coconut. Serves 8.

Bananas with Sour Cream & Coconut

4 bananas, cut on the diagonal into 1-inch slices. Sprinkle
    with lemon juice to prevent darkening.

1 cup sour cream

1 cup sweetened flaked coconut

Dip banana slices into sour cream and roll in flaked coconut, until slices are nicely coated. Use as a delicious edible garnish. Refrigerate until ready to use. As bananas tend to darken, you can prepare these earlier in the day, but not more than 12 hours before using.

Note: - Mold can be prepared 1 day earlier and stored in the refrigerator.

Apple Cream Mousse with Orange & Cinnamon

This is a very unusual mold that is simply delicious. It is a light version of apple cream pie, filled with apples and sparkled with orange and lemon.

   3 **apples, cored, peeled and grated**
1/2 **cup yellow raisins**
1/2 **cup orange juice**
1/2 **orange, grated**
   1 **tablespoon lemon peel**
1/2 **cup brown sugar**
   1 **teaspoon cinnamon**
   1 **teaspoon vanilla**

   1 **cup chopped toasted walnuts**

2 1//2 **cups apple juice**
   1 **package (6 ounces) orange gelatin**
   1 **cup cream, whipped**

Saute together the first 8 ingredients until the apples become soft. Add the toasted walnuts. Bring apple juice to a boil. Add gelatin and stir until gelatin is completely dissolved. Add apple mixture to the gelatin. Allow the mixture to cool and beat in the whipped cream.

Pour into a 2-quart mold and refrigerate until firm. Unmold on a lovely platter and decorate with a sprinkling of cinnamon. Serves 10.

Note: - If cream is added when gelatin is warm, then it will separate into 3 layers, which is just lovely and equally delicious.

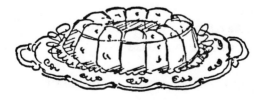

Mousse au Capuccino with Creme de Kahlua

This is probably one of the easiest mousses and very good, indeed. The only consideration is to fold in the whipped cream when the chocolate mixture has partially cooled. Other than that, it's a triumph of simplicity.

1/2 pound semi-sweet chocolate chips

1 cup whipping cream
1 tablespoon powdered instant coffee
3 egg yolks
1 tablespoon Creme de Kahlua or coffee liqueur
1 teaspoon Cognac

1/2 cup whipping cream
1 teaspoon sugar
1/2 teaspoon vanilla

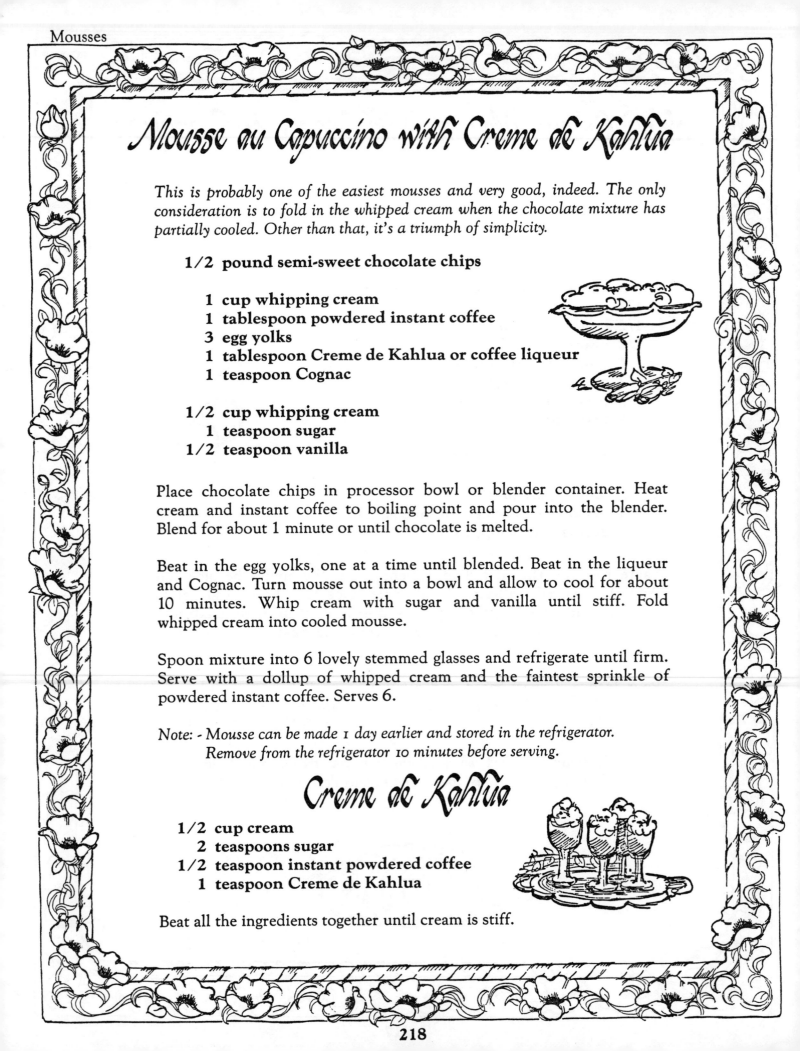

Place chocolate chips in processor bowl or blender container. Heat cream and instant coffee to boiling point and pour into the blender. Blend for about 1 minute or until chocolate is melted.

Beat in the egg yolks, one at a time until blended. Beat in the liqueur and Cognac. Turn mousse out into a bowl and allow to cool for about 10 minutes. Whip cream with sugar and vanilla until stiff. Fold whipped cream into cooled mousse.

Spoon mixture into 6 lovely stemmed glasses and refrigerate until firm. Serve with a dollup of whipped cream and the faintest sprinkle of powdered instant coffee. Serves 6.

Note: - Mousse can be made 1 day earlier and stored in the refrigerator. Remove from the refrigerator 10 minutes before serving.

Creme de Kahlua

1/2 cup cream
2 teaspoons sugar
1/2 teaspoon instant powdered coffee
1 teaspoon Creme de Kahlua

Beat all the ingredients together until cream is stiff.

Old~Fashioned Deep Dish Sour Cream Apple Pie

This super easy pie is so thoroughly delicious, you will enjoy making it often. The crust is assembled in seconds in a mixer and the tart, juicy apples are covered with a succulent sour cream topping.

Crust:
- 2 cups yellow cake mix (not the super-moist, pudding mix)
- 6 tablespoons butter
- 1/2 cup finely chopped walnuts

Filling:
- 3 apples, peeled, cored and thinly sliced
- 2 tablespoons lemon juice
- 1/2 cup apricot jam
- 1/2 cup yellow raisins
- 3/4 teaspoon cinnamon
- 4 tablespoons sugar

Topping:
- 1 cup sour cream
- 1 egg, beaten
- 3 tablespoons sugar
- 1 teaspoon vanilla

In the large bowl of an electric mixer, beat together the cake mix and butter until blended. Beat in walnuts. Press dough on the bottom and sides of deep-dish 10-inch pie pan, which has been lightly buttered. Bake crust in a 350° oven for 8 minutes.

Combine filling ingredients and stir until mixed. Place in cooked shell. Combine topping ingredients and pour mixture evenly over the apples. Return pie to oven and continue baking for 30 to 35 minutes or until top is a light golden color. Serve warm or at room temperature. Serves 8.

Note: - If you make this lovely pie a day earlier, store it in the refrigerator. Remove from the refrigerator about 1 hour before serving.

Old-Fashioned Sour Cream Apple Pie with Cinnamon

1 10-inch Pecan Cookie Crust

3 apples, peeled and thinly sliced
1/2 cup yellow raisins
3/4 teaspoon grated lemon peel
1/4 cup brown sugar
1/4 cup sugar
1 teaspoon cinnamon

1 1/4 cups sour cream
1 egg
4 tablespoons sugar

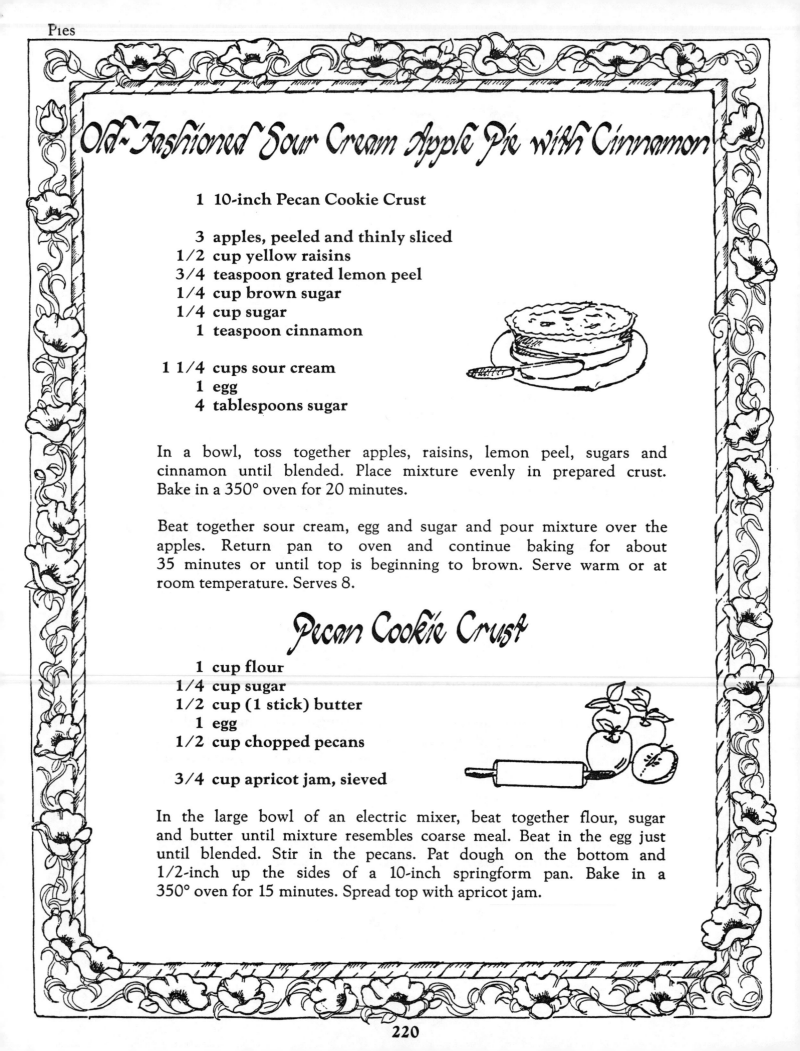

In a bowl, toss together apples, raisins, lemon peel, sugars and cinnamon until blended. Place mixture evenly in prepared crust. Bake in a 350° oven for 20 minutes.

Beat together sour cream, egg and sugar and pour mixture over the apples. Return pan to oven and continue baking for about 35 minutes or until top is beginning to brown. Serve warm or at room temperature. Serves 8.

Pecan Cookie Crust

1 cup flour
1/4 cup sugar
1/2 cup (1 stick) butter
1 egg
1/2 cup chopped pecans

3/4 cup apricot jam, sieved

In the large bowl of an electric mixer, beat together flour, sugar and butter until mixture resembles coarse meal. Beat in the egg just until blended. Stir in the pecans. Pat dough on the bottom and 1/2-inch up the sides of a 10-inch springform pan. Bake in a 350° oven for 15 minutes. Spread top with apricot jam.

Southern Chocolate Pecan Pie with Whipped Cream de Cacao

1 9-inch deep dish pie shell, baked in a 400° oven
  for 8 minutes

2 eggs
1 cup sugar

1/4 cup flour
1/4 cup cocoa

1/2 cup butter (1 stick) melted
1 teaspoon vanilla
2 tablespoons Creme de Cacao liqueur

1 cup semi-sweet chocolate chips
1 cup chopped pecans

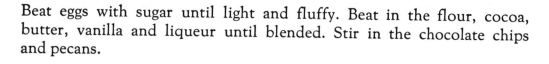

Prepare pie shell and place it on a cookie sheet.

Beat eggs with sugar until light and fluffy. Beat in the flour, cocoa, butter, vanilla and liqueur until blended. Stir in the chocolate chips and pecans.

Pour mixture into prepared pie crust and bake in a 350° oven for about 40 minutes or until filling is set. Allow to cool. Frost with Whipped Cream de Cacao or simply serve it with a dollup of whipped cream. Serves 8.

Whipped Cream de Cacao: Beat together 3/4 cup cream, 1 tablespoon sugar and 1 tablespoon Creme de Cacao liqueur until cream is stiff.

Note: - Pie can be prepared 1 day earlier and stored in the refrigerator. It could be frosted earlier in the day you are planning to serve it.

Deep Dish Apple Pie with Butter Crisp Nut Topping

4 to 5   apples, peeled, cored and thinly sliced
1/2   cup apricot jam
3   tablespoons lemon juice
2   tablespoons grated lemon peel
1/2   cup raisins
1/2   cup sugar

1   teaspoon cinnamon

In a 9-inch deep dish pie pan, toss together the apples, jam, lemon juice, peel, raisins and sugar. Spread evenly in pan and sprinkle top with the cinnamon.

Sprinkle top with Butter Crisp Nut Topping and pat it down to cover the fruit. Bake in a 350° oven for about 1 hour or until top is nicely browned. Allow to cool a little.

This can be served warm, or at room temperature, or cold. To serve, spoon into dessert dishes and serve with ice cream or a dollup of whipped cream. Serves 6.

Butter Crisp Nut Topping:
1/2   cup flour
1/2   cup sugar
1/4   cup butter (1/2 stick)

1   cup ground walnuts

In the large bowl of an electric mixer, at low speed, beat together the flour, sugar and butter until mixture resembles fine meal. Stir in the ground walnuts until nuts are evenly distributed.

Chocolate Almond Tart with Chocolate Mousse

1 cup flour
1/4 cup sugar
1/2 cup butter
1 egg
1/2 cup chopped almonds
1/4 cup grated chocolate
1/2 teaspoon almond extract

In the large bowl of an electric mixer, beat together flour, sugar and butter until mixture resembles coarse meal. Beat in the egg just until blended. Stir in the remaining ingredients until blended.

Pat dough on the bottom of a greased 10-inch springform pan. Bake in a 350° oven for about 25 minutes or until top is lightly browned. Allow crust to cool.

Pour Chocolate Mousse Filling into crust and refrigerate until firm.

Decorate top with Creme de Cacao Whipped cream and a few sprinkles of shaved chocolate. Serves 10.

Chocolate Mousse Filling

1 package (8 ounces) semi-sweet chocolate chips
(1 1/3 cups)
1 cup whipping cream
4 egg yolks
2 tablespoons Creme de Cacao Liqueur
1 teaspoon vanilla

Place chocolate in blender container. Heat cream to boiling point and pour into blender. Blend for about 1 minute or until chocolate is melted. Beat in yolks, liqueur and vanilla. Pour mousse into prepared crust.

Creme de Cacao Whipped Cream: Beat together 1 cup cream, 1 tablespoon sugar and 1 tablespoon Creme de Cacao Liqueur until cream is stiff ·

Note: - If dough is a little sticky, flour your fingertips.

Coconut Cloud Pie with Coconut Brandy Cream

Vanilla Crumb Coconut Crust:
1 1/4 cups vanilla wafer crumbs
1/4 cup coconut flakes
1/3 cup butter, melted
3 tablespoons sugar

Combine all the ingredients and pat them on the bottom and sides of a buttered 9-inch pie pan. Bake in a 350° oven for about 8 minutes or until top is very lightly browned. Set aside to cool.

Coconut Brandy Cream Filling

1 tablespoon gelatin
1/4 cup Cognac

4 eggs, at room temperature
1/2 cup sugar

1 1/2 cups cream, beaten until stiff with 3 tablespoons
sugar
1/2 cup toasted coconut

1/2 cup apricot jam
1/2 cup toasted coconut flakes

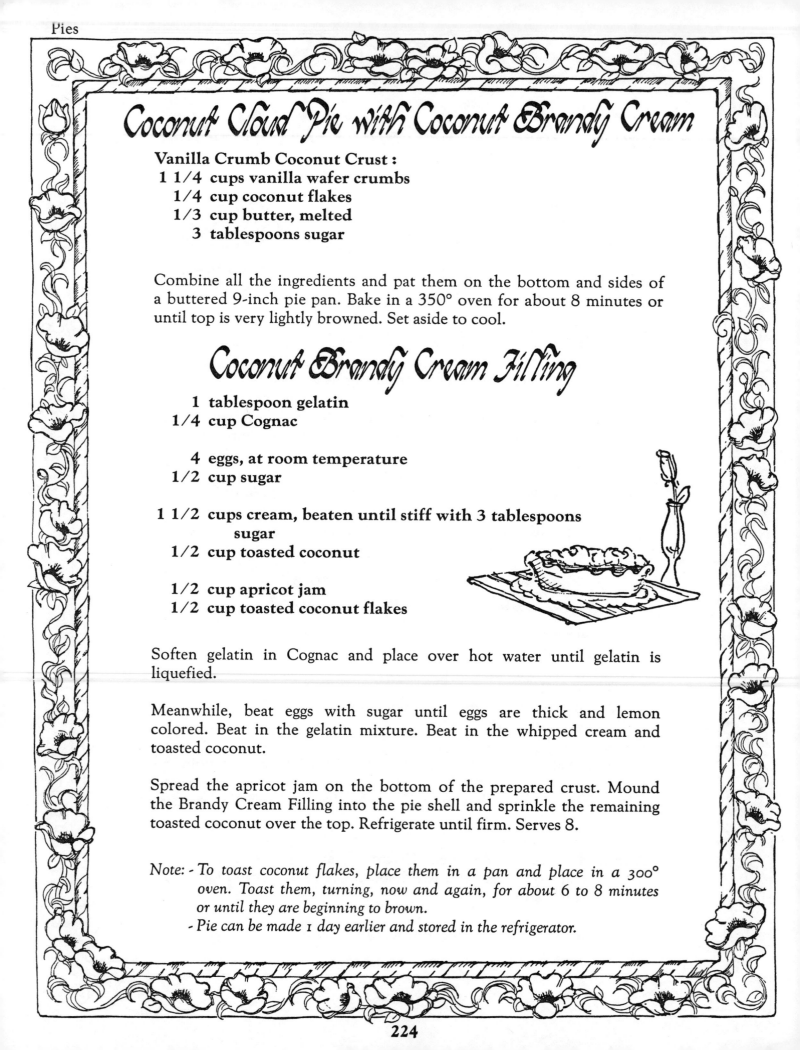

Soften gelatin in Cognac and place over hot water until gelatin is liquefied.

Meanwhile, beat eggs with sugar until eggs are thick and lemon colored. Beat in the gelatin mixture. Beat in the whipped cream and toasted coconut.

Spread the apricot jam on the bottom of the prepared crust. Mound the Brandy Cream Filling into the pie shell and sprinkle the remaining toasted coconut over the top. Refrigerate until firm. Serves 8.

Note: - To toast coconut flakes, place them in a pan and place in a 300° oven. Toast them, turning, now and again, for about 6 to 8 minutes or until they are beginning to brown.
- Pie can be made 1 day earlier and stored in the refrigerator.

Praline Pumpkin Pie with Bourbon & Cream

A simplified version of my very favorite Pumpkin Pie. The praline layer is on the top this time and the pumpkin is sparkled with bourbon.

- 1 **frozen deep-dish 9-inch pie shell, brush bottom with 2 tablespoons apricot jam**
- 1 1/2 **cups canned pumpkin**
- 1 **cup sugar**
- 3 **eggs**
- 3 **teaspoons pumpkin pie spice**
- 1 1/2 **cups half and half (you can use 1 1/2 cups cream if you want to splurge)**
- 2 **tablespoons bourbon**

Prepare pie shell by brushing bottom with 2 tablespoons apricot jam. Beat together the remaining ingredients until blended and pour pumpkin mixture into pie shell. Place on a cookie sheet. This will help pie to bake evenly. Pie can also be handled easily. Bake in a 400° oven for 20 minutes. Reduce temperature to 350° and continue baking for 35 minutes or until custard is set.

Allow pie to cool. Sprinkle Praline Topping over the pie and carefully broil until praline is bubbling. Be careful not to burn the praline. Serve at room temperature with a dollup of whipped cream. Serves 8.

Praline Topping

- 1 **cup brown sugar**
- 1 **cup chopped pecans**
- 1/4 **cup (1/2 stick) butter, melted**

Combine sugar, pecans and butter and mix until blended.

Note: - Pie freezes beautifully. Defrost overnight in the refrigerator.
- Remove from refrigerator about 30 minutes before serving.

Chocolate Chip Chocolate Pecan Pie

If you are looking for a grand dessert and one that is very unusual, this is a wonderful pie to consider. It is like a southern pecan pie, yet totally different in taste and character.

3 eggs
1 cup chocolate syrup
1 cup sugar
2 tablespoons flour
2 tablespoons melted butter
1 teaspoon vanilla

1 unbaked 9-inch frozen pie shell
1 cup coarsely chopped pecans
1 cup semi-sweet chocolate chips

In a large bowl of an electric mixer beat together first 6 ingredients until blended, about 1 minute.

Meanwhile, sprinkle nuts and chocolate chips into pie shell. Pour egg mixture into pie shell. Place pie on a cookie sheet and bake it in a 350° oven for about 45 minutes or until filling is set. Allow to come to room temperature. Serve small portions as this pie is rich. Serves 8.

Note: - Pie can be frozen. Wrap in double thicknesses of plastic wrap and foil. Remove wrappers while thawing.

Chocolate Satin Mousse Pie with Kahlua Cream

This is an especially attractive dessert which is not particularly difficult to prepare. The mousse filling is equally good served in individual crystal goblets with a dollup of whipped cream.

3/4 cup milk
  3 cups miniature marshmallows

12 ounces chocolate (use a good quality chocolate), broken into pieces
  1 tablespoon Kahlua liqueur
  1 cup cream

In the top of a double boiler, over hot, not boiling water, stir together milk and marshmallows until marshmallows are melted. Add the chocolate, stirring until chocolate is melted and mixture is blended. Allow to cool for about 1 hour in the refrigerator.

Beat cream with liqueur until stiff. Beat in cooled chocolate mixture until blended. Spoon into Chocolate Cookie Crumb Crust and refrigerate until firm. Decorate top with chocolate leaves and peaks of whipped cream. Serves 8.

Chocolate Cookie Crumb Crust:
1 1/2 cups chocolate cookie crumbs (use a good quality fudge cookie)
  1/2 cup melted butter
    1 tablespoon Kahlua liqueur
  1/4 cup grated chocolate
  1/4 cup chopped almonds

Combine all the ingredients and pat them on the bottom and 1″ up the sides of a 10-inch springform pan. Bake in a 350° oven for about 8 minutes or until crust is set.

Note: - Entire dessert can be prepared one day earlier and stored in the refrigerator until serving time.

Old-Fashioned Raisin Date Nut Pie

1 9-inch frozen pie shell, deep-dish variety
1/2 cup yellow raisins
3/4 cup chopped walnuts
1/2 cup chopped dates

3 eggs
1/2 cup sugar
1/2 cup honey
1/2 cup light corn syrup
1 tablespoon flour
2 teaspoons vanilla
1/2 teaspoon cinnamon (or more to taste)
1/4 cup melted butter

In a frozen pie shell, scatter raisins, walnuts and dates. Beat together the remaining ingredients until blended and pour into pie shell. Place pie on a cookie sheet and bake in a 350° over for about 45 minutes or until filling is set and crust is browned. Serve warm or at room temperature with a spoonful of whipped cream.

Orange Custard Tart

1 9-inch frozen pie shell. Remove from pie pan and place into a 9-inch tart pan with a removable bottom. This is only for cosmetic reasons and you can make the tart in the pie pan.

2 eggs
1/3 cup sugar
1 teaspoon vanilla
1/4 cup flour
1/4 cup orange juice
1/4 cup melted butter

2 oranges, remove peel and pith (white part) and cut into thin slices
1/3 cup melted apricot jam

Beat together eggs, sugar, vanilla, flour, orange juice and melted butter. Pour mixture into pie shell and bake in 350° oven for about 45 minutes or until custard is set. Arrange orange slices over custard and brush tops with heated apricot jam. Allow to cool and refrigerate. Serve with a dollup of orange flavored whipped cream. Serves 8.

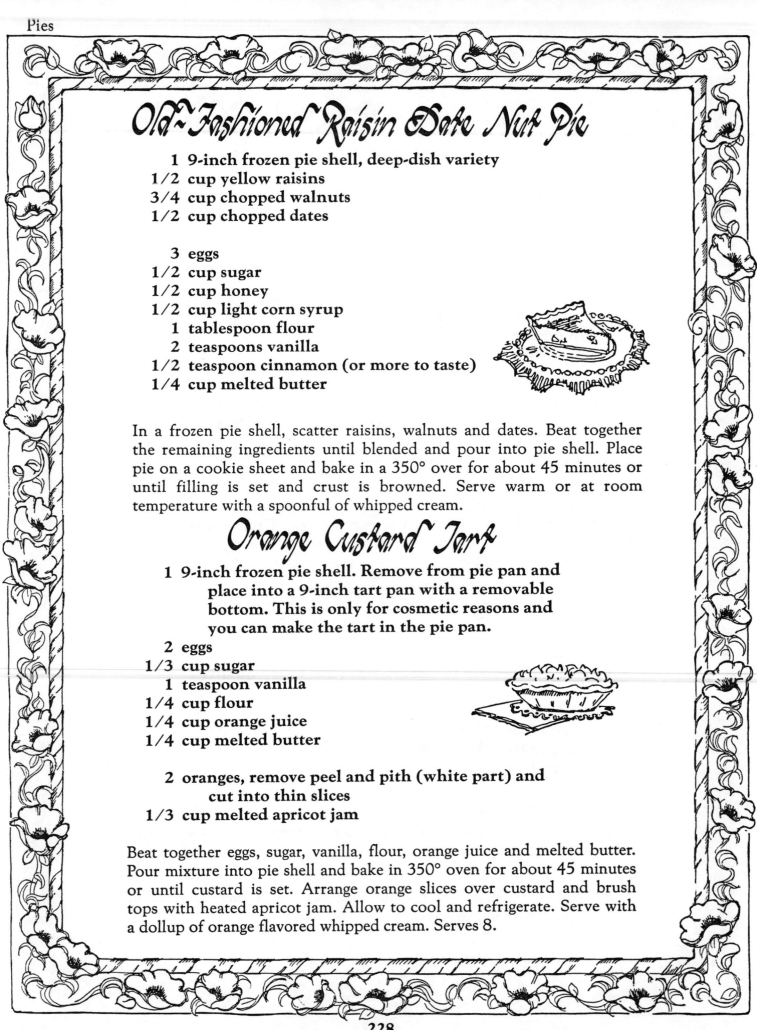

Easy 2-Minute Fudgy Brownie Pie with Chocolate Cream Frosting

This is my version of the 4-Minute Brownie Pie. It is a little moister with the addition of the chocolate syrup and a bit chewier because it is beaten for only 2 minutes, instead of 4.

2	eggs
1	cup sugar
1/2	cup butter, softened
2/3	cup flour
4 to 5	tablespoons sifted unsweetened cocoa
2	tablespoons chocolate syrup
1	teaspoon vanilla
1/8	teaspoon salt

1/2 cup chopped walnuts

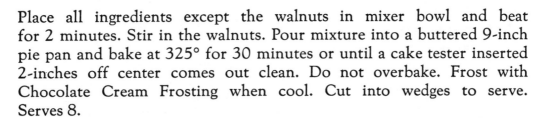

Place all ingredients except the walnuts in mixer bowl and beat for 2 minutes. Stir in the walnuts. Pour mixture into a buttered 9-inch pie pan and bake at 325° for 30 minutes or until a cake tester inserted 2-inches off center comes out clean. Do not overbake. Frost with Chocolate Cream Frosting when cool. Cut into wedges to serve. Serves 8.

Chocolate Cream Frosting:
3/4 cup semi-sweet chocolate chips
1/2 cup cream
1/2 teaspoon vanilla

Place chocolate chips in blender container. Heat cream to boiling point and pour into blender. Blend for 1 minute or until the chocolate is melted and frosting is smooth. Beat in vanilla. Pour frosting over pie and spread evenly.

Note: - If you do not have the time to make the frosting, here is a very easy (and delicious) way to make an "instant frosting". When you remove the brownies from the oven, sprinkle the top with 3/4 cup of chocolate chips. TURN OVEN OFF. Return pan to the oven for 1 minute or just until chocolate is softened. Spread chocolate evenly over the brownies. Allow to cool.

Old-Fashioned Honey Spice Pumpkin Pie

Sometimes, it feels good to go back to basics. This is a traditional, old-fashioned pie with a touch of honey and spice and everything nice.

1 deep dish frozen pie shell (9-inch). Prebake in a 375° oven for 8 minutes. Brush bottom with 2 tablespoons apricot jam.

- **1 can (1 pound) pumpkin**
- **3/4 cup brown sugar**
- **1/4 teaspoon salt**
- **2 teaspoons pumpkin pie spice**
- **2 eggs, beaten**
- **1 1/2 cups half and half (can use cream if you're not counting)**
- **1/4 cup honey**
- **1 tablespoon bourbon**

Prepare pie shell. Combine the remaining ingredients and beat until blended. Pour mixture into prepared pie shell and place pie on a cookie sheet. (This will help crust to brown better and will facilitate removing the pie from the oven.) Bake in a 375° oven for about 50 minutes or until a knife inserted in center comes out clean. Cool. Serve with a dollup of whipped cream flavored with bourbon. Serves 6 to 8.

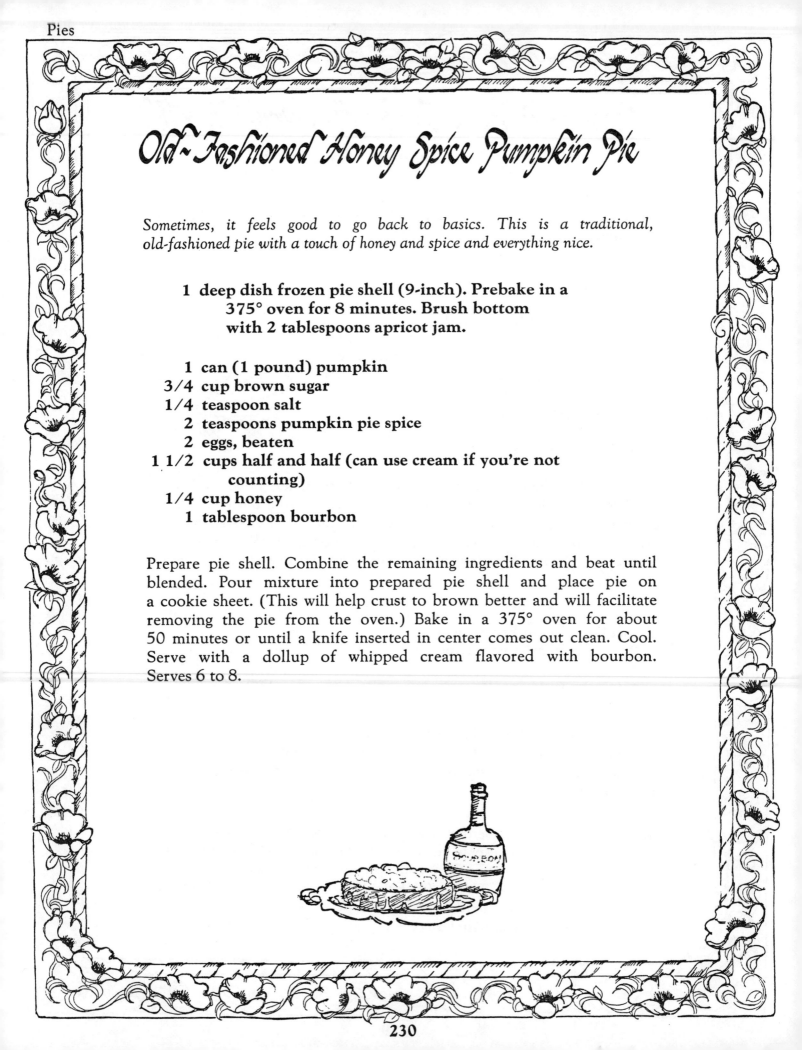

Lemon Meringue Pie with Vanilla Crust

This is a good old-fashioned Lemon Meringue Pie made just a little simpler (and I do believe, better) with a new-fashioned vanilla wafer crumb crust. The taste of vanilla, in combination with the lemon is simply delicious.

Vanilla Crust:
- 1 1/4 cups vanilla wafer crumbs
- 1 tablespoon grated lemon peel
- 1/4 cup sugar
- 1/3 cup butter, melted

Combine all the ingredients until blended and pat them on the bottom and sides of a buttered 9-inch pie pan. Bake in 350° oven for about 7 or 8 minutes or until top is very lightly browned. Set aside to cool.

Lemon Filling:
- 2 cups boiling water
- 2 tablespoons finely grated lemon peel
- 1/4 cup butter, softened
- 1/8 teaspoon salt
- 1/2 cup sugar

- 4 egg yolks
- 1 cup sugar
- 1/2 cup cornstarch
- 2/3 cup lemon juice

In a saucepan, stir together hot water, peel, butter, salt and sugar. Beat together, in large mixer bowl, the yolks, sugar, cornstarch and lemon juice until thoroughly blended.

Pour egg yolk mixture into hot water mixture and stir until blended. Place saucepan on low heat and cook and stir constantly until mixture has thickened. Do not boil. Pour filling into prepared crust.

Lemon Meringue Pie (continued)

Meringue:
- 4 egg whites
- pinch of salt
- 1/8 teaspoon cream of tarter
- 1/2 cup sugar
- 1 teaspoon vanilla

Beat whites until foamy. Continue beating and add salt, cream of tartar, sugar (1 tablespoon at a time) and vanilla until meringue is very stiff. Swirl meringue decoratively on top of lemon filling and cover every bit of crust. Bake in a 350° oven for 12 to 15 minutes or until top is lightly browned. Cool for 3 hours before serving. For easy cutting, use a wet knife. Serves 8.

German Chocolate Pecan Coconut Pie

- 1 regular frozen pie shell (9-inch). Prebake in a 375° oven for 8 minutes.

- 1 cup chopped pecans
- 1/2 cup coconut flakes

- 3/4 cup milk chocolate chips
- 1/4 cup (1/2 stick) butter, softened
- 1/2 cup sugar
- 3/4 cup cream, at room temperature
- 3 eggs, at room temperature
- 1 teaspoon vanilla

Prepare pie crust. Sprinkle pecans and coconut on bottom of crust. Heat together chocolate, butter and sugar until chocolate is melted. Cool slightly and beat in cream, eggs and vanilla until blended. Pour mixture into prepared pie crust and bake in a 375° oven for about 45 to 50 minutes or until a knife inserted in center comes out clean. Cool. Serves 6 to 8.

Chocolate Pie Glorioso

Chocolate lovers rejoice. This pie is as rich and devilishly delicious as you could imagine a chocolate pie to be. It has a heavenly mousse-like texture and is simply a delight for family dinners or the most elegant dinner parties. The pie can be served with a spoonful of whipped cream but that would really be gilding the lily.

> 12 **ounces semi-sweet chocolate chips**
> 1 **cup cream**
> 2 **tablespoons rum**
>
> 6 **eggs**
> 1/2 **cup sugar**
> 1 **teaspoon vanilla**

Place chocolate chips into blender container. Heat cream to boiling point and pour into blender. Blend for a few seconds until chocolate is melted. Blend in the rum.

In the large bowl of an electric mixer beat together the eggs, vanilla and sugar until the mixture is very light and fluffy, about 5 minutes. Beat in the chocolate mixture. Pour batter into a buttered and floured 9-inch pie pan. Place pie pan on a heavy duty cookie sheet and bake in a 350° oven for about 45 to 50 minutes or until a cake tester inserted in center comes out clean. Open oven door and allow pie to cool in oven for about 30 minutes. Remove from oven and refrigerate. Serve cold, and if you like, pipe a few rosettes of whipped cream over the top. Serves 8.

Note: - Pie can be made 1 day earlier and refrigerated.
- For an old-fashioned effect, place a doily over the pie and sprinkle lightly with powdered sugar that has been sifted.

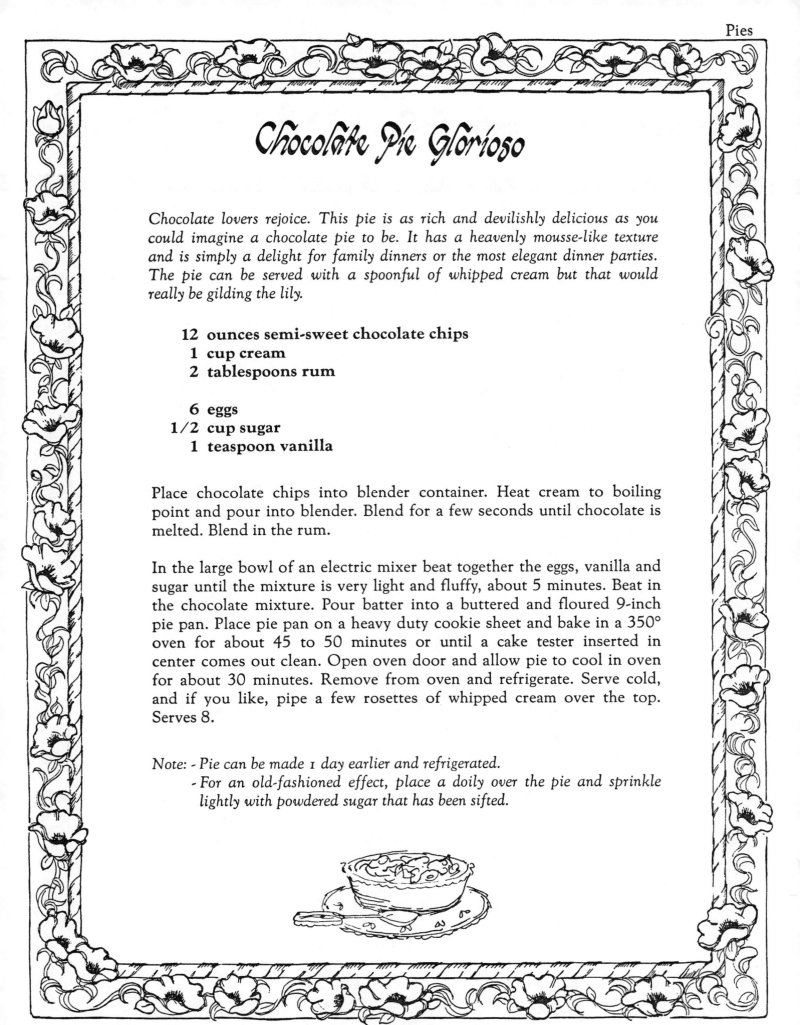

Ginger Snap Pumpkin Cake with Walnuts & Raisins

This is a very simple dessert that you can assemble in literally minutes. Although it is cakelike in character, it serves like a pie. The addition of nuts and raisins further enhances the spicy, gingery quality of this very delicious pumpkin pie cake. Served with large mugs of cider, it is especially good around the holiday times.

       3 eggs
     3/4 cup sugar
     2/3 cup canned pumpkin

   2 1/4 cups ginger snap cookie crumbs
   1 1/2 teaspoon pumpkin pie spice
       1 cup chopped walnuts
     1/2 cup yellow raisins
       1 teaspoon vanilla

Beat eggs with sugar until mixture is light and fluffy, about 5 minutes. Beat in the pumpkin until blended. Mix in the remaining ingredients on low speed until mixture is blended.

Pour batter into a buttered 9-inch pie pan and spread to even. Bake in a 350° oven for about 40 to 45 minutes or until a cake tester inserted in center comes out clean. Allow to cool and then frost with Whipped Cream with Orange Liqueur. Refrigerate for 4 to 6 hours. Overnight is very good, too. Serves 8.

Whipped Cream with Orange Liqueur

       1 cup cream
       2 tablespoons sugar
     1/2 teaspoon vanilla
       1 tablespoon orange liqueur

Beat cream with sugar until soft peaks form. Add the vanilla and orange liqueur and continue beating until cream is stiff.

Note: - If you are using a 9-inch foil pan, place it on a cookie sheet while baking.
- This lovely creation can also be frozen.

Grandma's Flaky Pastry Roll with Butter & Walnuts

Don't be discouraged to try this recipe if you are one of those who are afraid to work with yeast. Let me assure you, that nothing could be easier . . . as the yeast is simply beaten into the dough and needs no special attention or consideration.

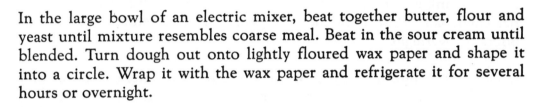

- **1 cup butter (2 sticks)**
- **2 cups flour**
- **1 package fresh yeast**

2/3 cup sour cream

In the large bowl of an electric mixer, beat together butter, flour and yeast until mixture resembles coarse meal. Beat in the sour cream until blended. Turn dough out onto lightly floured wax paper and shape it into a circle. Wrap it with the wax paper and refrigerate it for several hours or overnight.

Divide dough into 4 parts. Working one part at a time, roll it out on a floured pastry cloth until the dough measures about 10x10-inches. Spread 1/4 of the Butter Walnut Filling evenly over the dough. Roll jelly roll fashion ending with a roll that measures 3x10-inches and seam side down.

Place rolls on a lightly greased 12x16-inch pan so that you can bake the 4 rolls at one time. Bake in a 350° oven for about 35 to 40 minutes or until tops are lightly browned. Allow to cool and drizzle tops with Sour Cream Vanilla Glaze. Cut into slices at serving time. Yields about 36 one-inch slices.

Butter Walnut Filling: Beat together 1/2 cup butter, 1 cup flour, 1 cup sugar and 2 cups finely chopped walnuts until the mixture resembles fine meal. Do not overbeat or mixture will form a dough, which is very good but a bit more difficult to work with.

Sour Cream Vanilla Glaze: Stir together 2 tablespoons sour cream, 1 teaspoon vanilla and about 2 cups sifted powdered sugar until mixture is quite thick. Drizzle glaze over cooled pastry rolls.

Note: - You cannot substitute dry yeast for this recipe.
- Pastries freeze beautifully. Glaze after defrosting.

Easiest & Best Tart Apple Strudel with Cinnamon, Raisins & Walnuts

What a delightful combination of apples, cinnamon, raisins, lemon and tart apricot jam. The dough is flaky and tender and the essence of simplicity to prepare.

    1 cup butter, (2 sticks)
    2 cups flour
    1 cup sour cream

In the large bowl of an electric mixer, beat together butter and flour until the mixture resembles coarse meal. Add sour cream and beat for 30 seconds. Turn dough out onto wax paper that is heavily dusted with flour. Sprinkle a little more flour over the dough and shape it into a flattened ball. Wrap it in the wax paper and refrigerate it for several hours or overnight.

Divide dough into 4 parts. Working one part at a time, roll it out on a floured pastry cloth to measure about 10x10-inches. Spread 1/4 of Apple Filling over the dough, leaving a 1-inch edge without filling. Roll it up, jelly-roll fashion and place on a lightly greased 12x16-inch pan, and seam side down.

Bake in a preheated 350° oven for about 30 minutes or until top is golden brown. Cool in pan for 10 minutes and then continue cooling on a rack or brown paper bag. Sprinkle generously with sifted powdered sugar and cut into slices to serve. Yields 24 to 30 slices.

Tart Apple Filling

    2 apples, peeled, cored and grated
    3/4 cup apricot jam
    1 cup chopped walnuts
    4 tablespoons cinnamon sugar
    1 cup yellow raisins
    2 tablespoons grated lemon peel
    4 tablespoons flaked sweetened coconut (optional)

In a bowl, combine all the ingredients and stir until blended. Will yield enough filling to fill 4 strudels.

Old-Fashioned Apple Tart with Orange

Not quite a tart, or a cake, but somewhere in between, this is actually a nutty sponge cake layer, topped with apples and cinnamon sugar and vanilla glaze.

> **3** eggs
> **1/2** cup sugar
>
> **1/2** cup flour
> **1/2** cup finely chopped walnuts
> **1** tablespoon grated orange peel
> **1** teaspoon grated lemon peel
> **1** teaspoon vanilla
>
> **1** large apple, peeled, cored and very thinly sliced
> **2** teaspoons cinnamon sugar

Beat eggs with sugar until very light and fluffy, about 5 minutes. Beat in the flour, walnuts, peels and vanilla just until blended. Do not overmix.

Pour batter into a buttered 10-inch springform pan. Place apple slices over the batter and sprinkle top with the cinnamon sugar. Bake in a 350° oven for 30 minutes or until a cake tester, inserted in center, comes out clean.

Allow tart to cool in pan. When cool, drizzle with Vanilla Glaze. Cut into wedges to serve. Serves 6.

Vanilla Glaze: Stir together 1 tablespoon cream, 1/2 teaspoon vanilla and 1 cup sifted powdered sugar until mixture is a drizzling consistency.

Note: - Tart can be prepared 1 day earlier and stored in the refrigerator loosely covered with plastic wrap. Allow to come to room temperature before serving.

Apricot Tart with Almond Meringue & Butter Lemon Cookie Crust

This lovely tart has a cookie dough shell and is topped with fruity apricot jam and a meringue sparkled with almonds.

  1 cup fruity apricot jam, sieved

  2 egg whites
1/2 cup sugar
3/4 cup grated almonds (or almond meal, from
      health food stores)

Spread apricot jam over warm crust. Beat egg whites until foamy. Gradually beat in the sugar until meringue is stiff and glossy. Beat in the ground almonds. Spread meringue evenly over the jam. Return pan to oven and continue baking for about 25 minutes or until meringue is lightly browned. Cover pan with foil and allow to cool. Cut into wedges to serve. Serves 6 to 8.

Butter Lemon Cookie Crust

  3/4 cup butter
1 1/2 cups flour
  1/2 cup sifted powdered sugar

  2 egg yolks
  2 tablespoons lemon juice
  1 teaspoon grated lemon zest

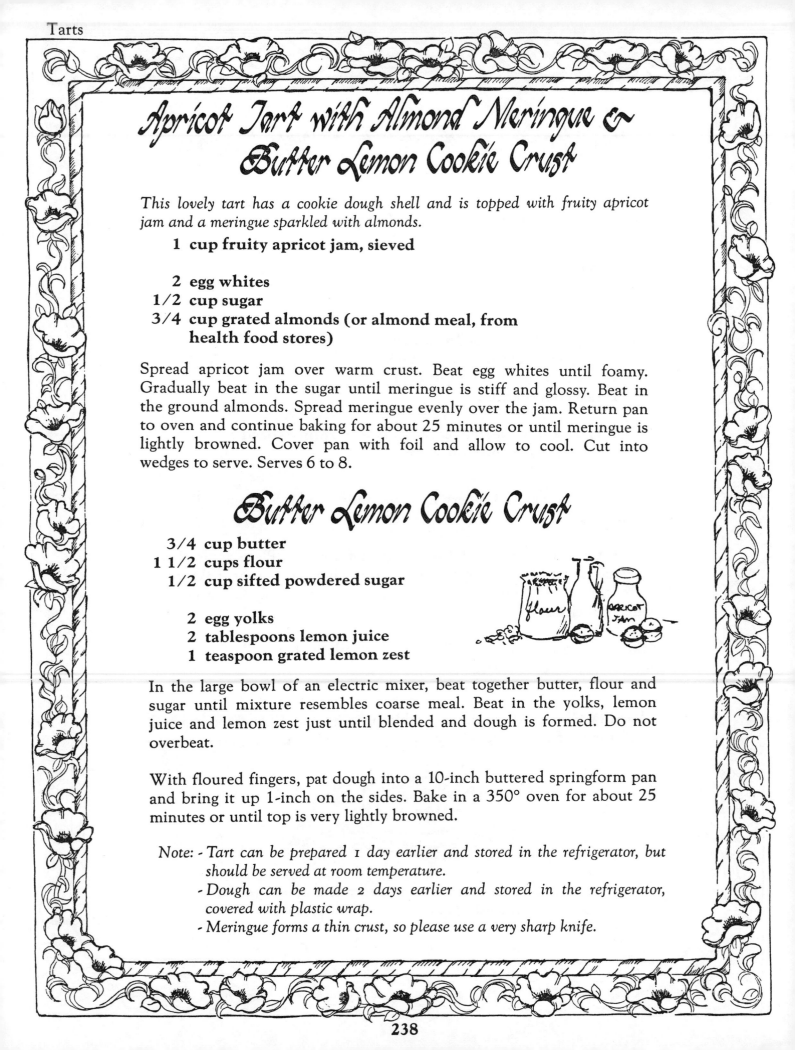

In the large bowl of an electric mixer, beat together butter, flour and sugar until mixture resembles coarse meal. Beat in the yolks, lemon juice and lemon zest just until blended and dough is formed. Do not overbeat.

With floured fingers, pat dough into a 10-inch buttered springform pan and bring it up 1-inch on the sides. Bake in a 350° oven for about 25 minutes or until top is very lightly browned.

Note: - Tart can be prepared 1 day earlier and stored in the refrigerator, but should be served at room temperature.
    - Dough can be made 2 days earlier and stored in the refrigerator, covered with plastic wrap.
    - Meringue forms a thin crust, so please use a very sharp knife.

Raspberry & Pecan Tart in Flaky Lemon Pastry

Tart raspberries, crunchy pecans and a flaky lemon pastry are a divine combination. And the little drizzle of Sour Cream Glaze is the perfect final touch.

1   10-inch Flaky Pastry Lemon Crust

1   cup seedless raspberry jam
1/2   cup finely chopped pecans

1/2   cup butter (1 stick)
3/4   cup sugar

2   eggs
1   teaspoon vanilla
1   tablespoon grated lemon peel
1   cup grated pecans

Stir together raspberry jam and pecans and spread evenly on the bottom of prepared Flaky Pastry Lemon Crust.

In the large bowl of an electric mixer, beat butter with sugar until creamy, about 2 minutes. Beat in eggs, one at a time, beating well after each addition. Stir in vanilla, lemon peel and pecans until blended. Pour nut mixture over the jam. Bake in a 350° oven for 40 minutes or until filling is set.

Allow tart to cool and then drizzle with Sour Cream Vanilla Glaze. Serves 8 to 10.

Flaky Lemon Pastry Crust (continued)

            1 cup flour
          1/2 teaspoon baking powder
          1/4 cup sugar
          1/2 cup butter (1 stick)
            1 egg
            1 tablespoon grated lemon peel

In the large bowl of an electric mixer, beat together flour, baking powder and sugar until blended. Beat in butter until mixture resembles coarse meal. Beat in the egg and lemon peel just until blended. (Do not overbeat.) Pat dough on the bottom of a greased 10-inch springform pan and bake in a 350° oven for 25 minutes or until top is lightly browned. Allow crust to cool.

Sour Cream Vanilla Glaze: Stir together 1 tablespoon sour cream, 1 teaspoon vanilla and enough powdered sugar until drizzling consistency.

Potpourri

Double Egg Nog Float with Kahlua

This is a delicious drink around holiday time. Serve it in a large, glamorous stemmed goblet. Place a cherry on top and use 2 pretty red straws.

    1 quart egg nog (from the dairy case in your market)
    1 quart egg nog ice cream
    6 ounces Kahlua liqueur

Divide the egg nog between 6 large stemmed goblets. Divide the ice cream between the 6 glasses. Float 1 ounce liqueur over each glass. Decorate with a cherry and serve with colorful straws. This simple drink can transform a quite ordinary evening into a party. Serve with some festive cookies.

Hot Apple Cider with Oranges & Cinnamon

Some evening soon, you might enjoy serving hot apple cider instead of the usual coffee and tea. Serve it in large mugs with some pumpkin cake or pumpkin bread with creamy butter.

    1 quart apple cider, unsweetened
    2 tablespoons dark brown sugar (or to taste)
    2 cinnamon sticks (or 1/4 teaspoon ground
        cinnamon)
    4 cloves
    1 orange, cut into slices. Do not peel.
    1 lemon, cut into slices. Do not peel.

Combine all the ingredients in a saucepan and simmer mixture for about 10 minutes. Serve cider hot. Discard fruit. Yields 4 cups.

Cappuccino Supreme with Kahlua & Brandy

Traditionally, Cappuccino is made with equal amounts of espresso coffee and hot milk. Served with a dollup of whipped cream and a sprinkling of cinnamon or nutmeg, it is very good indeed. However, the addition of liqueurs and cream adds a good deal of excitement and "spirit" to the occasion. Mixes can be prepared in advance, leaving only the boiling of the liquid at the last moment.

INSTANT CAPPUCCINO MIX

4 tablespoons instant espresso coffee
2 tablespoons cocoa
2 tablespoons sugar

Combine all the ingredients in a jar with a tight-fitting lid and shake to blend.

LIQUEUR & BRANDY BLEND

5 ounces Kahlua coffee liqueur
5 ounces Creme de Cacao liqueur
2 ounces Cognac or brandy

Combine all the ingredients in a jar with a tight-fitting lid and stir to blend.

LIQUID MIXTURE

4 1/2 cups water
1 1/2 cups milk
1 1/2 cups cream

Place all the ingredients in a saucepan and bring mixture to a boil.

To Serve: Place 1 teaspoon Cappuccino Mix into each cup. Add about 5 ounces hot milk mixture and 1 ounce liqueur blend to each cup. Stir. Top with a dollup of whipped cream. Sprinkle lightly with cinnamon or nutmeg or shaved chocolate. This recipe is planned to serve 12.

Note: - Cappuccino Mix can be stored for weeks and is very nice to have on hand. Use it as you would instant coffee.
- Liqueurs can be combined and stored indefinitely.

Coffee Punch with Brandy & Cream

You will enjoy serving this punch with dessert. It is a grand choice for a backyard picnic.

       8 cups strong coffee, chilled
1 1/2 cups milk
          sugar to taste (about 3 to 4 tablespoons)
       2 teaspoons vanilla

   1/4 cup brandy
   1/4 cup Kahlua liqueur
     24 coffee ice cubes*
   1/2 gallon mocha ice cream
       1 cup cream, whipped

Combine coffee, milk, sugar and vanilla and refrigerate until ready to serve. Pour mixture into a punch bowl and stir in brandy, Kahlua and coffee ice. Float ice cream and whipped cream on top. Sprinkle with cinnamon and powdered instant coffee. Yields about 24 (4 ounce) servings.

*To Make Coffee Ice: Fill ice cube tray with freshly brewed coffee and freeze until firm. Remove from freezer at serving time.

Company Spiced Tea with Cinnamon & Cloves

If you are preparing tea for a crowd, this is a wonderful recipe to consider. Simply boil water and add tea mix to taste.

- 1/2 **cup instant tea**
- 1/2 **teaspoon ground cinnamon**
- 1/2 **teaspoon ground cardamon**
- 1/2 **teaspoon ground cloves**
- 1/2 **cup sugar**

Place all the ingredients in a glass jar with a tight-fitting lid and shake to blend. Use from 1 to 2 teaspoons for each cup of boiling water. This recipe will yield about 24 cups.

Spiced Apple Cider with Oranges & Cinnamon

- 1 **quart apple cider**
- 1 **quart orange juice**
- 2 **tablespoons brown sugar (or more to taste)**
- 1/2 **teaspoon ground cinnamon (or 2 cinnamon sticks)**
- 6 **whole cloves**
- 1 **orange, unpeeled, cut into slices**
- 1 **lemon, unpeeled, cut into slices**

Combine all the ingredients in an enamel pot and simmer mixture for about 10 minutes. Strain and discard fruit. Serve in large mugs with fresh orange slice and a cinnamon stick (optional) in each mug. Yields 8 cups.

Note: - This is especially good served with Pumpkin Cake.

Pink Champagne Punch with Pineapple Sherbert

Don't be misled by the simplicity of this recipe. This is a beautiful punch, colorful and exciting. It is the essence of simplicity to prepare, but no one will know, unless you tell.

4 bottles pink champagne (4/5 quart, each) chilled
1 quart ginger ale, chilled

1/2 gallon pineapple sherbert

    strawberries, pineapple slices, orange slices, lemon slices

    24 pretty ice cubes*

At serving time, pour chilled champagne and ginger ale in a pretty punch bowl. Float sherbert, fruit and pretty ice. Yields about 24 (4 ounce) servings.

***To Make Pretty Ice:** In each cube section of an ice tray, place a strawberry (with the green stem), or a maraschino cherry, or 2 small grapes. Fill the ice cube tray with ginger ale and freeze until firm. Remove from freezer at serving time.

Holiday Spiced Wine with Oranges & Raisins

This is a lovely drink on a frosty night when you're sitting around a crackling fire. Set a tray with some cookies and sit back and relax with your guests. In no time, all's well with the world.

        2 **cups orange juice**
        1 **orange, remove stem and cut into thin slices, then**
              fourths
        1 **cup yellow raisins**
    1/2 **cup black currants**
        1 **cup chopped apricots**
    1/4 **cup sugar**
    1/2 **teaspoon cinnamon**
    1/2 **teaspoon ground cloves**

        3 **bottles (25 ounces, each) California Burgundy**
        1 **bottle (25 ounces) California Port**

Combine first eight ingredients in a saucepan and simmer mixture for about 20 minutes or until apricots are tender. (This can be done ahead.)

Just before serving, place all the ingredients in a large enamel pot and heat slowly, just to warm. Do not boil. Ladle into little glass mugs and serve with some of the apricots and raisins in each glass. Yields about 3 quarts or about 25 servings, 4 ounces, each.

Note: - Taste for sugar; you may like it sweeter.

Hawaiian Cici Colada

1 cup vodka
2 cups pineapple juice
1/2 cup half and half
1/2 cup coconut syrup

6 ice cubes

In a blender container, blend vodka, pineapple juice, half and half and coconut syrup. Add ice cubes, one at a time, blending well after each addition. Pour into pretty stemmed glasses and decorate with pineapple spears. Serves 4.

Mai Tai

1 cup light rum
3 tablespoons orange liqueur
1 cup pineapple juice
1/2 cup orange juice
2 tablespoons lemon juice

6 ice cubes

In a blender container, blend rum, orange liqueur, pineapple juice, orange juice and lemon juice. Add ice cubes, one at a time, blending well after each addition. Pour into pretty stemmed glasses and decorate with pineapple spears and orange slices. Serves 4.

Las Margaritas Mejicana (Lime Margaritas)

Coarse Kosher Salt
1 egg white
1 cup lime juice
1 cup tequila
1/4 cup triple sec
2 cups ice chips

Rub the rims of 8 stemmed glasses with grapefruit juice and dip the rims into coarse salt. Set aside. Place the remaining ingredients in a blender container and blend until foamy. Pour into prepared glasses. Decorate with a thin wedge of lime. Yields about 8 (4 ounce) servings.

Kir Gallique

2 cups dry white wine
2 tablespoons Creme de Cassis liqueur
4 strips of lemon peel
8 ice cubes

In a glass pitcher, stir together white wine and liqueur. To serve, divide mixture between 4 glasses. Add 2 ice cubes and a twist of lemon peel to each glass. Yields 4 (4 ounce) servings.

Holiday Egg Nog with Brandy & Kahlua

3 egg yolks
3 tablespoons sugar

3 egg whites
3 tablespoons sugar

1 cup milk
1/2 cup cream, whipped
1/4 cup brandy
1/4 cup Kahlua liqueur

Beat yolks with sugar until thick and creamy. Beat whites with sugar until stiff. Fold together and stir in the remaining ingredients. Chill. Serve with a dash of nutmeg. Serves 6.

Grapefruit Margaritas

Coarse Kosher Salt
1   **teaspoon egg white**
1   **cup grapefruit juice**
1   **cup tequila**
1/4   **cup triple sec**
2   **cups ice chips**

Rub the rims of 8 stemmed cocktail glasses with grapefruit juice and dip into coarse salt. Set aside. Place the remaining ingredients in a blender container and blend until foamy. Pour into prepared glasses. Decorate with a thin wedge of grapefruit. Yields about 8 servings.

Sangria Roja (Sangria with Red Burgundy)

1/2   **gallon Burgundy wine**
1   **cup lemon juice**
1   **cup orange juice**
1   **orange, thinly sliced**
1   **lemon, thinly sliced**
3   **pineapple slices, cut into spears**
1   **quart club soda**
1/4   **cup sugar or to taste**

Combine all the ingredients and stir to blend. Add ice cubes and serve. Yields about 1 gallon.

Note: - If you prepare this earlier in the day and store it in the refrigerator, then add the club soda at serving time.

Hot Mexican Chocolate with Cinnamon

        4 cups milk
    1/2 cup water
        3 tablespoons cocoa
        4 tablespoons sugar
    1/3 teaspoon cinnamon
        4 teaspoons Creme de Cacao liqueur (optional)

Combine all the ingredients in a saucepan and simmer mixture for 2 or 3 minutes. Serve with a dollup of sweetened whipped cream and a sprinkling of cinnamon. Serves 6.

Sangria Blanca (Sangria with White Wine)

    1 bottle dry white wine (Chablis, Chenin Blanc)
    1 cup ginger ale
    1 cup orange juice
    2 tablespoons lemon juice
    2 tablespoons orange liqueur

Peach slices, orange slices, strawberries

In a large pitcher or punch bowl, stir together first 5 ingredients. Float fresh fruit on top and refrigerate for several hours. About 10 minutes before serving, chill with about 16 ice cubes. Yields about 1 1/2 quarts or 12 servings.

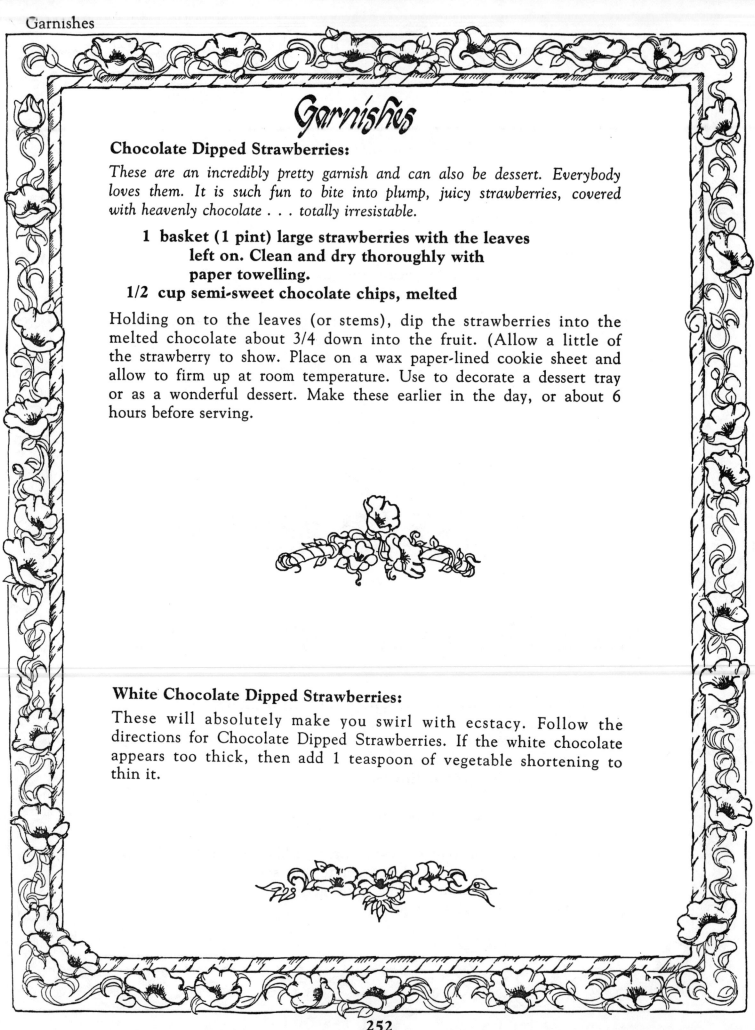

Garnishes

Chocolate Dipped Strawberries:

These are an incredibly pretty garnish and can also be dessert. Everybody loves them. It is such fun to bite into plump, juicy strawberries, covered with heavenly chocolate . . . totally irresistable.

> **1 basket (1 pint) large strawberries with the leaves left on. Clean and dry thoroughly with paper towelling.**
> **1/2 cup semi-sweet chocolate chips, melted**

Holding on to the leaves (or stems), dip the strawberries into the melted chocolate about 3/4 down into the fruit. (Allow a little of the strawberry to show. Place on a wax paper-lined cookie sheet and allow to firm up at room temperature. Use to decorate a dessert tray or as a wonderful dessert. Make these earlier in the day, or about 6 hours before serving.

White Chocolate Dipped Strawberries:

These will absolutely make you swirl with ecstacy. Follow the directions for Chocolate Dipped Strawberries. If the white chocolate appears too thick, then add 1 teaspoon of vegetable shortening to thin it.

Chocolate Leaves:

There are few garnishes that can be made that are more attractive or more appealing than chocolate leaves. They add a bright and festive touch and will elevate a dessert to celestial heights.

14 camellia or lemon leaves, rubbed, tubbed and scrubbed clean. (You can use any non-toxic or non-poisonous leaves.) Dry thoroughly with paper towelling.
1/2 cup semi-sweet chocolate chips, melted

Place about 1 heaping teaspoon of chocolate on the **back** of the leaf and spread it evenly with the back of the spoon. (A small spatula can also be used.) Cover the leaf evenly, and try not to get the chocolate on the front of the leaf. Place the leaves, chocolate side up, on a wax paper-lined cookie sheet and refrigerate until chocolate is firm. These can be prepared several days before serving.

To remove, peel the leaf off the chocolate and use to decorate desserts.

Marshmallow Gardenias:

Cut large-size marshmallows into 3/8-inch thick slices. Roll slices out on sifted powdered sugar. Pinch tips to form petals. Using about 5 or 6 petals, skewer or thread petals on a flat, wooden tooth pick and shape them into a flower. Break the tooth pick, leaving about 3/8-inch on top. Cover this with a small slice of yellow gumdrop.

These are just lovely on a pastry tray. They can be used to decorate a sweet mold or mousse. Set the gardenias on green leaves for a beautiful effect. If you are serving a chocolate dessert, place the flowers on chocolate leaves for a smashing effect.

Frosted Crackling Grapes:

Grapes and leaves are made exciting by frosting. Brush fruit and leaves with beaten egg white. Heavily cover the fruit and leaves with sugar and set aside to dry at room temperature. You can use powdered sugar, granulated sugar, colored sugar or multi-colored sugar for different and unusual effects. The multi-colored sugar gives the appearance of stained glass.

Gumdrop Flowers:

Use many colored gumdrops for a bouquet of spring flowers. With a sugared rolling pin, roll out small gum drops to flatten. Pinch ends to form petals. Assemble with a tooth pick. like the Marshmallow Gardenia. Place on mint leaves or other green leaves.

Lemon, Orange and Grapefruit Baskets:

With a sharp knife, cut into the center of a lemon, in a zig-zag, saw tooth fashion. Cut all the way to the center. Separate the lemon halves and place little sprigs of parsley in the lemon to fill the basket with greens. Cut a small slice from the bottom of the lemon, so the basket will stand straight. A small vegetable flower is a nice addition. Use the same technique for oranges or grapefruits. If you own a "V" shaped knife, then simply cut into the center of the lemon with continuous "V's".

Daisies:

Cut jicama into 1/4-inch thick slices. Cut into the jicama slices with a daisy-shaped cookie cutter. For the center, use a thin slice of carrot, half of a black olive, a round slice of mushroom or a small round of lemon or orange peel. Fasten with a piece of tooth pick, but do not let it show. Daisies can be cut from turnips, but I prefer using jicama. These are just lovely on an hors d'oeuvre tray or part of a vegetable basket. Use with green leaves.

Roses:

Roses can be made with the peel of fruits or vegetables. Peel an orange, grapefruit, lemon or tomato in one continuous line, starting from the top and working to the bottom. Use a sharp knife and thinly peel the fruit or vegetable. The width of the peeling would depend on the size rose desired. The wider the peel, the larger the rose. Don't be too accurate. Peel can be wavy. Now, reroll the peel and shape it to resemble a rose. Fasten with a tooth pick and set on green leaves.

Chrysanthemums:

Peel an onion and trim off the stem. Cut a thin slice off the top. With a sharp knife, cut onion in half, starting from the top and cutting almost to the bottom. Cut in half, then half again, then half again. Place onions in water and refrigerate. If colored chrysanthemums are desired, then tint the water with food coloring.

Radish Roses:

Radishes are a bright and colorful decoration for a vegetable platter. Cut off a thin slice from the top and stem. Shape the petals by cutting a thin slice from the top and going down, almost to the bottom. Depending on the size of the radish, cut 4 or 5 petals along the sides. Store in the refrigerator in cold water and the petals will open into flowers.

Radish Fans:

Cut off a thin slice from the top and stem. Now, lay the radish on its side and cut thin slices from the top, going almost to the bottom. Store in the refrigerator in cold water and fans will open.

Carrot Curls:

With a vegetable peeler, cut thin slices of carrot, starting at the top and working down to the bottom. Shape these slices into curls and skewer with a tooth pick. Place the slices in cold water overnight. Before serving, remove the tooth picks and use to decorate a vegetable platter.

Carrot Flowers:

With a sharp knife, cut off a "V" shaped strip down the length of a peeled carrot. Repeat this, at even distances, 3 or 4 times depending on the size of the carrot. Cut the carrot crosswise into thin slices. Slices will be shaped like a flower.

Cucumber Flowers:

These are nice for a vegetable basket. Peel a cucumber and run the tines of a fork on the sides, starting from the top and going down to the bottom. Now, cut the cucumber into slices and each slice will be scalloped.

Zucchini Flowers:

Peel the zucchini with a vegetable peeler, starting on the top and going down to the bottom. Peel off a 3/4-inch strip; then leave a 1/4-inch strip of green peel. Work your way around the zucchini, leaving a strip of peel every 3/4-inch. Now, cut out the green areas in a "V" shape and this will form the petals. Cut the zucchini into slices and each slice will form a flower.

Green Onion Frills:

Green onion frills are especially attractive and add a frivolous quality to a vegetable platter or basket. You can frill the bulb and the leaves of the onion. Cut varying sizes of leaves. Now, lay the leaves flat and with a very sharp knife, cut the thinnest slices down the length of the leaf or bulb, without cutting all the way across. Place the onions in cold water and refrigerate overnight. The cut edges will curl into pretty frills.

The Index

Additional Copies of
GREAT BEGINNINGS AND HAPPY ENDINGS
can be purchased at your local bookstore or
directly from:

RECIPES-OF-THE-MONTH CLUB
P.O. Box 5027   Beverly Hills, CA 90210